Praise for PROCRASTINATION

"Trying to kick the procrastination habit? In their practice treating procrastinators, [these] California psychologists . . . have pinpointed several causes."

—*USA Today*

"An exploration of what causes people to procrastinate and various procrastination styles. . . . Fascinating."

—*Fitness*

"Dr. Burka and Dr. Yuen . . . get procrastinators to feel better about themselves. . . . In learning to reduce their delaying tactics, procrastinators have much to gain in addition to faster performance and enjoying life more."

—*New York Times*

"Procrastination can be deadly to just about every aspect of your life . . . Burka and Yuen . . . offer hope for those prone to delay."

—*Boston Herald*

"*Procrastination*'s basic message: A tendency to be tardy is neither a bad habit nor moral failing [but] a 'complex psychological prob' caused by fear."

—*U.S. News and Worl'*

"Warmly and even humorously written, made. . . . Burka and Yuen did not procr remedies which have been successful in thei.

—*Honolulu Star-Bulletin*

"Burka and Yuen see procrastination as more than just laziness. For some, it's closer to a psychological block that keeps them from doing what needs to be done."

—*San Jose Mercury-News*

PROCRASTINATION

PROCRASTINATION

Why You Do It,
What to Do About It Now

JANE B. BURKA, PHD &
LENORA M. YUEN, PHD

Da Capo
∞
LIFE
LONG

A Member of the Perseus Books Group

Designed by Trish Wilkinson
Set in 10.5-point Minion by the Perseus Books Group

Library of Congress Cataloging-in-Publication Data

Burka, Jane B.
    Procrastination : why you do it, what to do about it now / Jane B. Burka
& Lenora M. Yuen. — Rev. ed.
        p.   cm.
    Includes bibliographical references and index.
    ISBN 978-0-7382-1170-1 (alk. paper)
    1. Procrastination. I. Yuen, Lenora M. II. Title.
BF575.P95B87 2008
155.20'32—dc22   2008034692

Published by Da Capo Press
A Member of the Perseus Books Group
www.dacapopress.com

Da Capo Press books are available at special discounts for bulk purchases in the U.S. by corporations, institutions, and other organizations. For more information, please contact the Special Markets Department at the Perseus Books Group, 11 Cambridge Center, Cambridge, MA 02142, or call (800) 810-4145, ext. 5000, or e-mail special.markets@perseusbooks.com.

LSC-C

20 19 18 17 16 15

Contents

Acknowledgments

We are grateful to all the people in our private practices and our Procrastination Groups and Workshops for deepening our understanding of procrastination. Hearing their stories, understanding their struggles, and helping them progress has been one of the great joys of our professional life. Their words, phrases, and stories have significantly enriched this book.

We appreciate the support and encouragement of the many friends and colleagues who helped make this book possible. Carol Morrison offered wise editorial advice as well as frequent personal boosts. Ken Rice graciously shared his extensive research on perfectionism. Barbara Blasdel, Karen Peoples, and Leslye Russell are members of a writers' group that provided psychological guidance and inspiration along with editorial eyes and contact creativity. Apologies to the many friends who remained supportive even while being neglected. Barbara Kaplan, Gerson Schreiber, Ingrid Tauber, Kathy DeWitt, Virginia Fredrick, Beth Herb, Anna Muelling, and members of the Lindemann Study Group and the Stanford Professional Women's Book Club offered steady encouragement with open hearts and great patience for many canceled meetings. Our dear friend Taraneh Razavi opened not only her heart to us, but her wonderful beach house where we spent many weekends working with a magnificent view of the Pacific Ocean. Taraneh, we don't know how we would have done it without your generosity.

The editorial staff at Da Capo Press provided both leadership and responsiveness. Our editor, Jonathan Crowe, has been unfailingly gracious and supportive of this project; his kind and respectful guidance was a pleasure. Renee Caputo is just what we would want a production manager to be: clear, efficient, and on time. Jennifer Swearingon is a wonderful copyeditor, and that means a lot coming from two recovering perfectionists, one of whom had an English-teacher mother.

Immense love and gratitude to Paul and Reece for each being that special combination of family and friend. You were steadying influences when necessary and always generous well-wishers. And to John, Nick, Chloe, and Obi—thank you for your patience, your tolerance, your editorial suggestions, and for being the best family ever. It is a privilege to share the planet with you.

Finally, in the first edition of this book, we had to acknowledge our indebtedness to Federal Express, which enabled us to meet numerous deadlines at the last minute. This time we thank all who made the Internet accessible to the technologically challenged and those who developed the "Track Changes" editing program for manuscripts. What a difference twenty-five years makes!

A Note to Our Readers

People who write books are supposed to be very knowledgeable about their subjects. We know procrastination from the inside out: between us, we have been through many all-nighters, spent long years struggling with our doctoral dissertations, paid late tax penalties, and made up elaborate scenarios to excuse our delays (a story about a death in the family is our most extreme example).

In addition to two lifetimes of personal experience, we have had many years of professional experience working with procrastinators. We began in 1979 when we were on the staff of the Counseling Center at the University of California at Berkeley where, to the best of our knowledge, we created the first group treatment program for student procrastinators. In our Procrastination Groups, we saw patterns and themes emerge again and again. While each individual's struggle was unique, there were many striking similarities among them. We learned, for example, that our plan to start the week off by holding the group on Monday mornings from nine to eleven was completely unrealistic—no one even showed up until ten o'clock!

When we offered Procrastination Workshops to the general public, we were once again reminded of the nature of the beast. We almost canceled our first workshop one week before the scheduled date because too few people had registered. In the end, we had to move to a larger room when two-thirds of the group signed up at the last minute.

For thirty years now, we have worked with individuals in our private practices of psychotherapy and psychoanalysis, exploring issues of procrastination in depth for extended periods of time. Our patients have opened their hearts and minds to us, and we have been the fortunate beneficiaries of their courage.

All of these experiences have reinforced our idea that procrastination is not primarily a time management problem or a moral failing but a complex psychological issue. At its core, problem procrastination is a problem with one's relationship to oneself, reflecting a shaky sense of self-esteem. In our first book, we called it a problem of self-worth. Now we emphasize that self-worth is rooted in the capacity for acceptance, which includes acceptance of our biology, our history, our circumstances, and our many human limits.

Why, after twenty-five years, did we decide that the time is right for an update of our book? We want to place procrastination in the context of our current culture and add new perspectives to our formulation of what procrastination is all about. In addition to having a deeper psychological understanding of the issues, we have new information from other fields, such as neuroscience and behavioral economics, that contributes to the understanding of procrastination.

Twenty-five years ago, there was virtually no research on procrastination, but now there are research findings that clarify what leads to procrastination. In 2007, psychologist Piers Steel at the University of Calgary published a review of almost 800 studies on procrastination,[1] including our 1983 book, which was one of the earliest resources cited. Steel ultimately identified four main issues that make procrastination more likely—low confidence in succeeding, task aversiveness, distractibility and impulsiveness, and having goals and rewards be too far off in the future. We were pleased to see that these research findings supported our clinical observations and suggestions, but we think there is more to procrastination than meets the research eye.

The world has changed dramatically since we wrote the first edition of *Procrastination*. The Internet was not available to individuals in the early 1980s, and the personal computer was not commonplace. We wrote in pencil on yellow pads, typed our drafts on IBM Selectric typewriters (with the thrilling "erase" key), and exchanged chapters in person. Getting our manuscript to the publisher required many mad dashes to the Federal Express office for overnight delivery. (If we missed the 6:00 P.M. closing time downtown, we were well aware that there was always the 8:00 P.M. option at the airport.) Now computers are our pads and pencils, our research libraries, and our mail carriers.

At that time, there were no Blackberries, PDAs, cell phones, or iPhones. Technological advances now allow us to work 24/7, but they also tempt us to procrastinate 24/7! No matter the time or place, at work or at home, we can lose ourselves for hours while we surf the Internet—reading the news, researching ad infinitum, blogging, watching sports, fantasizing about vacations or pornography. There's something for everyone.

In fact, over the years there has been an increase in avoidance behavior, with the Internet as the single most powerful cause.[2] Now, information is both limitless and instantaneously available; there is far more information than we can manage, let alone use. Too much information, too many decisions, too many options—this overabundance of information leads many of us into procrastination paralysis.

As we write today, we see that procrastination is even more complex than we once thought—an interweaving of not only individual psychological, behavioral, and emotional issues, but also social, cultural, and technological dynamics, biological and neurological predispositions, and universal human tendencies. We therefore regard the complexity of procrastination with even greater respect.

In writing this book, we believe now, as we did twenty-five years ago, that loosening the grip procrastination holds over your life requires both understanding what leads you to put things off and finding some way to take action. You may be aware of how delaying works *against* you, but we imagine you are less familiar with how procrastination works *for* you, and until you can see the function that procrastination serves in your life, you'll probably put off trying our techniques, just as you've put off so many other things. If you don't understand why you delay, all the practical techniques in the world aren't likely to help. Yet, even if you've searched your soul and believe you thoroughly understand your reasons for procrastinating, you still won't get anywhere unless you *do* something to overcome it. (Reading about techniques may be interesting, but reading is not doing.) So figuring out how to take action in new ways is vitally important.

In Part One of this book we untangle the many and varied roots of procrastination; then in Part Two we offer suggestions that can help you take action. Our aim is not to do away with procrastination. There are plenty of times when it's in your best interest to put something aside and not attend to it. Rather, we hope this book will lead you to the freedom of choice that comes from self-acceptance. We want our readers to lessen their tendency to delay by being happy with their humanity, accepting their strengths and weaknesses, and being able to be with themselves liking the company they keep. We don't suggest that you give up setting ambitious goals, striving for excellence, or taking on new challenges. But the fear, shame, dread, and self-loathing that go along with conflicted attempts to take action are surely worth banishing.

We no longer procrastinate the way we once did. Although Lenora does file a tax extension every year, it is a planned event, not a frantic, desperate solution to last-minute panic. And despite the fact that it took Jane five months to take her new PDA out of the box, she now manages to handle most of her responsibilities sooner rather than later. And while our first book was delivered two years past the publisher's deadline, this time we needed only a four-week grace period! We can attest to the fact that change is possible, though we also know it's not easy.

In this book, we want to accompany you through the challenges of procrastination into a world of psychological growth, acceptance, and action. We have given voice to many of the people with whom we've worked. To protect their confidentiality, we've changed all names and identifying information; the procrastinators we describe are composites of several people we've known. In sharing their stories, we hope you will better understand your own. It is in knowing your story, the narrative of your own life, that you will find the context for your procrastination. We believe this is crucial, for when we accept ourselves as we really are, rather than as we wish to be, we are most able to act in our best interest and not live at the mercy of procrastination.

PART ONE

UNDERSTANDING PROCRASTINATION

KNOW THYSELF

About four weeks into our first Procrastination Group at UC-Berkeley, a student said with surprise, "Procrastination is like a dandelion. You pull it up and think you've got it, but then it turns out the roots are so deep, it just grows back." While for some people, procrastination is like a flower easily loosened and removed, for many it is a patch of dandelions whose roots are deep and tangled. We can only talk about these roots one at a time, so we must separate them in an artificial way. But in life, these roots grow simultaneously, interweaving and shaping each other as they grow. Human experience, like some weeds, is complex.

The emotional roots of procrastination involve inner feelings, fears, hopes, memories, dreams, doubts, and pressures. But many procrastinators don't recognize all that's going on under the surface, because they use procrastination to avoid uncomfortable feelings. Underneath the disorganization and delay, most procrastinators are afraid they are unacceptable in some basic way. As painful as it is to judge yourself for your procrastination, self-criticism may be easier to tolerate than the feelings of vulnerability and exposure that come with trying your best and then landing in the territory of your fears. We know this is uncomfortable territory, but when you avoid your feelings, you are always unbalanced, picking your way through a field of buried emotional land mines, fearful about when you will stumble into the next explosion. We therefore invite you to explore this territory with us, to look at fear of failure, fear of success, fear of being controlled, and fear of intimacy or separation in relationships, because we believe that when you know what you feel and understand why you feel it, you are likely to be more confident, solid, at ease with yourself, and then able to proceed without procrastinating.

Another root of procrastination is the procrastinator's complicated relationship to time. Procrastinators often have a "wishful thinking" approach to time or see it as an opponent to outwit, outmaneuver, or outlive. This attitude toward time fuels more procrastination. If your "subjective time" is in conflict with "clock time,"[1] it is difficult to anticipate deadlines, work steadily toward a goal, or predict how much time you need to get things done. In addition, your sense of time may have created trouble in relationships with other people whose subjective experience of time is more naturally aligned with clock time. And when you have conflict with others about time, you might be tempted to procrastinate all the more.

The biological roots of procrastination include your body, your brain, and your genetic inheritance. All play a role in your procrastination. The field of neuroscience has exploded with exciting discoveries that may help you understand your procrastination in a new way. What happens in your brain influences what you avoid, and what you avoid (or don't avoid) affects the structure and function of your brain. Because of this "neuroplasticity," the brain is always changing, and therefore your biological tendencies do not have to be a fixed impediment to your progress.[2]

The interpersonal roots of procrastination encompass your family history, your social relationships, and your place in your current culture. Family dynamics from your past probably continue into the present and play a role in maintaining a dynamic of procrastination that no longer serves you. Social and cultural concerns may also contribute to your tendency to procrastinate, and it's important to understand their influence on your sense of yourself and your relationships with others.

We encourage you to explore and understand these emotional, biological, and social influences without criticism or blame. One of the themes of our book is that it can be exciting and interesting to learn from your experience—not denying it, forgetting it, or judging it, but accepting what is and making the most of it. Learning about the roots of your tendency to delay lays the foundation for utilizing the techniques to overcome procrastination that we offer in Part Two.

1

Procrastination
Nuisance or Nemesis?

It's New Year's Day—time for your annual resolutions. But after a long night of celebration, and with all the Bowl games on TV, who has time for serious reflection? By the end of January, when one friend has already lost ten pounds on her new diet and another has begun working on his taxes (who *are* these people?), you decide that the time has finally come for you to make your own resolution: "I'll never procrastinate again!"

Procrastination. The word conjures up different images for each of us. If you are among the fortunate who are not severely afflicted, you may imagine a person lying in a hammock, contentedly drinking iced tea instead of mowing the lawn. But if procrastination has been a problem for you, the images are probably less pleasant: a desk so cluttered, you can hardly see it beneath the rubble; the faces of old friends you've been meaning to write to for years; memories of school days that turned into all-nighters; a project that even now is waiting to be done. . . .

The dictionary definition of the verb "procrastinate" is "to postpone, put off, defer, prolong." The word comes from the joining of two Latin words: *pro,* meaning "forward," and *crastinus,* which means "belonging to tomorrow."[1] Forward it to tomorrow, otherwise known as "I'll do it later." Procrastination has been a problem since ancient times. The Egyptians had two words that translated as "procrastinate," and both were related to survival.[2] One denoted the *useful* habit of avoiding unnecessary work and impulsive effort, thus conserving energy. The other denoted the *harmful* habit of laziness in accomplishing a task that was necessary for subsistence, such as failing to till the fields at the appropriate time of year in the Nile flood cycle. In 1751, Samuel Johnson wrote about procrastination while a messenger waited to deliver the essay Johnson was late in submitting: "The folly of allowing ourselves to delay what we know cannot be finally escaped is one of the general weaknesses which, in spite of the instruction of moralists, and the remonstrances of reason, prevail to a greater or less degree in every mind."[3]

Procrastination has been on the rise since we wrote our first book. In 2007, estimates of procrastination in college students ran as high as 75 percent, with 50 percent of students reporting that they procrastinate consistently and consider it a problem. In the general population, chronic procrastination affects 25 percent of adults.[4] Over 95 percent of procrastinators would like to reduce their delaying ways,[5] since they suffer both in terms of their performance and their sense of well-being. If we want to stop procrastinating, why is it so difficult to do so? Research does not provide a simple answer to the mystery of why we procrastinate. There is no "typical" profile of a procrastinator, because "the network of psychological variables seems complex."[6]

One cause can be put to rest: research has shown that intelligence bears *no* relationship to procrastination,[7] so you can forget the idea that you're putting things off until your brilliance kicks in, or that being a procrastinator means you're stupid. Men procrastinate only slightly more than women, and there is evidence that procrastination abates as we get older. Perhaps people don't want to waste the time they have left, or they have stepped off the competitive escalator, or maybe they are finally comfortable with who they are and what they've accomplished—or not.

Procrastination plagues people of all occupations. Under the constant pressure of grades and other evaluations, a student puts off writing papers and studying for exams, only to cram for days when time is finally running out. Self-employed people have only themselves to rely on to stay in business—yet many find it's easy to delay when no one is watching to make sure they follow through. In increasingly competitive corporate settings, some people slow down instead of trying to keep up with the fast pace. Those irritated by bureaucratic red tape may file things under "pending," rather than complete the requisite (boring) busywork. At home, the possibilities for procrastination are endless. Who isn't nagged by an unfinished project, such as cleaning out the basement, painting the bedroom, or deciding on a new cell phone plan?

HOW CAN I TELL IF I'M PROCRASTINATING?

People often wonder how they can differentiate between true procrastination and simply putting things off either because they don't have time to do everything or because they're naturally relaxed and low-keyed. This is an important distinction. One way to tell whether procrastination is a problem for you is whether you find it troublesome. At one end of the continuum of distress about procrastination are people who procrastinate but don't suffer much. Here are some examples.

Some people thrive on keeping very busy, loaded with projects and activities; living from one deadline to the next, they love intense pressure and wouldn't choose to live any other way. There are also people who like to take life easy. It may take them a long time to get something done, but they're in no hurry to get around to it; they aren't especially driven or pressured. At times, people deliberately *choose* to procrastinate. They might decide to put something off because it's low on their priority list or because they want to think things over before making a decision or taking action. They use procrastination to give themselves time to reflect, to clarify options, or to focus on what seems most important.

We all have moments when everything seems to happen at once and we can't help but fall behind temporarily. There might be one day when the relatives arrive for a visit, the kids need chauffeur service, the refrigerator breaks down, and the tax receipts are due at the accountant's the next day. At times like these, something's got to give—it would be impossible to get everything done on time. People who acknowledge that there are limits to what they can expect of themselves are not likely to feel overly distressed when they can't do everything.

Some people don't suffer from their procrastination because it occurs in areas that are of little consequence to them. The important things get done more or less on time. Procrastination is part of their lives, but in a minor way.

Others don't suffer because they don't anticipate any problems, and they don't admit they're procrastinating. They may be overly optimistic about how long it takes to complete a task, consistently underestimating how much time they need. Some are "socially active optimists"[8] who use the distraction of social activity to procrastinate and have fun doing it. Outgoing and extroverted, they are (overly) confident about postponing now and being successful later.

INTERNAL AND EXTERNAL CONSEQUENCES

At the other end of the distress continuum are people whose procrastination creates significant problems. There are two ways procrastination can be troublesome. People who procrastinate may suffer *internal* consequences, feelings that range from irritation and regret to intense self-condemnation and despair. To an outside observer, many of these people appear to be doing just fine. They may be highly successful, like the lawyer who heads his own firm or the woman who is able to manage three children, volunteer work, and a full-time job. But inside they feel miserable. They are frustrated and angry with themselves because procrastinating has prevented them from doing all they think they are capable of. Although they appear to be doing well, they suffer inside.

Procrastination may lead not only to internal suffering but to significant *external* consequences. Sometimes these external consequences come as a shock, if you haven't even thought about possible repercussions. Some are mild, like a small penalty for a late payment.

But many procrastinators have endured major setbacks at work, at school, in relationships, or at home and have lost much that is important to them. A lawyer was disbarred because she missed too many court deadlines. We know a man whose wife left him because she got fed up with the way his procrastination at work interfered with family activities. The last straw came when he had to cancel their anniversary trip to Hawaii in order to meet a work deadline. An accountant told his manager that he missed his deadline because his wife was in the hospital. When the manager called his home and his wife answered, he was fired for his deception. A mortgage broker spent his time helping others learn new computer software instead of reviewing mortgage applications. He lost his job, had to move his family to a less-expensive neighborhood in the middle of the school year, and was unemployed for several months.

THE CYCLE OF PROCRASTINATION

Many procrastinators find that their delaying seems to have a life and will of its own. They compare the experience of procrastination to living on an emotional roller coaster. Their moods rise and fall as they attempt to make progress, yet they inevitably slow down. When they anticipate starting a project and then work toward its completion, procrastinators undergo a sequence of thoughts, feelings, and behaviors that is so common that we call it the "cycle of procrastination."

You have your own unique experience of this cycle. Your cycle may be drawn out over a period of weeks, months, or even years, or it may occur so rapidly that you move from the beginning to the end in a matter of hours.

1. "I'll start early this time."

At the outset, procrastinators are usually very hopeful. When you first undertake a project, the possibility exists that *this* time it will be done in a sensible and systematic way. Although you feel unable or unwilling to start *right now*, you may believe the start will somehow spontaneously occur, with no planned effort on your part. It is only after some time has elapsed and it becomes apparent that this time may *not* be different after all that your hope changes into apprehension.

2. "I've got to start soon."
The time for an early start has passed, and illusions of doing the project right *this* time are fading. Your anxiety builds and the pressure to begin intensifies. Having almost lost hope for the spontaneous start, you now begin to feel pushed to make some effort to do something soon. But the deadline is not yet in sight, so some hope remains.

3. "What if I don't start?"
As time passes and you *still* haven't made a start, it is no longer a question of the ideal beginning, or even of the push to get going. By now, any remaining optimism has been replaced by foreboding. Imagining that you may *never* start, you may have visions of horrible consequences that will ruin your life forever. At this point you may become paralyzed, a number of thoughts circling around in your head:

   a. *"I should have started sooner."* You may look back over the time you have lost, realize it's irretrievable, and chastize yourself with this self-reproach. You regret the behavior that has brought you to the edge of this precipice, knowing you could have prevented it if only you had started sooner. As one procrastinator put it, "I have the experience of constant lament."
   b. *"I'm doing everything but . . ."* It is extremely common for procrastinators at this stage to do everything and anything *except* the avoided project. The urge to reorganize the desk, clean the apartment, or try out new recipes suddenly becomes irresistible. Previously avoided but less onerous tasks cry out to be done *now*. In no time you are busy accomplishing things, happily absorbed in any activity that is not *it*, soothed by the rationalization, "Well, at least I'm getting *something* done!" Sometimes distracting activity seems so productive that you actually believe you are making progress on The

Project. Eventually, however, it becomes clear that *it* still isn't done.

c. *"I can't enjoy anything."* Many procrastinators try to distract themselves with pleasurable, immediately rewarding activities. You may watch movies, play games, get together with friends, or spend the weekend hiking. Although you try hard to enjoy yourself, the shadow of the unfinished project looms. Any enjoyment you feel rapidly disappears and is replaced by guilt, apprehension, or disgust.

d. *"I hope no one finds out."* As time drags on and nothing is done, procrastinators begin to feel ashamed. You don't want anyone to know of your predicament, so you may create ways to cover up. You may try to look busy even when you're not working; you present the illusion of progress even if you haven't taken the first step; you might hide—avoiding office, people, phone calls, and any other contact that might reveal your secret. As the cover-up continues, you may invent elaborate lies to cover up your delay, feeling increasingly fraudulent. (When people offer condolences on your grandmother's death, you know she's alive and well, playing bridge in Florida.)

4. *"There's still time."*

Even though you feel guilty, ashamed, or fraudulent, you continue to hold on to the hope that there's still time to get the project done. The ground may be crumbling away underfoot, but you try to remain optimistic, waiting for the magical reprieve that still might come.

5. *"There's something wrong with me."*

By now you are desperate. Good intentions to start early didn't work; shame, guilt, and suffering didn't work; faith in magic didn't work. The worry about getting the project done is replaced by an even more frightening fear: "It's *me*. . . . There's something wrong with *me!*" You may feel that you're lacking something fundamental that everyone else has—self-discipline, courage, brains, or luck. After all, *they* could get this done!

6. The Final Choice: To Do or Not to Do.

At this point you have to decide either to carry on to the bitter end or to abandon the sinking ship.

Path 1: Not to Do

a. *"I can't stand this!"* The tension has become unbearable. Time is now so short that the project seems totally impossible to do in the minutes or hours remaining. Because you cannot stand the way you feel, the effort required to pull through seems beyond your capability and your tolerance. Thinking, "I can't stand this anymore!" you decide the pain of trying to finish is too great. You flee.

b. *"Why bother?"* At this late stage in the game, you may look ahead at all that's left and decide it's simply too late to pull it off this time. There's no way in the world you can complete the project as initially planned—it can't be done well with so little time remaining. Any efforts you make now can't create what you had envisioned, so why bother even trying? You give up.

Path 2: To Do—On to the Bitter End

a. *"I can't wait any longer."* By now, the pressure has become so great that you can't stand waiting another minute. The deadline is too close or your own inertia has become so painful that it's finally worse to do nothing than it is to take action. So, like a prisoner on a death row, you resign yourself to your unavoidable fate . . . and you begin.

b. *"This isn't so bad. Why didn't I start sooner?"* To your amazement, it's not as bad as you had feared. Even if it is difficult, painful, or boring, at least the project is getting done—and that's a tremendous relief. You might even find that you enjoy it! All your suffering seems so needless. "Why didn't I just do it?"

c. *"Just get it done!"* The end is almost at hand. There's not a second to spare as you race the clock in order to finish. When you play the perilous game of brinksmanship, you no longer have the luxury of extra time to plan, refine, or improve what's done. Your focus is no longer on how well you could have done it, but whether you can get it done at all.

7. "I'll never procrastinate again!"

When the project is finally either abandoned or finished, the procrastinator usually collapses with relief and exhaustion. It's been a difficult ordeal. But at long last, it's over. The idea of going through this process even once more is so abhorrent that you resolve never to get caught in the cycle again. You vow that next time you'll start early, be more organized, stay on schedule, control your anxiety. Your conviction is firm—until the next time.

So the cycle of procrastination comes to an end with an emphatic promise to renounce this behavior forever. Yet in spite of their sincerity and determination, most procrastinators find themselves repeating the cycle over and over again.

THE ROOTS OF PROCRASTINATION

When we ask procrastinators to speculate about the factors that have led them down the path of delay, they often tell us, "We live in a competitive society! Everyone is expected to perform perfectly all the time. You just can't keep up with all that pressure." We are indeed bombarded by demands that could keep us occupied 24/7 in our drive to be successful. And the cultural definition of success means having lots of money, power, prestige, beauty, brilliance—having it all. In short, success is defined in terms of perfection. But the implicit message is, "If you don't have it all, there's something wrong with you." As the culture pulses at such a hectic pace, touting impossibly high standards, is it any wonder that so many of us run for the cover of procrastination?

But there must be more to becoming a procrastinator than simply being exposed to a high-pressured, perfection-conscious society. If that were all there was to it, then everyone would have trouble with procrastination. There are many people who respond to cultural pressures by exhibiting different signs of distress than the inability to produce—such as overworking, depression, psychosomatic illnesses, alcoholism, drug addiction, and phobias. And then there are people who thrive on 24/7 pressure.

To understand how you have chosen procrastination as your primary strategy for coping, we must look to the more personal dimensions of your life. We'd like you to consider when it all got started.

Earliest Memories

Do you remember the first time you procrastinated? What were the circumstances? Did you put off doing something for school or was it something your parents told you to do? How old were you? High school . . . elementary school? Even earlier than that? How did the situation turn out, and how did you feel about it? Here are a few examples of some early memories procrastinators have described to us:

I remember it was in the second grade, when we were assigned our first paper. We had to write two paragraphs about mountains and hand it in the next day. As soon as the teacher assigned it, I remember feeling scared—what was I going to say? All that night, I worried about it, but I didn't do it. Finally, the next morning over breakfast, my mother wrote it for me. I copied it and handed it in. At the time, I felt relieved. But I also felt like a liar. I got an "excellent" on the paper.

I don't remember any incident exactly. It's more a fuzzy sense of my mom telling me to do something, and my feeling, "No, I won't do it!"

I used to hurry through my homework so I could go out and play. My father checked it over before I could leave. He would always find something wrong with how I'd done it, and I'd have to do it over. Or else he'd give me something else to do before I could go out. Finally, I realized it didn't matter how fast or how well I did my homework—

he just wanted to keep me busy so that I couldn't leave until he was ready to let me. After that, I stopped trying to finish quickly. I just daydreamed and dawdled around.

Fifth grade. I'd always done well in school, and all the teachers liked me. That year, a group of girls in my class formed a club, and they wouldn't let me join because I was the teacher's pet. They made fun of me for being a goody-goody. I felt as though I was contaminated. And I remember making a conscious decision that I would never be the teacher's pet again. So I stopped working and started procrastinating. Just like that.

For many, the earliest symptoms of procrastination occurred in school—the first formal introduction of a young child to our larger, competitive society. The tracking systems of many schools emphasize academic ability as the major factor for distinguishing between students, so you may have identified yourself as an A, C, or F kid based on which class you were in. The social cliques that form in school are often based on these distinctions as well. The "brains," the "jocks," and the "partyers" may mock the children in the other groups in order to establish their own distinct places in the hierarchy. Experiences at the hands of one's peers can have a powerful effect on a person's academic and social confidence. Long after school years have passed, many adults still think of themselves in terms of how they were labeled as children.

People may also continue to think of themselves in terms of the learning issues they had in school—trouble with reading or math, distractibility, difficulty processing information, or speech problems. Even though their skills may have improved over the years, they don't feel completely safe from the possibility that someone will discover their deficits. Procrastination may have been a strategy for covering up weak areas.

Perhaps procrastination gave you some special protection in the classroom. Your teacher could say, "I wish you'd try harder," but could never say, "You just don't have what it takes," because the teacher never saw what you *had*. Unfortunately, people sometimes forget that grades do not measure intellect alone. They also measure a child's ability to concentrate, to cooperate, and to use imagination freely.

Whenever you started procrastinating, you know how hard it is to stop. In addition to functioning as a strategy for self-protection, procrastination is based on deeply held beliefs about life. We have heard these ideas expressed so often that we call them the Procrastinator's Code.

THE PROCRASTINATOR'S CODE

I must be perfect.

Everything I do should go easily and without effort.

It's safer to do nothing than to take a risk and fail.

I should have no limitations.

If it's not done right, it's not worth doing at all.

I must avoid being challenged.

If I succeed, someone will get hurt.

If I do well this time, I must always do well.

Following someone else's rules means that I'm giving in and I'm not in control.

I can't afford to let go of anything or anyone.

If I show my real self, people won't like me.

There is a right answer, and I'll wait until I find it.

These assumptions may be familiar to you, or they may be operating outside of your awareness. Either way, these are not absolute truths; they are personal perspectives that pave the way for procrastination. If you think you should be perfect, then it may seem safer to procrastinate than to work hard and risk a judgment of failure. If you are convinced that success is dangerous, then you can protect yourself and others by procrastinating and reducing your chances of doing well. If you equate cooperation with giving in, then you can put things off and do them when *you* are ready, thus maintaining your sense of control. Or, if you believe that people won't like the real you, then you can use procrastination to withhold your ideas and to keep people at a safe distance.

The beliefs that make up the Procrastinator's Code reflect a way of thinking that keeps procrastinators from making progress. Self-critical, apprehensive and catastrophic thoughts can make it impossible to move beyond the inevitable obstacles of daily living. Realizing that you are thinking unrealistically is one step toward overcoming procrastination, but there is more to the Procrastinator's Code than just unrealistic thoughts.

We think that people who procrastinate in a problematic way do so because they are afraid. They fear that if they act, their actions could get them into trouble. They worry that if they show who they really are, there will be dangerous consequences to face. They are afraid, underneath all the disorganization and delay, that they are unacceptable, so much so that they may hide not only from the world but even from themselves. As painful as it is to endure self-inflicted criticism, contempt, and disgust, such feelings may be easier to bear than the feelings of vulnerability and exposure that come with taking a clear look at who they really are. Procrastination is the shield that protects them.

2

Fear of Failure
The Procrastinator on Trial

M any people who procrastinate are apprehensive about being judged by others or by the critic who dwells within. They fear they will be found lacking, their best efforts won't be good enough, and they won't meet the mark. This concern reflects a fear of failure, and we believe that procrastination may function as a strategy for coping with this fear.

FEAR OF FAILING:
THE SEARCH FOR PERFECTION

David is a lawyer with a large corporate firm. He was an academic star in college and was accepted into a competitive law school. He struggled often with procrastination, sometimes staying up all night to write his briefs or study for exams. But he always managed to do well. With great pride he joined a prestigious law firm, hoping eventually to be named a partner in the firm.

Although he thought a lot about his cases, David soon began to postpone doing the necessary background research, making appointments with his clients, and writing his briefs. He wanted his arguments to be unassailable, but he felt overwhelmed by all the possible angles, and sooner or later he'd get stuck. Although he managed to look busy, David knew he wasn't accomplishing much, and he was plagued by the feeling that he was a fraud. As a court date drew near, he would begin to panic because he hadn't allowed enough time to write an adequate brief, much less a brilliant one. "Being a great lawyer means everything to me," said David. "But I seem to spend all my time worrying about being great and very little time actually working at it."

If David is so concerned about being an outstanding lawyer, why is he, by procrastinating, avoiding the work that is necessary to help him achieve what he wants so badly? David's procrastination helps him avoid facing an important issue: Can he in fact be as outstanding a lawyer as his student record promised? By waiting too long to begin writing up his research, David avoids testing his potential. His work will not be a reflection of his true ability; rather it demonstrates how well he is able to produce under last-minute pressure. If his performance doesn't live up to his (and others') expectations, he can always say, "I could have done a lot better if I'd just had another week." In other words, the verdict of failure so frightens David that he is willing to slow himself down, even occasionally to the point of disaster, to avoid letting his best work be judged. He is terrified that his best would be judged inadequate.

Why would anyone go to such self-defeating lengths to prevent a judgment of failure on a task, whether it be writing a legal brief, updating a résumé, selecting gifts for friends and relatives, or buying a new car? People who have inhibited themselves because of their fear of failing tend to define "failure" in a very broad way. When they are disappointed by their performance on a task, they think not only that they have failed on that task, but also that they have failed as a person.

Dr. Richard Beery, who was our colleague at the University of California at Berkeley Counseling Center, observed that people who fear failure may be living with a set of assumptions that turn striving for accomplishment into a frightening risk. These assumptions are: (1) what I produce is a direct reflection of how much ability I have, and (2) my level of ability determines how worthwhile I am as a person—that is, the higher my ability, the higher my sense of self-worth. Thus, (3) what I produce reflects my worth as a person. Dr. Beery formulated these assumptions into the following equation:

Self-worth = Ability = Performance

In essence, this equation translates into the following statement: "If I perform well, that means I have a lot of ability, so I like myself." Or, "If I don't perform well, that means I have no ability, and I feel terrible about myself." It's not simply how well you did at a particular time on a particular day under particular circumstances. Your performance is a direct measure of how able and worthwhile you are—forever.

For many people, *ability* refers to intellectual competence, so they want everything they do to reflect how smart they are—writing a brilliant legal brief, getting the highest grade on a test, writing elegant computer code, saying something exceptionally wise or scintillating in a conversation. You could also define ability in terms of a particular skill or talent, such as how well one plays the piano, learns a language, or serves a tennis ball. Some people focus on their ability to be attractive, entertaining, up on the latest trends, or to have the newest gadgets. However ability may be defined, a problem occurs when it is the sole determinant of one's self-worth. The performance becomes the *only* measure of the person; nothing else is taken into account. An outstanding performance means an outstanding person; a mediocre performance means a mediocre person. Period.

For David, writing a legal brief for a case is the performance that measures not only his ability to be a good lawyer but also his value as a human being. If he works hard to prepare the brief and it isn't brilliant, he will be devastated—it means he is a *terrible* person who can't do *anything*. "I don't think I could stand it if I went all out and the brief still wasn't good enough," David confessed.

As Dr. Beery pointed out, procrastination breaks the equation between Ability and Performance:

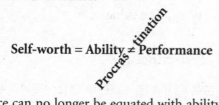

$$\text{Self-worth} = \text{Ability} \underset{\text{Procrastination}}{\neq} \text{Performance}$$

Performance can no longer be equated with ability because complete effort has not been made. This means that regardless of how the performance eventually turns out, the connection between Self-worth and Ability can still be preserved. For example, if David is disappointed or criticized for his brief, he can reassure himself with the thought, "Well, I could have done better if I'd started sooner and given myself more time to do it." Or, if he manages to do well in spite of procrastinating, he can feel even more pleased with himself, thinking, "Look how I pulled this one out of the fire. Just imagine how well I could do if I *really* worked at it!"

Procrastination allows people to take comfort in believing that their ability is greater than their performance indicates, perhaps even maintaining the belief that they are brilliant or unlimited in their potential to do well. As long as you procrastinate, you never have to confront the real limits of your ability, whatever those limits are.

Some people would rather suffer the consequences of procrastination than the humiliation of trying and not doing as well as they had hoped. It is more tolerable to blame themselves for being disorganized, lazy, or uncooperative than to view themselves as being inadequate and unworthy—the failure they fear so deeply. And it is the fear of *this* failure that is eased by procrastination.

People who worry about being judged inadequate or unworthy usually are afraid that is exactly what they are. If they take a realistic look at themselves and judge themselves to be lacking, they face another fear. They fear they are unlovable. As one procrastinator put it, "If I don't do well, who would want me? Who could love me if I have nothing to offer?" Because this woman thinks that her ability, reflected by her performance on tasks, will determine whether or not she deserves to be loved, the consequences of not measuring up are much greater than simply "failing" in terms of her performance—it means failing as a person and being unwanted by all.

The World of a Perfectionist

Often without realizing it, people who procrastinate are perfectionists. In an attempt to prove they are good enough, they strive to do the impossible, thinking that they should have no problem at all reaching their lofty goals. They usually put unrealistic demands on themselves and then feel overwhelmed when they are unable to meet them. Discouraged, they retreat from the demands by procrastinating.

Most procrastinators don't understand how they could possibly be considered perfectionists when everywhere they turn they find evidence of how they have messed up. Gary, a self-employed Web site designer, sees himself this way: "I always do things in a half-baked way. I do a rushed job at the last minute and sometimes I don't even see projects through to the end. How in the world can I be a perfectionist?"

Psychologists have identified two types of perfectionists, *adaptive* and *maladaptive*.[1] If you are an adaptive perfectionist, you have high standards, and you believe your performance lives up to them. This kind of successful perfectionism feels like an essential part of your identity and is a basis for self-esteem.[2] However, if you are a maladaptive perfectionist, you, too, have high standards, but you are disappointed in yourself. In maladaptive perfectionism, there is a discrepancy between your standards and the way you view your performance, so you are prone to be self-critical and are more vulnerable to feeling depressed and having low self-esteem.[3]

Maladaptive perfectionists are excessively concerned about making mistakes.[4] As psychologist David Burns pointed out, people who are high achievers generally are *not* intractable perfectionists.[5] The champion athlete, the extremely successful businessperson, and the Nobel Prize-winning scientist usually know there will be times when they will make mistakes or when they will have a bad day, and their performance will suffer a temporary setback. Although they strive for high goals, they are also able to tolerate the frustrations and disappointments of sometimes failing to meet those goals. They know that they can improve their efforts, and they work hard to do so.

In contrast, the perfectionistic procrastinator usually expects more of herself than is realistic. A woman who hasn't exercised in years wants to be in top physical condition in two weeks. A first-time novelist wants the first draft of his writing to be of publishable quality. A college freshman who has not mastered time management or study skills expects to get all As his first semester. A young man wants every phone call to land a date; a salesman expects to turn every customer into a sale. As a result, the high standards that are intended to motivate people toward accomplishment often become impossible standards that hinder their efforts. An important question to ask yourself is: Are you setting standards for yourself that enable you to make progress, or do your standards lead you to become discouraged, frustrated, and stuck? It's not how high your standards are that makes you a maladaptive perfectionist; it's how far below your standards you perceive your performance to be, how unrealistic and inhibiting your standards are for you, and how harshly you judge yourself for not meeting them. When perfectionism becomes a problem, procrastination is likely to become a problem.[6]

There are several beliefs cherished by perfectionists who procrastinate. These beliefs may be operating even though you're not aware of them, and they may even seem noble and reasonable. But they can make your life extremely unsatisfying and pave the way for procrastination rather than progress.

Mediocrity Breeds Contempt. For some procrastinators the thought of being ordinary can be so intolerable that they want everything they do to be outstanding. They wish not only for ideal careers and relationships but also to make a masterpiece of the letter they write or the garden they plant. If you expect your everyday performance to be up to the level of your ideal picture of yourself, then whatever you do is bound to seem mediocre in comparison. You devalue the average, the ordinary, the regular, regarding them with contempt. Since mistakes and flaws are an inevitable part of the human condition, people who can't bear the ordinary find comfort in procrastination. When an ordinary performance can be attributed to the last-minute rush, they can continue to believe their ideal could have been reached, if they'd had more time. This allows perfectionists to avoid feeling contempt for themselves when they are simply average.

Excellence without Effort. The perfectionist believes that if one is truly outstanding, even difficult things should be easy. Creative ideas should flow ceaselessly! Studying should be pure intellectual joy! Decisions should be made immediately with total certainty! Using such impossible standards, a person who must work hard, or even exert a moderate amount of effort to get something done, is likely to feel inferior. A college physics major said, "If I can't solve a problem instantly, I feel stupid. I understand the concepts and I'm pretty smart, so I *should* be able to see the answer right away—I get so mad at myself that I can't stand sitting there. I play video games."

The expectation that one should be able to catch on instantly, no matter how complex the material, brings many procrastinators to a grinding halt. Their disappointment at having to work hard prevents them from making the effort required to grapple with the material and master it. Instead, they avoid it by delaying. In the long run, their need to be smart keeps them ignorant. After all, if you can't stand not knowing, you can't learn.

Going It Alone.   Perfectionists often feel they should do everything by themselves, believing it's a sign of weakness to get help of any kind. There is no flexibility to consider what might be best for the situation, no room to admit that sometimes you don't have the answer, that you can't do it all by yourself, or that it just might be more fun to have company. Even when it would be more efficient to get help, many perfectionists are bound and determined to work, and suffer, in isolation. They may even take pride in this splendid isolation. Or they may come from a culture that does not endorse asking for help, where needing help is seen as a sign of weakness and a source of shame. When the burden finally becomes too heavy, procrastination becomes a source of relief. Unable to do everything all by themselves, they resort to delay.

There Is a Right Way.   This is one of the most cherished notions held by perfectionists. They believe there is one correct solution to a problem, and it is their responsibility to find it. Until they've discovered the right solution, they are reluctant to take *any* course of action or commit themselves to anything. So, rather than take the risk of making the wrong choice, they do nothing.

Consider the case of Charles and Brenda who wanted to move from their small town to a larger community. They knew the decision would change the course of their lives forever, and they wanted to be absolutely sure they were doing the right thing. They made long lists of pros and cons for each town they were considering. Since they could never feel absolutely certain that any one location would be the perfect place to live, work, and raise children, they never made the move. As long as Brenda and Charles put off deciding where to live, they can hold on to the illusion that there is a perfect solution and they can make a perfect choice.

Perfectionists fear that if they make a wrong decision, they will think less of themselves and their feeling of regret will be intolerable. But underneath this apprehension is a belief that they can (and should) be omniscient—able to read the future and guarantee how things will turn out. It is a childhood fantasy that grown-ups know everything (how *did* your parents figure out that you were lying any-way?) and most of us harbor the wish that someday we, too, will know and control everything. It is indeed hard to accept the reality that we are neither omniscient nor omnipotent—and neither were our parents.

I Can't Stand to Lose. (Or: What, Me Competitive?)

On the surface, it appears that many procrastinators are not competitive. Their constant delaying takes them out of the running, so they don't really compete—or do they? Randy, a contractor who often delays submitting bids until it is too late, made a typical comment: "I'm not interested in competing for jobs. I'll find a job without going through that conventional rigmarole—I like to run on my own track." The truth is that many perfectionists hate losing so much that they avoid any activity that would bring them into direct competition with others. Like Randy's refusal to play the game, an apparent disinterest in competition covers the feeling that competition is dangerous. Randy hates to lose because not winning means he has failed, and failing means he is worthless. He can't lose because he never really enters the race.

Procrastination can be a form of "self-handicapping."[7] You make winning so much harder for yourself, like playing golf with only one hand, that you then have an excuse for your dismal score: "Hey, I was only playing with one hand!" People who "choose to lose" procrastinate to such an extent that they guarantee failure, yet they still imagine that they could have won if they had tried—like the bachelor who brags about all the hot romances he could have if only he had the time to make phone calls, or the student from another country who puts off mastering English, so that papers are graded down because of the quality of the language and not because of the quality of the ideas. Self-handicapping is a backhanded way to protect your ego and your self-esteem: I lost, but I did it to myself.

All or Nothing.   The all-or-nothing view of life is common among perfectionists who procrastinate. A person who believes that he or she must do everything usually has difficulty appreciating any progress made toward a goal: as long as the project is incomplete, it seems that nothing at all has been accomplished. As one perfectionist put it, "It's either gold or it's garbage." No wonder it's so tempting to give up in despair before reaching the end!

The all-or-nothing notion can affect a person's initial formulation of goals, leading him or her to attempt to do everything at once because anything less seems insufficient. For instance, we asked Steve to select a goal that he wanted to accomplish during a one-week period of time. Initially, he wanted to work out at his health club every day during the week. Although he had joined the club more than a year earlier, he had never once used his membership. It took some work, but we finally convinced Steve that the goal of going to the club every day was pretty unrealistic. Reluctantly, Steve modified his goal, deciding that he would be doing well if he went to the club three times during the week. A week later, Steve was very discouraged because he had used the gym *only* twice. Even though Steve worked out more in that week than he had during the entire previous year, he felt as if he'd accomplished nothing.

With an all-or-nothing attitude, you can become discouraged for many reasons, including:

You don't accomplish *everything* you set out to do.
You don't do things *exactly* as you had planned.
You do something well but not *perfectly*.
You don't get as *much* recognition as you feel you deserve.

In situations like these, you can feel as though you accomplished nothing, because what you have done isn't exactly what you envisioned. If you can only be satisfied with perfection, you are doomed to be disappointed. After all, going after perfection is like chasing the horizon: you keep going, but you can never really get there.

Perfection is an ideal that is relinquished very, very gradually. Even if you can agree intellectually that perfectionistic standards are unrealistic and counterproductive, you may still find it hard to accept the fact that you aren't now, never have been, and never will be perfect.

For most perfectionists, accomplishment represents much more than simply achieving goals or being remarkable. In many of their families, being outstanding seemed to be the most reliable strategy for earning recognition, acceptance, and love—accomplishments were valued above all else, and being second best seemed of no value at all. Other perfectionists never enjoyed the satisfaction of winning approval. Although accomplishments were highly valued, their ability to achieve was doubted, criticized, or undermined. They may try to dispel doubts by striving to be perfect, believing that if they're ever going to earn respect and love, perfection is their only hope.

Mindsets

Our observations about the perfectionism of procrastinators have been supported by the extensive research of Stanford psychologist Carol Dweck. Her research on how people cope with failure led her to identify two different mindsets, the Fixed Mindset and the Growth Mindset.[8] The perspective of a Fixed Mindset is that intelligence and talent are attributes you are born with; they are fixed and permanent. Success is all about proving your ability, validating that you are smart or talented. And it's something you have to prove over and over again, as each new set of challenges enters your life. If you have a Fixed Mindset, there is no room for mistakes in any situation, because mistakes are evidence of failure that prove you're not really smart or talented after all. If you were, you would not have to work at it—whatever "it" is; having to make an effort is evidence of deficiency. And because each performance is seen to be an eternal measure of your ability, failure feels dangerous; it defines you forever.

You can see how fear of failure springs from the Fixed Mindset and leads, in turn, to procrastination. When things get hard, people with a Fixed Mindset retreat and lose interest. They don't want to do anything that might prove their inadequacy—or, we would add, their unworthiness. Procrastination protects people from taking a risk that might result in failure, which from a Fixed Mindset perspective would be a life sentence of inadequacy.

Contrast this with Dweck's second mindset—the Growth Mindset. The central belief in this mindset is that abilities can be developed; with hard work and effort you can get smarter and better over time. In a Growth Mindset, effort is what makes you smart or good at something; it is what "ignites ability and turns it into accomplishment."[9] From this perspective, you don't have to be good at something immediately. In fact, it's more interesting to do things you're *not* good at, because that's a way to stretch yourself and to learn. People with a Growth Mindset don't just seek challenges; they thrive on them. Failures may hurt or disappoint, but they don't define a person. In fact, failure becomes a reason to redouble effort and work harder, rather than to give up, retreat, and . . . procrastinate.

Adopting the Growth Mindset is one way to undo the self-worth equation. Not only does performance not reflect your value as a person, but performance is no longer a central concern! What matters is what you learn, what you feel excited about, and how you've improved, while outcome moves to the background. The definition of "ability" is no longer a fixed entity; it is something that can change and develop. There's no longer anything to prove. As Dweck asks so compellingly, "Is success about learning—or proving you're smart?"[10]

The writer May Sarton has described the Growth Mindset beautifully. "In the middle of the night, things well up from the past that are not always cause for rejoicing—the unsolved, the painful encounters, the mistakes, the reasons for shame or woe. But all, good or bad, painful or delightful, weave themselves into a rich tapestry, and all give me food for thought, food to grow on."[11]

THE FATE OF THE IMPERFECT:
CONSEQUENCES REAL AND IMAGINED

Perfectionists tend to think in absolute terms about what they do. In addition, they often think catastrophically; they take one small event, such as a mistake, and exaggerate the consequences until the repercussions are staggering. They react to one incident as if it were the beginning of the end, certain that disaster is just around the corner. You can see the Fixed Mindset at work in this kind of scenario.

These catastrophic expectations are even more intimidating when they are nameless and vague: "My life will be miserable if I'm not perfect!" But in what *specific* ways would life be miserable? It is often both interesting and helpful for procrastinators to articulate the nameless fantasies of dread that haunt them. Ask yourself the question, "What would happen if I weren't perfect?" In addition to the general sense of doom you might feel at the thought of being less than exceptional, what specifics do you foresee? How bad would things get? What chain of events would lead up to the final catastrophe?

Here is an example from a man whose expectations careened from perfection to mediocrity to disaster. Ethan, a middle-level manager in banking, was, in outward appearance, very successful. He had a secure job, a devoted wife, and a comfortable home. Yet he always felt in jeopardy of losing everything. Ethan feared that he would be fired if he didn't maintain exceptional job performance in every area—making decisions, managing his subordinates, projecting the budget, running meetings—everything.

This demand to be in top form all the time grew into a pressure greater than Ethan could bear, and he began to procrastinate, putting off paperwork and phone calls, delaying personnel decisions, and postponing preparation for meetings. He feared his procrastination would be discovered and it would lead to his being fired.

From one incident of imperfection, Ethan anticipated total disaster: "If I don't have my agenda ready for Thursday's conference, I'll run a lousy meeting, and everyone will see that I'm not as competent as I pretend to be. I'll be fired from my job and blackballed from the rest of the banking community—who would want to hire a lazy procrastinator? If I can't get another job making as much money, my wife will be furious and she'll leave me for someone else. I'll be alone with no family and no future. I'll have nothing to live for. I might even do myself in. Now I feel too depressed to work on my agenda. I need a drink."

Although you can probably see that Ethan's picture of the cataclysmic consequences of one meeting is blown far out of proportion, to him the danger seems real. Disaster feels so imminent that Ethan becomes paralyzed and unable to do any work.

This kind of catastrophic thinking is extremely undermining, especially if you don't realize that you're doing it. If you can learn to step back and take a careful look at what you are anticipating, you can challenge the "inevitability" of your "fate." Ethan, for example, began to contest his conclusion that running a so-so meeting would lead directly to his being fired. He eventually saw there was a big difference between running a mediocre meeting and losing his wife, his job, and his hope for the future.

The next time you find yourself slipping into a paralysis of perfectionism, consider playing out your worst-case scenario for that situation. Perhaps as you do, you can remind yourself that, although these fantasies are your fears, they are almost certainly exaggerated. And if you can take your thoughts a step further to shift from Fixed to Growth Mindset, you might begin to see that you can view imperfection in an entirely new light—as an impetus to improve or to learn something new, instead of as a death warrant.

3

Fear of Success
Hello Procrastination,
Good-bye Success

We each have to define "success" for ourselves. For some, it is measured by societal standards of job status, financial stability, or personal power. For others, success implies a more relational achievement, such as a loving relationship or a happy family. An internal experience of success might be living mindfully or feeling content. Clarry Lay, a researcher in academic procrastination, defines success as "the timely pursuit of your intentions."[1] By this definition, any of us can feel successful whenever we do what we say we're going to do. "The timely pursuit of your intentions" will gradually lead you toward any other measure of success, and at the same time, it allows you to feel successful just for trying. Procrastinators, however, have trouble following through on their intentions in a timely way, so they feel like failures every time they let themselves down—again. Yet, if they can shift into a Growth Mindset, appreciating their efforts toward improvement, they can see that *getting better* at the timely pursuit of intentions *is* success.

Even when procrastinators manage to achieve outward success, they can't fully enjoy it. The potential pleasure in success is dampened by the close calls, the last-minute scramble, the all-nighters that required Herculean efforts. Even if no one else knows they've barely pulled success out of the fire, *they* do—and for them that means they still haven't really succeeded. They criticize themselves for their lack of success and wish they could be free of the chains of procrastination that hold them back. But in their self-deprecation, they often miss an important issue: perhaps they are actually afraid of being successful and are using procrastination to avoid the perils of success.

ARE YOU AFRAID OF SUCCESS?

It's easier to identify the desire for success than the fear of it, but if you recognize yourself in any of the following scenarios, you may harbor a fear of success. Do you sometimes slow down on a project that's going well? Do you feel anxious when you receive a lot of recognition? When your manager suggests a promotion, do you start to wish you were invisible? Do compliments embarrass you or leave you feeling apprehensive and wary? If you are successful in one area of your life, do you mess up in another? When things are going just fine, do you assume the other shoe is about to drop? If you have more opportunities to be successful than others in your family, do you worry about losing your connection to your relatives? These are just a few experiences that point to a fear of success.

Jane remembers the first time she considered this counterintuitive notion. She entered college as an English major, but when she took a psychology course in group dynamics, she immediately felt at home. She discovered that her mind had found its element. Her required three-page papers turned into such detailed ten-page outpourings that she was often late turning in her weekly assignments. She did so much research for her final paper that she did not finish it on time, and she received an incomplete in the course. The professor called Jane into her office and expressed concern that a strong student was jeopardizing a high grade. "I think you're afraid of . . . " and Jane assumed the next word would be "failure," but the teacher said, "*success.*"

What a shock! It had never occurred to Jane that she could be afraid of doing well. She had found a subject that fit the way her mind naturally worked, but there would be complications. The class had solidified Jane's decision to switch her major to psychology, which would force her to meet a new set of students and teachers. She would follow an entirely different career path from the one she had envisioned. Even though Jane had found her calling, she didn't feel free to pursue it fully, not only because it meant change, but because it anointed her as being really good at something, and that didn't fit her self-image at the time. (She thought only her older brother could inhabit the role of being really good at something.) Her anxiety about being successful was unknown to her, but it was demonstrated by her procrastination.

Why are some people unable to pursue success wholeheartedly, whatever success means to them? It can be baffling to find yourself undermining the very success you desire. We think many procrastinators are conflicted about being successful, as Jane was. They fear the downside of success often without even being aware of it. Most people who fear success *want* to do well, but because of unconscious worries, the desire fails to turn into reality.[2] These worries may be so subtle that they are not always known directly. Psychologist Susan Kolodny says the conflict "sometimes manifests itself instead as an inexplicable shift in mood, an attack of self-doubt or guilt, a wave of hope or despair, as if something had been whispered almost within earshot and we aren't sure what, or by whom."[3]

The important question for all of us is not whether we are ambivalent about success, but whether our conflict about success is so intense that it gets in our way. Does it stop us from moving forward and taking risks that could enrich our lives? Does it lead us to restrict ourselves to such an extent that we lose our spontaneity, our curiosity, and our desire to master new challenges?

CULTURAL PRESSURES

Cultural norms, gender roles, and economic opportunities have influenced all of us with respect to our possibilities for success, creating advantages for some and limiting others. For many procrastinators, they also create conflict. For example, we are bombarded by demands that could keep us occupied 24/7, and some people use procrastination to resist the cultural pressure to be everything and to have it all. On the other hand, some people who want it all find that procrastination gets in the way of having it.

Cross-cultural pressures can have an inhibiting effect on success. People who left their homelands and moved to our country may feel that succeeding in the high-pressured, competitive American culture means abandoning the traditions and values of their native lands. Caught between a desire to assimilate and loyalty to their heritage, they may use procrastination to avoid making an impossible choice.

Although notions of "masculine" and "feminine" have become less rigid, they may still contribute to procrastination. Women who want to be successful in "a man's world" may fear being labeled ambitious and aggressive—too "masculine"—and put off doing what it takes to be competitive. Men who feel pressured to be "masculine" may avoid success because they fear they would have to give up the "feminine" sides of themselves—to be tender, to have doubts and insecurities, to need comfort.

These are all significant factors, but they do not tell the whole story. We must also consider the more personal concerns that lead men and women to avoid success and to rely on procrastination as their way out. We present below some common psychological predicaments that reveal a fear of success.

COMMON REASONS FOR AVOIDING SUCCESS

Success Demands Too Much: I Have to Retreat

Some people worry that success will require too much of them, more than they can afford to give. Because working toward success demand a lot of time, effort, and dedication, there are those who believe they are not up to the task. It feels safer to hold back, to retreat. Here are some possible variations.

Competition: Take It or Leave It. By delaying, procrastinators appear to be disinterested in competitive struggles and indifferent to the rewards of victory. Procrastination gives the impression that they can "take it or leave it," because they don't make an all-out effort.

People who are afraid of failure choose not to compete because they are afraid of losing or being exposed as weak or inadequate. People who are afraid of success, however, choose not to compete because they are afraid of winning. They procrastinate to hide their ambition, because they think there's something wrong with being competitive in the first place. So they put off sending an application until it's too late to be considered for a position; they delay training for a marathon run and thus cannot be a serious competitor in the race; they postpone studying, saying "grades aren't all that important," and take themselves out of the running for a scholarship for graduate school.

Shaun is an architect whose lifelong dream has been to have his own architectural firm. He is a creative thinker, but he delays laying out the designs he plays with in his head. As a result, he is always behind schedule. Other designers ask him for advice informally, but no one wants to work with him on a project because he can't meet deadlines. Shaun is anguished by his inhibition. "I hate myself when I don't get my vision into the computer. My great ideas exist only in my head, where no one else can see them. If the others really did like my drawings, I'd be proud but uncomfortable. It makes me nervous when I hear a lot of compliments. I'll never be able to start my own firm if I keep this up." Shaun is undermining his talent, and his attention is focused on his bad habits and his self-disgust. But this preoccupation may be a distraction. Although Shaun spends a lot of energy feeling bad about what he isn't doing, he rarely thinks about what awaits him on the other side of his goal. What if he *could* consistently show his designs and he *did* ultimately have his own architectural firm?

We asked Shaun to consider the "dangers of improvement"[4]; in his situation, the possible downsides of having his own firm. "I would be in the spotlight. Everyone would pay attention to whether my business was successful or not. And once you've produced one really interesting design that gets built, people expect everything you do to be innovative. To do that, I'd really have to put pressure on myself and work nonstop. I might never have any free time to have fun and be lazy." By procrastinating, Shaun diminishes his chances for success, giving him a buffer from the possibility of being exposed and trapped—forced to live a high-pressured life he thinks he doesn't want.

This worry about escalating expectations is a common anxiety for those who fear the pressures of success. One procrastinator expressed it vividly: "It's like being a competitive high jumper. You train for months, get yourself ready physically and mentally, you keep trying over and over to clear the bar and break the record. Then, when you finally do jump higher than you ever have before, what do they do? *They raise the bar.*"

Commitment Phobia. An indirect method of staying out of the spotlight and avoiding competition is to delay making commitments. If you don't commit, you can't move forward in any one direction, and you can't rush headlong into success. As Zach said, "Success is like an escalator. Once you get on, there's no place to get off except at the top." Procrastinators who worry about getting stuck on the escalator refuse to take that first step. Instead they may spread themselves over numerous interests and activities and end up busy yet frozen, unable to progress toward any one specific goal.

Procrastinators who fear failure have trouble making commitments because they worry that they will make a mistake and commit to the wrong thing. Those who fear success worry that making a commitment will sweep them into the competitive process and move them into the contest for success before they're ready. Procrastination is their way to step on the brakes.

I'll Turn into a Workaholic. Some procrastinators who fear success worry that if they stop fooling around and get down to work, they will work all the time and never be free to fool around again. Against their will, they'll somehow be transformed into workaholics who toil endlessly and whose lives are a succession of productive days and nights.

A freelance writer explained how procrastination saves her from this dismal fate: "If I start three weeks ahead of time, I'll be working solidly for three entire weeks. I might as well wait until I have only three days, so I only kill myself for three days. That way I can at least have a life for two and a half weeks." It's as if the work, of its own accord, takes over and turns her into an automaton, whether she likes it or not: "Once I get into working, there'll be no stopping me. I'll think of people as interferences who get in my way, and I won't want anything to do with them. Then they won't want anything to do with me."

What we find so intriguing about this perspective is the implication that success invariably leads to a loss of control and a loss of choice in one's life. Procrastinators often assume that, because their delaying seems to operate outside of their control, their working would become just as unmanageable. They fear that without compulsive procrastination, they would be doomed to compulsive work. The fear of morphing into a workaholic suggests that you worry success will create a sense of helplessness instead of a sense of power: you will no longer be yourself, you will turn into someone you don't like, and you won't be able to keep this alien "you" from taking over.

Success Is Dangerous: Somebody Always Gets Hurt

Many people who procrastinate to avoid success expect to be punished for their desire to win. You may fear you will be criticized, accused of being "selfish" or "full of yourself." Then there's the loser to contend with—someone might be hurt and withdraw from your relationship or may become angry enough to retaliate against you for winning. Whatever happens, someone ends up feeling bad—hurt, diminished, or left behind. Going after success feels like entering a dangerously aggressive world. These fears may be somewhat based on reality if you are in fact competing with someone who would be a sore loser, or they may be imaginative worries. Either way, these concerns feel real. Fear of causing harm and being harmed can be a powerful inhibitor to doing your best and may become an invitation to procrastinate, as you keep your competitive desires hidden from others, or more importantly, from yourself.

I Could Hurt Someone Else.   Have there been times when you have belittled or hidden something good that's happened to you because you didn't want to offend someone else? Maybe you kept the A you got for your last-minute paper a secret from your friends who got Bs and Cs, even after working hard. Or you didn't tell your father about your latest salary increase because you don't want him to know that you're already earning more than he does.

You may be concerned that your good news will be bad news to someone else. In some cases, of course, keeping your success to yourself is simply courteous: no one likes a braggart. But many procrastinators have taken more extreme measures than simply downplaying their success to protect someone's feelings. They have diminished themselves in order to prop up someone else. When you assume that being successful means that you are hurting someone else, success becomes equated with aggression. You may use procrastination to hold yourself back, so that you won't have to live with guilt.

Teresa went to work to augment the family income. Her husband, Tony, was a building contractor whose business had hit hard times. Teresa started making good money on commissions at her sales job. But instead of capitalizing on her success, she got so far behind on her paperwork that her job was threatened. "It would almost have been a relief to lose my job," she said. "I was afraid to tell Tony about my commissions because I didn't want to hurt his pride. It wasn't his fault that his business was bad and I was making more money."

Although we may worry that our success will hurt other people, they may actually be stronger and more generous than we give them credit for. It may be a distortion in our own thinking, a misreading of the reality around us, that sets us up to assume that our achievements will inevitably hurt someone else. Some people can enjoy the success of others without feeling deprived, diminished, wounded, or left behind. Maybe Tony would have been happy for Teresa if she had let herself do well.

Success can bring both joy and pain to those you love. For example, it may be difficult to let yourself be successful when you expect that your success will carry you away from your family and culture. College students whose parents have not gone to college face this difficult dilemma. They are aware of the sacrifices their parents have made to give them greater opportunities; they want to make their families proud and to be in a position to help the family. At the same time, they are entering a social and intellectual culture their parents have not experienced, and the more they succeed, the more the differences grow. "I love my family, but I feel I'm leaving them behind, and I know that hurts them," said Luis, a junior whose procrastination was affecting his grades. Luis's father worked two jobs and his mother cleaned houses and spoke little English. "It's awkward when I go home. They don't understand what I'm studying or what school is like. It feels like I'm gaining an education but losing my family." Procrastination can be an expression of anxiety and guilt about moving beyond a loving family.

I Could Get Hurt.   One danger many people foresee in achieving success is that they would get what they want—and then would be attacked. Someone, somewhere, will challenge or criticize them, and they don't feel strong enough to fight back. Andre's procrastination keeps him in a job far below his capabilities. When he was hired, Andre and his manager expected that he would rise through the ranks into middle management. Instead, Andre put in minimal effort and was never promoted. "There are a lot of aggressive people in this company. If I move up, I'd have to make decisions and people would fight me and criticize my ideas; I'd just as soon stay out of their way."

If Andre were content with his position, he would have no problem—he'd have found a comfortable niche for himself. Not everyone has to zoom up the ladder of success. But Andre wasn't satisfied. "I'd really like to have a chance to run things and I have some ideas for improvements. But management would see me as a troublemaker and they'd make my life difficult." Andre lives with a view that it's a dog-eat-dog world, and as the dogs get bigger, the bites get worse.

Since he expects to be attacked, he protects himself by delaying; he doesn't get promoted, and he never has to fight.

As children, many of us have learned that our successes can indeed trigger retaliation: if the drive to pursue our own goals threatened an angry parent or a competitive sibling; if our accomplishments were consistently mocked or ignored; if our success took us away from our family; if we feared being punished for having unacceptable thoughts or wishes. Recurrent experiences like these can create a worldview in which success seems a setup for retribution.

Success Is Off-Limits:
There's Something Wrong with Me

Sometimes people feel that there is something fundamentally wrong with them, a basic fault[5] that is so profound and deeply engrained that it precludes any real success or contentment in their lives. This idea of being basically flawed is a construction, an idea, not a fact, but we understand how compelling this feeling can be and how it can lead to pervasive procrastination.

I Don't Deserve Success. Procrastination can be used as punishment for "bad" things people have done—or think they've done. We've met procrastinators who feel guilty for unethical or hurtful things they have actually done, such as lying, cheating, manipulating, or defrauding someone. But many people feel guilty for actions that are really not very serious, or for situations that aren't truly their responsibility. In their guilt, however, they do not differentiate between real crimes and imagined ones.

One hard-core procrastinator felt guilty about the unhappiness he had inflicted on his family growing up. "I was a big bully," he said. "Especially after my parents divorced, I used to have blowups that made my mother cry and my little sister run and hide. I had fun tormenting my sister. I was mean, and it's unforgivable. So now it's my turn to be tormented."

Procrastination can be used as punishment for an imaginary "crime." Damien's wife died in a car accident. Although he was also injured in the crash, Damien survived and appeared to make a full recovery. However, after the accident, Damien stopped progressing in his job with the power company. Damien understood that his grief affected his work. In addition, he felt responsible for his wife's death, despite the fact that the crash had been caused by another driver.

Damien suffered from survivor guilt. As the one who lived, he felt he did not deserve to have a happy or fulfilling life. Three years later, he was still blaming himself and still stagnating. Although the stagnation of his life was unsatisfying, he didn't realize that procrastination was serving as the punishment for his "crime" of surviving.

Some people experience survival guilt for escaping a chronically bad situation if they leave others behind. They feel guilty because their lives are improving while others they care about continue to suffer. For example, many college students who have moved away from difficult family situations feel guilty for abandoning younger siblings who are still living at home, coping with parents who may be depressed, abusive, alcoholic, or negligent. These students find themselves procrastinating in school, unable to allow themselves academic success. They feel they don't deserve to be free while the rest of the family remains trapped.

Sometimes the people you can't allow yourself to abandon are work colleagues. In a negative work environment, people often band together to complain about how bad things are, to get support from each other that they can't get from their managers, and to validate their experience. They form tight bonds, like soldiers in foxholes. Some of them commit themselves to getting out, but some put off looking for a new job or work in a desultory way, eroding the confidence needed to land a better job—as well as their chances of receiving a decent recommendation. They can't bring themselves to get into a better situation because they feel guilty about leaving their friends behind.

Sadly, the guilt most procrastinators feel is far out of proportion to their "crimes." Often, there is not even any crime to speak of, other than wanting to extend oneself and have a life of one's own, and it is this wish that generates guilt. Asserting the right to your own life may bring you into conflict with your family system or with cultural values. In some cultures, having a life of one's own is less important than taking care of family members and putting the needs of the community first.[6] Whereas in the United States, the individual is the primary social unit, in many other cultures, the family is the central social unit, and the individual does not expect to pursue success if it comes at the expense of the family.

Lilly is from an Asian family that moved to California when she was five. Her parents owned a small grocery store, where she worked every afternoon during high school. Lilly won a scholarship to college, majored in economics, and planned to go to business school. In her junior year, her mother fell ill, and Lilly offered to move back home. Her mother encouraged her to stay in school, but her father expected Lilly to return home to care for her mother and help out in the market. Lilly agonized over what she should do. She wanted to fulfill her mother's dream of being well educated and successful, but she also wanted the approval of her father. Unable to make a decision, Lilly became distracted in school and put off doing her work. Her grades suffered to such an extent that she was in danger of losing her scholarship and being forced to leave school. Lilly's difficulty working reflected her conflict about whether to go on with her academic life or fulfill her obligation to her family. In effect, her procrastination was making the decision for her.

Success Just Isn't in the Cards for Me.   Some people have such a low opinion of themselves that they can't incorporate success into their self-image. Feeling inadequate, unprepared, or unappealing, they don't expect to succeed at anything, so they simply don't try in the first place.

Rachel, for example, is a shy person who remains in the background, both at work and in relationships. She wears clothes that hide her shape, and hers is the face that gets lost in the crowd. Although she fantasizes about having a satisfying job and a loving marriage, Rachel avoids opportunities for either. "Happy marriages and great jobs are for other people, not for me, so why should I even bother trying?" sighs Rachel.

When Rachel did manage, after many delays and incomplete attempts, to get a new job, she could not enjoy it. Since she believes success has no place in her life, she sees any accomplishment as a fluke, a random stroke of luck; success can vanish at any moment. Rather than dream of success and be disappointed, Rachel avoids both hope and disillusionment by assuming that success is not meant for her. It doesn't fit her self-concept.

There are two aspects to the self-concept: "me" and "not me." For Rachel, happiness was "not me." Rachel's low opinion of herself does not fully match the way other people see her; her friends can see her "potential," but Rachel is stuck with her own self-concept. She has identified herself as "a loser," and her procrastination keeps that identity intact.

In making herself almost invisible, Rachel communicates that she is barely there. In fact, she's not sure she has a right to exist at all. Rachel was the fourth daughter in her family, and immediately after her birth, her father had a vasectomy. He often said, "I had one girl too many." Rachel lives with a deep feeling of not being welcomed into life, just because of who she was, one girl too many. If you're not even supposed to exist, then you're certainly not supposed to thrive and succeed. Procrastination reflects Rachel's feeling that she has no place in the world.

What If I'm Too Perfect? At the other extreme from Rachel, there are people who worry that if they stop procrastinating and go full speed ahead toward success, it would come to them too easily. They would have "everything," but they would achieve it with so little effort that they would be the object of everyone's envy.

In contrast to the fear of failure, in which the procrastinator assumes, "I *should* be perfect, but I'm afraid I might not be good enough," in this particular form of fear of success, the procrastinator assumes, "I *am* perfect, but I shouldn't be. I have to hide it."

Kim, an attractive woman with a loving husband and two thriving children, expressed her dilemma in this way: "People seem to think I have everything—a great marriage and family, lots of friends, enough money, and time for volunteer work. I can tell that a lot of people envy me, and it's an ugly feeling. The one thing I don't have, though, is a college degree. I would like to go back to school and get a degree in art history. Then I would really feel as if I had it all. But then the envy would be even worse! It's safer to be lacking something."

Like Kim, people who worry that they are too perfect feel they need a tragic flaw, one that provides protection against envy and makes them feel they have problems just like everyone else. The fatal flaw reassures them that they are not really so different, and therefore they can be accepted and loved.

But why do they have to prove they're no different? After all, even though they may feel they *could be* perfect, nobody *is* perfect. Why is it so important for people to maintain this illusion about being perfect? The sense of superiority that goes along with feeling "too perfect" is a cover for a deeper sense of inferiority that quietly haunts people like Kim. Even though they may procrastinate to hold themselves back and be "like" everybody else, they nevertheless depend on feeling "special" just to feel adequate. They believe they would indeed be special if they stopped procrastinating. As long as they believe they are flawed *by their own choice*, they can maintain the belief that they still are perfect.

So, perhaps you have been using procrastination to avoid success because you harbor one or more of these fears. The theme common to all of them is the belief that you must choose between having success and having love. If you become an uncaring workaholic, who would be your friend? If you achieved an undeserved success, wouldn't you be shunned for being presumptuous? If you are too perfect, who would accept you as one of the gang? If you expect your success to create problems in your relationships, you may not want to risk alienating the people around you.

How did you come to conclude that your success would push people away? Perhaps your accomplishments had an unsettling impact on your family, or you assumed they did. For example, you may have sensed that when you accomplished something, a sibling felt jealous or left out; the family may have seemed out of balance; your parents may have even seemed threatened. Eventually, you may have concluded that everyone would be better off, and you would be most accepted, if you accomplished less rather than more. Whether this idea comes from your direct experience or lives in your mind without being tested, it can have the powerful effect of inhibiting your efforts to achieve success.

As you consider the relationship between your procrastination and your fear of success, try to stand back and take a more objective look at your situation. It may help to remind yourself that just because you fear something doesn't mean it's true now and forever. If you can challenge the assumption that at the first sign of success everyone will leave you, then you may be surprised to notice that there are some people who will not use your success against you. They will delight in your success and celebrate it with you. However, some people may resent your success—perhaps even some of the most important people in your life. If so, the question you must confront is: Can you make progress for yourself in spite of their resentment or their retreat from you? Are you strong enough to survive without their total support?

Remember that success does not come all at once. As you begin to resolve the anxieties that lead you to procrastinate, you will make progress toward your goals. As you move ahead, your conflicts about succeeding can kick up again. Improvements represent a threat to the ways we have been organized to defeat ourselves. Don't be surprised when you take two steps forward and one step back, or one step forward and two steps back! As you see that you can live with success— and without the disasters you've been anticipating—you will be more able to move ahead.

We understand that success might have its dangers for you. We know these dangers are powerful. It's natural to feel apprehensive when you're making a change in your life, even when the change is for the better. Achieving your idea of success—whether it be going back to school, exercising and losing weight, getting a new job, finding a good relationship or leaving a bad one—will inevitably involve facing change. Change may feel risky. When you make a change, you encounter the unknown in yourself, in your relationships, and in the world. But we think you may be in a better position than you realize to tolerate the risks. You *can* change and adapt to new circumstances, even to success.

4

The Procrastinator
in Combat
Fear of Losing the Battle

You're building up a new business and you need more clients, but when you get a message from someone you don't know asking you to call back at 1:00 P.M., you feel indignant. The caller isn't giving you much leeway. You delay returning the call, finally calling back at 3:00 P.M., even though you were free at 1:00 P.M.

Last month's utility bill arrives, and as always, it's higher than you'd like. You resent the rising costs of energy, and you think about recent media reports about the big profits being made by the utility company. Though your checking account balance is more than adequate to cover the payment, you hold on to your check for so long that you have to deliver it in person to prevent the company from shutting off your electricity. When you finally do it, you have a feeling of satisfaction for having made the company wait for its money.

Your wife asks you for the twentieth time to finish a chore you've been putting off. You promise you will do it, but you never actually get around to it. Eventually, she becomes frustrated and angry about the delay, which she feels is an act of hostility. You resent her nagging.

In situations like these, procrastination has little to do with preventing you from making your best effort. The reasons for your procrastination aren't tied to success or failure. Another, quite different fear is at work here.

THE BATTLE FOR CONTROL

While it is important for all of us to feel that we have some control over our lives, it is also important that we be able to follow rules that are not of our own making and accommodate the requirements of others. People who are particularly sensitive to feeling controlled, however, may rebel against every rule and resist every request; for some, procrastination becomes their way to feel they are in control.

As you consider your own procrastination, do any of the above scenarios sound familiar? Proud of your independence and determined not to compromise yourself, you want to prove that no one can force you to act against your will. Procrastination is a way to say, "No! You can't make me do this!" That caller was presumptuous for assuming you would obediently jump through his hoop, so you return the call on your terms. Utility companies may be very powerful, but they can't make you pay the bill on time. You'll do the chore when you're good and ready, not when your spouse tells you. Procrastination has become a strategy for fighting a battle—a battle for control, for power, for respect, for independence and autonomy.

Fighting a battle through procrastination might be such an automatic and reflexive way to defend yourself that you may not even be aware you're doing it. Since using procrastination to be in control may or may not be conscious, take some time to consider whether you procrastinate when you are expected to comply with "the rules." Do you toss parking tickets into the glove compartment? Do you ignore credit card due dates and then feel resentful when you are charged a late fee? We won't even bother asking about how seriously you take the April 15 tax "deadline," which all procrastinators know can be turned into an extension until October, but have you actually paid your taxes? If you're on probation at school or with your employer, have you shaped up, or are you still way behind?

We'd also like you to think about what impact your procrastination has on the people around you. Are there people who are inconvenienced by your delays? Do you ask others to make special arrangements for you because you're late? Is anyone thwarted by your procrastination, unable to carry out a plan because you didn't get your part finished on time? Does anyone have to do more work because you didn't do yours?

Consider, too, how people respond to your procrastinating. Do they become irritated by your lateness? Frustrated with your excuses? Angry because you didn't do what you promised? Do they give up trying to influence you and eventually let you do things your own way? Without realizing it, you may be using your procrastination to assert your independence. You may be more of a fighter than you think, and procrastination may be your way to battle for control.

Let's look at some of the themes that come up when people do battle-by-procrastination.

Rules Are Made to Be Broken. There are undoubtedly times when obeying rules is tedious for you, and you feel an urge to break free. For some people, this occurs only in a limited number of specific situations; others feel they are constantly subjected to rules against which they want to rebel. Whether you fight against rules occasionally or constantly, you probably feel restrained by directives that seem to be too confining for your sense of who you are.

A public relations specialist recalled his experience in high school and junior college. "When the class was given an assignment that was open-ended, like writing a short story about anything we wanted, I didn't have any trouble doing it. But when the teacher told us what to write about, I felt there was no room for me to express my own individuality or to be creative. I would end up asking for an extension, and then writing about something different from what was assigned anyway. Somehow, this helped me feel that I wasn't just a cow in a herd of cattle, even though I was usually graded down for not following directions."

Rules come in the form of restrictions or expectations imposed on us by external forces—the time we're supposed to be at work in the morning, the law that says we can't drive faster than the speed limit, the policy on returning merchandise. If you feel that following a rule somehow makes you unimportant or indistinguishable from others, then you may feel compelled to break it. As one procrastinator said, "The rules of mortal men do not apply to me."

Rules can also come from principles you have internalized from important people in your life. These "rules to live by" can remain in effect long after they were created and long beyond their usefulness, but they remain battlegrounds for procrastination. Adrienne describes her rebellious experience: "When I feel that I *should* sit down and write thank-you notes or clean up the kitchen, I instantly have this feeling of not wanting to do it. I don't want my whole life to be spent doing chores. My mother always made me write thank-you notes the minute I opened a present, and I had to spend hours cleaning the house every Saturday morning while my friends were out playing soccer. Those are two things I invariably put off, and when I do, I feel wonderful, like I've given myself room to breathe." Even though Adrienne now lives two thousand miles from her mother, the pressure of these rules is as strong as if she were still a teenager living at home. Procrastination increases her sense of freedom and reassures her that she is not a prisoner of these injunctions.

The rules you break may be your own. You might decide you want to follow a 1,200 calorie diet every day for two weeks, but you put off going to the grocery store to buy what you need. If you do get around to filling your kitchen with vegetables and low-fat mayonnaise, you don't get around to eating them. You might "sneak" a candy bar (as if you're not looking?), so that you don't feel so restricted. Even though the idea for the diet was originally your own, it feels like an external demand you have to fight in order to feel free. When a project you choose to accomplish for your own good reasons becomes disconnected from your internal desire, when a "want" is transformed into a "should," it seems to exist outside of you, and you forget that it was your idea in the first place!

Power to the Underdog. Battle-by-procrastination also occurs in situations where there is a formal hierarchy of power—and you aren't on top. The very fact that there is someone in a position of authority over you may leave you feeling small and helpless. This reaction is common in highly authoritarian corporate, academic, and family settings where, to enhance their own sense of power, subordinates delay responding to their superiors.

Perhaps you delay turning in reports or put off preparing presentations for your teacher or your boss, even though you may be on time doing things for friends. If, as you delay, you worry about whether your report or presentation will be good enough, or about how it will compare to others, your procrastination probably has more to do with fear of judgment than with fear of losing the battle. But if you find yourself thinking, "This is a ridiculous assignment. I shouldn't have to do this!" or, "Why should I do it *her* way?" then you are more likely battling for power. In situations like these, procrastination can act as an equalizer. Your superior seems less powerful, because she or he wasn't able to force you to be on time. You feel you have more control because you've done things on *your* terms—late.

Get Off My Back. There are times when a person feels restricted not so much by rules or someone else's power but by a sense of intrusion. Procrastination becomes a way to resist that intrusion. You might feel that someone has invaded your personal territory, like a woman who resented her neighbor's insistent request for a secret family recipe. "She had no business asking for it! She knows it's a secret." Rather than saying "No" to the request, the woman told the neighbor that she could have the recipe—and then kept "forgetting" to write it down. "Eventually, after I'd procrastinated for over three months, my neighbor gave up and stopped asking. I was so relieved to finally have her out of my hair!" A simple request can feel like an intrusion if you don't believe you can refuse it; procrastination may seem to be the only way you can say "No."

Sometimes people feel intruded upon by a task they see as an unnecessary imposition on their time and energy. Think of how you feel when, in early January, those inevitable tax forms arrive in the mail. Said one procrastinator: "As soon as those forms arrive, they seem to take up all the space in the house. So I put the forms in a drawer and forget about them. That way I can still enjoy the rest of my life—at least for a while."

Maybe even things *you* have asked for feel like intrusions. After putting it off for months, a young man finally created an online advertisement to sell his car. Receiving thirty responses on the first day the ad ran, he didn't answer even one. "It was just too much! All those people were after me, wanting something. I felt like telling them to go away and leave me alone. Of course, that was ridiculous because I'm the one who placed the ad. But when people responded, I felt as though I'd been invaded, so I just didn't answer."

Beat the Clock. In contrast to the safety procrastination can provide from intrusion, there are times when procrastination *increases* a person's enjoyment of danger and risk. People who love risk describe the thrill of being "on the brink." They feel elated when they take a situation to its limits and emerge victorious. They might get this thrill from driving race cars, playing the stock market, rock climbing, working for a start-up company, or engaging in high-risk behaviors such as gambling or dangerous sex. The excitement comes from flirting with danger and surviving by your own wits and skill. Your senses must be totally alert since you risk your job, your security, or your life at every turn.

Some procrastinators feel a similar sense of risk when they delay until the last possible moment. They take things so far that their lives and well-being are jeopardized. As one procrastinator described, "It's like walking along a very narrow cliff and trying to see how close you can get to the edge before falling off. You never know whether you're going to make it this time or not." How much lateness will your professors put up with before flunking you? How long can you delay work for a client before being dismissed from the job or sued? How much will your spouse tolerate before becoming infuriated with you and deciding to leave? Finally, when there seems to be no chance for escape, these procrastinators act. If they are lucky, they survive, elated and triumphant.

The Taste of Revenge. Procrastination can also sweeten the victory of revenge. If you feel hurt, angered, slighted, or betrayed by someone, you can use procrastination to retaliate. Perhaps a colleague said something critical about your work; perhaps your spouse doesn't pay as much attention to you as you would like; perhaps your manager changed the rules without warning. Procrastination can become your means of inflicting some pain or discomfort on those who hurt you.

For example, your manager needs your quarterly sales report so that he can prepare for his meeting with the company president. When you delay, your boss looks bad to his boss and, inwardly, you are delighted. Or, suppose you haven't studied very hard for a class because you felt the teacher wasn't putting enough time into planning the lectures. You miss the final but are able to convince your teacher to give you a make-up exam. She now has to create a new exam just for you and must schedule time to be with you while you take it.

The Ultimate Battle. The most profound of all battles-by-procrastination is the battle against reality. Some of us are simply unwilling to accept that what is, is. We can't stand limits; we can't stand that we can't control other people; we can't stand that we're not going to be rescued. Sometimes people invent how they think things *should* be and then live according to their vision, as if it were reality. Lindsay, a computer programmer, had trouble keeping jobs. She came late and left early. She asked a lot of questions of her coworkers and manager rather than take the time to figure out solutions for herself. When she started a temporary job, she assumed she would be kept on permanently without having to work hard to prove herself. Recently, Lindsay applied for a job that required knowledge of a computer language she didn't have, but she figured they would train her on the job. After all, it was obvious that she was smart and a quick learner, so she shouldn't have to bother spending her time and money to take courses to upgrade her skills. Lindsay spent money as if she already had her next job instead of accepting the limitations of living on unemployment checks. The word "budget" was not in her vocabulary, but "Can you lend me money until I get a job?" was. People were always telling Lindsay to "get real," and Lindsay's response was, "I hate reality." She clung to her version of how things should be and procrastinated on dealing with things as they were. Some people just cannot accept the facts of their situations, and their procrastination is a fight against a reality they don't like.

THE ISSUE OF AUTONOMY

As you can see, procrastination is often a declaration of one's independence, a way of saying, "I am a person in my own right. I can act in the way I choose for myself. I do not have to go along with your rules and your demands." People who use procrastination to resist control may be trying to preserve their sense of individuality and reassure themselves that they are living life on their own terms.

While some procrastinators measure their worth by their experience of success or failure, these procrastinators rely on feeling autonomous as the measure of their self-worth. The self-worth equation that we described in the chapter on fear of failure applies here, too, though with some modification. The procrastinator again defines self-worth in terms of performance, but in this case, it is by *not* performing, that is, by procrastinating, that self-worth is enhanced. *Not doing* is a demonstration of the procrastinator's ability, rather than a way to avoid testing it. The difference here is in the definition of "ability." For people who fear judgment, "ability" refers to how well they are able to do on a given task. For those who fear losing the battle, "ability" refers to how well they are able to resist control and defy any attempt to restrict their autonomy.

Self-worth = Ability (to be autonomous, defy control)
= Performance (on *my* terms, via procrastination)

When we understand that procrastination is a battle for more than just control, that it is a battle for self-worth and self-respect, we can understand why losing the battle evokes such intense and powerful fear—and why these procrastinators are so stubbornly resistant to change. If your sense of self-worth is based on your ability to defy influence by others, every encounter can take on exaggerated importance. A single, small defeat can leave you feeling as though you have compromised yourself, that your ability to be an autonomous individual is in doubt. Life may therefore have become a battleground on which you fight every rule, argue about anything, or ask for special consideration in large and small ways. In the back of your mind, you may be always assessing who is stronger, who is in control, who has the upper hand. You are ready, at the least provocation, to rebel against authority and assert your own influence in the situation.

Sam, an accountant and hardcore procrastinator, is a case in point. His major concern in life is making sure that he is not controlled by anyone. "I am my own man," he asserts. "I know I'm supposed to be at work at eight or have an audit report prepared for a client by a certain date. That's just it—I'm *supposed* to. I hate that word. If I go ahead and do it, I feel weak, so I don't do it or I do it late. That way, I can show them who's in charge—*me!*" Sam not only delays fulfilling work responsibilities, he also resists the smallest request or expectation from anyone. If Sam's wife, Eileen, asks him to do an errand on the way home, he invariably "forgets." Sam regards taxes, monthly bills, and late notices as nuisances. Saying that he won't let his life be governed by such trivialities, he pays his bills only when he feels so inclined—usually once every six months. Sam even fights when no one is involved but himself. He has run out of gas on the freeway because driving out of his way to look for gas while the indicator reads "empty" makes Sam feel as though he's giving in to the petty requirements of everyday life. So he doesn't do it.

Some procrastinators are so determined not to lose the battle that they are willing to pay a very high price to win. Sacrificing something of great personal significance may seem a necessary price to pay for a sense of personal power and the feeling of leading a life of one's own. Jessica has diabetes and is extremely overweight. The feeling that she *can't* have chocolate or that she *must* go for a walk is so noxious that she puts off exercise and weight loss even though she knows she's putting her health at risk.

Does all this sound far-fetched to you? Before you conclude that this talk of battle and extreme consequences is not relevant to your own situation, consider the story of another procrastinator. Courtney didn't realize she was caught in a struggle for independence that was diminishing her life.

Courtney is an intelligent thirty-four-year-old woman who presently works as a department store sales clerk. As a child, Courtney's life was managed by her mother, who also took credit for Courtney's good grades, bragging about her successes as if they were her own. Courtney's father, a prominent attorney, viewed her academic success as enabling her to attend law school and join his firm. When Courtney went away to college, she finally felt free. She did a lot of socializing and very little studying and ultimately flunked out of school. "I couldn't figure it out then. I actually enjoyed most of the classes, especially the sciences. I even thought about going to medical school to become a pediatrician. I know I had the ability to make it. But there seemed to be another part of me that wanted to destroy that possibility."

It wasn't until years later that Courtney realized her procrastination in school had something to do with her reaction to her parents' control over her. Growing up, she felt she had no life of her own, with her mother directing her activities and her father deciding what her future would be. "I refused to give them the satisfaction of making me into what they wanted. The sad part is that I really *wanted* to do well in school and to make something of my life. At the time I didn't think it was possible to do well and maintain my self-respect at the same time. If I had felt more secure about my independence, I wouldn't have had to work so hard to prove it. I wish I could have believed then that doing well in school didn't have to mean that my parents were controlling me."

By procrastinating, Courtney gave up the possibility of a professional career in order to prove that she could resist her parents' attempts to direct her life or take credit for her success. But Courtney's behavior was not truly independent because her choices were organized by her reactions to her parents: although she did not do what her parents wanted, she also did not do what *she* wanted. Years later, Courtney regretted the compelling forcefulness of her need to prove her autonomy. Courtney can now embark on a new path in her mid-thirties, but she has many regrets.

The Secret Battle

When a need for autonomy is the overriding theme in a person's life, the process of making decisions and committing oneself to a person or to a course of action can be very difficult. Committing yourself to a relationship, putting your thoughts into writing, or carrying out a business decision may mean that you are making your interests known, exposing your preferences for all the world to see. But once you've done that, you are no longer completely in the driver's seat. For procrastinators who fear losing the battle, exposing what they want, think, or feel leaves them feeling vulnerable to others. Their concern is not that, once exposed, they will be judged as lacking ability or as being too successful but rather that they will be disempowered, their weaknesses ruthlessly probed. Battling in secret seems a much safer course of action—or inaction.

Jeremy, who puts off everything from dating to deciding on a career path, described his experience this way: "I think of life as a poker game. I want to find out what cards the other person has before I make a play. Until I find out, I keep my cards close to my chest and try not to reveal a thing. So, I won't ask a woman out until she's let me know she's really interested in me. I refused to request a transfer at work because I didn't want people to know which department I was really interested in. I hold off making any decision because once I choose, I've given away my position, and someone could take advantage of that."

Procrastinating on decisions and commitments can be an indirect way of protecting yourself, since people can't get a clear idea of where you stand and so can't pin you down. As soon as you make a decision or commitment, however, you may begin to feel trapped or exposed.

Your sense of safety, which depends on being unknown and elusive, evaporates. Your only protection seems to reside in avoiding any commitment, big or small. That way, you can shift to something else at the slightest intimation that someone might try to control you. Escape is always at hand.

Procrastinators who avoid fighting out in the open don't want to let anyone know that they are vying for power because if they do, they risk exposing their weakness and vulnerability, thus increasing the risk of losing. And, when you fight secretly, your opponent doesn't *know* that a battle is on and so has less chance to mobilize his efforts against you. Your chances of winning improve.

Additionally, fighting secretly allows you to appear to be cooperating with others and thereby keep up a "nice guy" image. You can actually be extremely frustrating to others, but when you are indirect about it, they can't call you on it. Take Tom, for example: whether it be ordering the supplies needed at work or doing an errand for his girlfriend, Tom is consistently behind schedule. Because he's also very busy and overcommitted, he always has a convincing rationale for his lateness. His schedule was so incredibly tight that he just *couldn't* have done it any sooner. Tom is genuinely sorry for his delay, and he then is so generous in offering to make it up that most people swallow their irritation and try to be friendly in spite of the inconvenience they've suffered. In the end, Tom is doubly frustrating—he's constantly thwarting other people, and he won't admit to it.

If you fight indirectly, even if someone *does* confront you about your behavior by saying that you're making things difficult or that you're being hostile, you can deny it. After all, you haven't actually done anything overtly hostile or competitive: You were just late. And you can fall back on your old friend, procrastination, claiming that you're just so disorganized and unable to keep track of time that you couldn't do all that you intended. This way, not only can you hide your actual feelings, but you can also claim that your behavior is beyond your control. If you *could* be on time, you *would,* but procrastination always seems to get the better of you. It's not your fault! It's because of procrastination! You let people see your procrastination but you don't reveal that you're fighting.

The indirectness of procrastination can also protect you from admitting the power of your own anger. Expressing your anger indirectly may be a way for you to keep your emotions under control. Perhaps you've come to believe that all of your feelings should be kept under wraps. Any expression of irritation or anger might show that people can get to you, that someone can push your buttons. Your opponent would then know how to get to you the next time.

A Philosophy of Defense

Whether procrastination is used to fight minor skirmishes or to wage full-out war, people whose main concern is winning or losing the battle seem to make several basic assumptions about the world and their power to influence it.

The World Is an Unpredictable Place. For the embattled procrastinator, uncertainty lurks everywhere. Relationships with other people are not to be trusted. You never know whether someone will encourage and support you, or attempt to control and manipulate you. Rather than allow yourself to be lured into believing the best, you feel safer if you simply assume the worst. Since you can't predict whether you'll be helped or hurt, the world seems not only unpredictable but dangerous. No wonder you feel you must conceal weakness and never reveal your neediness or dependency.

If Someone Else Is Strong, Then I Must Be Weak. The person who fights by procrastinating often feels powerless in relation to someone who is strong. The other person may have a lot of actual power, like your manager or professor. Or the other person may have a lot of personal power, such as your assertive spouse or your opinionated friend. But if you interpret someone else's strength as automatically meaning that you are weak, you are exaggerating the other's power in your own mind. You see the other person as having control over your life, telling you what to do and when to do it. Decisions seem to be made without your input; rules are laid down arbitrarily, and your opinions don't seem to count much one way or another. Your opponent seems too big, too strong, and too powerful to yield to someone as weak and small as you. Feeling unable to engage as an equal, you resort to balancing the power through procrastination. The other person controls you only to the extent that you actively perform your duties and tasks. If you stop doing them, you take back some of the power. Because of this change in the balance of power, you can feel assured that you won't be obliterated by the other. You can stand your ground.

Cooperation Is the Same As Capitulation.   For some of you, the mere *idea* of cooperating evokes a feeling that you are surrendering yourself and a fear that you might be giving up your power. Going along with someone else's rules or agreeing to do something someone asks of you makes you feel that you are capitulating. The idea of choosing to comply because you want to, or because it's necessary in order to obtain a goal that you seek, may not occur to you. Instead, cooperation makes you feel as though you have been forced to compromise yourself against your will.

Thwarting My Opponent Is More Important Than Getting What I Want.   Thwarting your opponent can become such a primary concern that it outweighs all other considerations, including getting what you want for yourself. (Remember Courtney and her parents.) It's as if you're saying, "If you want me to do it, I won't do it, even if I might actually want to do it." You get more satisfaction from frustrating or defying someone else than from accomplishing what is important for your own life. Some procrastinators, in fact, are so focused on defeating the other person that they don't even *know* what they want. They only know that they don't want what other people want for them! The irony in all of this is, of course, that if you are procrastinating to say, "Screw you!" to someone, the person who is really getting screwed is you.

The Roots of the Struggle

You may remember things about your upbringing that help you understand how you have come to view the world as a battleground in the first place, regarding people as opponents who have the potential to control or disempower you. Many procrastinators who are sensitive to feeling controlled grew up in situations that did not encourage mastery and control over their own lives. Children may experience strict discipline, overcontrol of their toilet training, intense interest that feels intrusive, constant criticism that undermines confidence, limits on spontaneity and creativity—all of which inhibit their moves toward independence. Many of these battles are far beyond memory because they began in the earliest years of life when there may have been struggles around feeding, sleeping, and independent exploration.

It is always a challenge for a parent to balance a child's natural drive for independence with the parent's need for the child's cooperation, in order to support both the child's developing self-expression as well as the child's need for guidance and limits. Some parents have difficulty enjoying their child's excited moves toward self-determination, especially if the parent experiences separation anxiety or needs to feel in control at all times.

An overly controlled child lives through thousands of small encounters with parents in which the child's autonomy is discouraged or even ridiculed. Each single encounter may seem unremarkable, but when these moments occur repeatedly over many years, they have a tremendous impact. A child who doesn't have confidence in his autonomy cannot develop a secure self. The child begins to feel that there is something wrong with wanting to be independent. He comes to expect that his attempts to be autonomous will be met not with encouragement and support but with restrictiveness. For such a child, one way to survive is to do battle and to use procrastination for protection.

Once you recognize that procrastination is linked to your sensitivity to being controlled, you can use your resistance as a warning signal. When you feel the urge to resist, you can ask yourself, "What am I reacting to?" There will be times when your resistance is well founded:

someone is, in fact, trying to control you, restrict your individual effort, or take advantage of you. There will be other times when your alarm sounds in reaction to your own apprehension instead of to the realities of the situation. A request is not necessarily a bid for control; a rule does not have to be a prison from which there is no escape. And it's even possible that cooperating can be fun!

If you are compelled to fight every battle that comes along, you are not truly free or powerful. To be truly free, you must be able to choose which battles to fight and which to cede. Herein lies authentic power and the sense of being your own person.

5

The Comfort Zone
Fear of Separation and Fear of Intimacy

Procrastination can do more than protect a person from judgment or provide a covert way to engage in battle. Delay and postponement can also regulate the degree of closeness a person maintains with other people, preserving whatever interpersonal distance seems safest and most comfortable.

How deeply involved with others should we be? We all have to make choices about how many relationships to maintain, the degree of our commitment to each, how much time we spend with others, and how much time we need to be alone. Just as some people's lives are dominated by their need for approval or the desire to be independent, others' are dominated by their need to find a "comfort zone" for closeness. Moving out of that comfort zone—being too close or too far away—can be so uncomfortable that people go to great lengths to stay within it. Procrastination is a device they use to regain their relationship equilibrium.

FEAR OF SEPARATION:
I'LL NEVER WALK ALONE

When we talk about feeling more secure by being connected to someone else, we usually mean the preference most people share for having close relationships, seeking companionship, support, and love from others. Here, however, we focus on a need that springs from anxiety, a fear that you're not safe and can't survive on your own. It's not only that you want someone else around but that you don't feel complete unless you're part of someone else and they're part of you. When people feel they can't manage on their own, it can be very difficult to engage in activities that lead to independent functioning. Let's look at some ways people rely on procrastination when they're not sure how solidly they can stand on their own two feet.

Help Wanted.   When people feel unsure of the validity of their ideas, or feel unable to generate ideas of their own, they depend on the ideas of others. We're not referring to brainstorming with someone or getting feedback, but rather relying on another person to provide a viewpoint or a structure that can be adopted as one's own.

Many college students, for instance, devote weeks to gathering research for a term paper but never actually write it because they are afraid to offer a perspective of their own. They know how to consult outside resources, but when they try to look inside themselves, they come up empty-handed. Some college students received a lot of help during high school from their parents, who structured their time and oversaw their work. Gi was from a well-educated Korean family who placed tremendous importance on getting a good education. When Gi was in high school, her parents insisted on designated study hours, discouraged her from extracurricular activities, and monitored her social life. When Gi got to college, where she had to figure everything out for herself, she didn't feel prepared to function independently; yet asking for outside help felt shameful. Her confusion and isolation led to procrastination and poor grades, the opposite of what she'd hoped for.

People may feel they need the presence of another person to get going. They are afraid that without a partnership, they can't activate themselves. Cynthia explained how this dependency affected her: "In a group, I'm full of ideas, I have a lot of motivation, and I get things done. But when I'm alone at my desk, I feel as if my brain has died.

My mind is blank, and I start surfing the Internet. I need someone to provide the spark that gets me thinking, because if I'm left on my own, I have no thoughts."

Trying Harder to Be Number Two.   Some people feel comfortable in a secondary position under someone else's wing. They are looking for a guide, a mentor, a cheerleader, someone to make them feel safe. They avoid doing things that would propel them into the number one position, where they fear feeling too separate and alone.

For example, many graduate students postpone taking their oral exams or have difficulty finishing their dissertations because they don't want to give up the protection of the university or leave their faculty advisors. They don't feel confident that they can manage successfully in the "real" world, and graduate school feels like their final opportunity for guidance and tutelage.

People may also procrastinate when they don't want to leave the boss who first mentored them in the workplace, or the person with whom they first had a serious relationship because they don't feel confident that they can survive independently. This is particularly lamentable when a relationship actually offers little in the way of protection, support, guidance, or nurturance. Although they may actually be diminishing their lives by remaining in the relationship, it seems preferable to be with *someone* than to be alone in the world. Fear of separation prevents them from making a break that might ultimately be in their own best interests.

S.O.S.   Some people use procrastination to dig themselves into a deep hole in the hope that someone else will come along and dig them out. They create a procrastination emergency as a way to ask for help. The ultimate rescue for a procrastinator is to have someone else do your work for you. How many times have you hoped that if you just wait long enough, or if you're in deep enough trouble, someone would magically appear to do the horrid thing for you? Sometimes it happens! A high school senior waited so long to write his senior thesis that his graduation was threatened. At the eleventh hour, his father finally wrote most of the paper for him. The son interpreted this bailout as a sign of his busy father's love, and when he got to college, the son continued to e-mail assignments to his dad for help. It was their special connection, but it also reinforced the son's fear that he wasn't able to think on his own.

A divorced woman we know procrastinates on all financial matters, from paying bills to saving money to preparing her taxes. She finally realized that she'd always expected the man in her life to handle the finances. Doing it for herself meant that she was really on her own and no one was taking care of her, and this triggered her fear that maybe no one would ever take care of her again. If she didn't do the financial work, surely someone somewhere would appear, calculator in hand, to rescue her from having to manage on her own.

Occasionally, you may succeed in relinquishing responsibility for yourself and find someone who will rescue you, but there is often a high price to pay. Although you might enjoy the gratification of being helped or rescued, you never learn what you can do for yourself.

Keeping the Past Alive.   However procrastination functions for you, to the extent that it keeps you in familiar patterns and reenacts your usual relations with other people, it mitigates the feeling of being separate. This procrastinating pattern keeps the past alive in the present.

Dan, an appliance repairman, frequently gets into tangles with his supervisor, Marty. Marty complains that Dan doesn't arrive at appointments on time, he doesn't submit requisitions for replacement parts until he's run out of his supply, and he turns in his weekly time sheets late, disrupting the accounting and payroll departments. Although Marty is unaware that he is being cast in a familiar role, Dan is very much at home when someone puts him in the doghouse. His mother used to get after him constantly for things like coming home late to dinner and keeping the whole family waiting, or leaving his laundry unwashed until he discovered that he hadn't a single pair of clean underwear left. When Dan hears his supervisor roar, "This whole business doesn't revolve around you, you know!" it plays a familiar tune for Dan, whose mother used to say, "You're not the only one in this family!" As long as people currently in your life seem to echo people from your past, you don't really ever separate from those early relationships.

A Constant Companion.   When you're in the throes of delaying, facing unfinished projects, unresolved decisions, or unpaid bills, you probably carry the burden of procrastination with you wherever you go. If you do have some emancipated moments, the memory of your obligations can return to spoil your freedom in an instant.

While procrastination can be a constant burden, it can also be a constant companion in your life, reminding you of all you have to do. In this way, it may keep you from feeling lonely or abandoned, since you are always accompanied by mental lists of projects that you neither complete nor let go. Even though you may feel plagued by all you carry, when you procrastinate, you never have to say "good-bye" to anything.

Of course, there are better companions than your endless list of obligations. Get a dog. Make a friend. Keep a journal. Procrastination is a lousy companion: faithful, but as you know, quite a troublemaker.

FEAR OF INTIMACY: TOO CLOSE FOR COMFORT

People who fear separation derive great security from being close, close, close. In contrast, people who fear intimacy are more comfortable keeping their distance. They are alert to the possibility that someone might be moving in on them, crowding them, tugging at them, making demands of them. They rely on their radar system, constantly scanning their surroundings for signals of encroachment. Anxiety is activated as soon as someone appears on the edge of the radar screen, and they rapidly mobilize to retreat. Procrastination can be their means of escape.

Give 'Em an Inch, They'll Take a Mile.   Some people believe that relationships will drain them. They fear that others will never be satisfied and will demand more and more, until they are eventually depleted.

Wally was an auto mechanic who realized he was in the wrong job, but he put off looking for a new one. "If you're in a job where you work with a lot of people, they start to expect things from you. They want to get to know you, find out about your life, go out after work. If I worked in a place like that, I'd be aggravated all the time. The guys here know to leave me alone, and that's how I like it."

Of course, there were times when Wally was lonely and wished he were in a job he really liked; but the thought of having to "train" new people to keep their distance was so unappealing that Wally stayed in his familiar, if lonely, territory. He had the same reaction when he thought about inviting someone to his house. "If I invite somebody over for a beer," said Wally, "he'll stay too late. I'd never get him to leave." Since Wally feels unable to state his limits, he becomes resentful when the other person inadvertently oversteps his unspoken boundaries.

What's Mine Is Yours—So What's Left for Me?   If you stopped procrastinating and actually finished something, you'd then have the pleasure of taking the credit for your accomplishment, right? Well, not necessarily. Some procrastinators expect that, at the culmination of all their hard work and effort, someone else will take the credit. We all know people like that. At a party, you may hear someone else telling *your* joke as if it's an original. You may work for a boss who gets ideas from his employees but submits them to his manager as if they were his own. For some people, being robbed of their deserved credit is so painful and upsetting, they would rather procrastinate than give someone else the opportunity to steal what rightfully belongs to them. Because their sense of self is so intimately tied to their accomplishments, being robbed of the credit feels like being robbed of their identity.

Procrastination can be used as a protection from having your interest appropriated by someone else. Anna had been unable to choose a career and described how she had become hesitant to reveal, even to herself, what she was really interested in. She remembered that she had once announced to her family that she wanted to take piano lessons. Suddenly, she found herself enrolled not only in piano lessons but also in sight-reading and music composition classes. She was flooded with books on music, classical CDs, and posters of famous pianists. "All I wanted was to learn to play the piano like my friends, and the next thing I knew I was caught up in a whirlwind of music that had nothing to do with me. Somehow the idea had captured my mother's imagination, and she jumped in and took over. That taught me a lesson: when I want something, I have to keep it to myself."

Like Anna, some procrastinators unfortunately end up being so protective of their interests and accomplishments that they lose sight of what they actually want for themselves. If you are afraid that your interests, once made known to a predatory world, will be appropriated, you may go through life shut off from your true desires.

The Second Time Around.　Some people postpone getting involved in relationships because they have decided that they will not risk repeating bad experiences from the past. If you once had to stand by helplessly as your parents criticized, abandoned, ignored, or otherwise hurt each other, you may have concluded that settling down with someone is just asking for trouble. Maybe you have had your own painful relationships that left you scarred. So, you delay asking for dates, put off improving your appearance, avoid meeting new people, and shun activities that might lead to intimate involvements. Procrastination feels like an ally that protects you from getting hurt again.

The Werewolf Within.　There are those who worry about the kind of person they will turn into under the pressure of an intimate relationship. They worry that behind a Dr. Jekyll persona, there lurks a Mr. Hyde. You might reveal a dark side of your nature that most people don't get close enough to observe. Perhaps, in an intimate relationship, you would be as demanding and judgmental of others as you are of yourself. You may worry that closeness could unleash a destructiveness, a "monster" that you otherwise keep under wraps. It may be hard to imagine that someone could accept your ugliest moments. Could anyone know what you're really like on a long-term, day-by-day basis and still want to be around you? As long as you avoid getting involved in intimate relationships, you never have to find out.

It's Better Not to Love Than Lose.   People who avoid intimate relationships may not let themselves know just how much they long for closeness. If they let themselves develop a close relationship, they might discover how emotionally needy they really are. They might open up their own Pandora's box, and in it they would find a deep and powerful longing for emotional intimacy that would be overwhelming and insatiable.

Deep down, they are hoping for the perfect relationship with a mate who will unconditionally accept every facet of their behavior. Yet they suspect the truth, that complete and total acceptance is impossible in any human relationship. So, rather than face the reality of imperfect relationships, they avoid them altogether. It may seem best to keep the box closed right from the start, and procrastination is their strategy for doing that.

———————

Whether your anxiety stems from a fear of separation or fear of intimacy, procrastination may be your way of maintaining the boundaries of your comfort zone. But relying on postponement and delay for your comfort does not address the more fundamental issue of how you approach relationships. All relationships involve issues of boundaries and intimacy that have to be worked out. You can approach these issues as opportunities for growth. Resolving differences can be a way to learn and stretch yourself, both as an individual and as a partner in a relationship. Procrastination may keep other people at the comfortable distance you feel you need, but it prevents you from growing as a person.

You may find that it is possible to be both dependent and independent in a relationship—in fact, it is *important* to be both. What makes a good relationship reassuring is that it provides a reliable, safe place to obtain comfort. What makes it fulfilling is that it permits, indeed encourages, each person to develop and grow as a separate individual. A good relationship needs a balance.

6

Do You Know
What Time (It) Is?

"What time is it?"
        "The deadline is today?!"
    "I'm only fifteen minutes late; why are you so upset?"
    "I'm not wasting my life—my real life hasn't started yet."

Sound familiar? The fears we have described are interwoven with the procrastinator's relationship with time. Many procrastinators live within their own versions of the passage of time, and often, the procrastinator's ideas about time do not match "clock time." In Chapter 13, we'll talk about some things you can do to improve your relationship with clock time. Here we want to look at the psychological and emotional experience of time, so you can better understand your own personal relationship with time and how that might play a role in your procrastination.

On the surface, time seems to be something we can all agree on. In the present, it's three o'clock; five minutes ago, it was 2:55; and five minutes from now, it will be 3:05. Sound obvious? Guess again.

OBJECTIVE TIME
AND SUBJECTIVE TIME[1]

Philosophers and scientists have never been able to agree about the nature of time. Aristotle took a tree-falling-in-the-forest approach and wondered, would time exist if there were no one there to measure it? Newton believed that time was absolute and that it occurred whether anyone was around to notice it or not. Kant pointed out that, although we can't perceive time directly, we do have an experience of time. Then came Einstein, for whom past, present, and future were all illusions. Most procrastinators would love for time to be an illusion, because time is what brings deadlines closer. However, illusion or not, whether we like it or not, time passes.

The ancient Greeks referred to two aspects of time—*chronos*, or clock time, and *kairos*, a "time in between," a moment outside of *chronos* time that is significant and meaningful. A similar distinction is made today. "Objective time" is measured by clock and calendar, inexorable and predictable: we all know that April 15 comes around every year; the movie starts at 7:15 and if you're not there, you miss the beginning. And each birthday marks the passing of a calendar year that takes us farther from the beginning of life and brings us closer to the end of life.

In contrast, we each have our own unique sense of time passing, which is not quantifiable or communally shared. This is "subjective time," our experience of time outside of clock time. Sometimes we experience time passing swiftly; at other times it crawls ever so slowly. When you are engaged in your favorite activity, whether it be surfing the Internet, fixing your car, or luxuriating in bed before you get up, time passes so quickly that you can't believe it. But when you are anxiously waiting for a return phone call or working on an assignment you don't enjoy, the minutes feel like hours.

Having a uniquely subjective sense of time can help you feel like a one-of-a-kind individual, honoring your internal clock and your body's unique biorhythms, supporting the feeling of being a singular self among the masses. Subjective time might help you disengage from the linear view of hours and years to follow the rhythms of the natural world of seasons and cycles.[2] Instead of feeling constricted by the constraints of clock time, you can breathe more freely in the elasticity of subjective time.

A variation of subjective time, "event time,"[3] refers to orienting your sense of time around the occurrence of an event. Sometimes, these events occur in nature, such as seasons, tides, floods, or storms (for example, before the hurricane versus after the hurricane). You are using event time when you think, "I'll go to the meeting after I finish this memo"; "I'll leave for the airport as soon as I've straightened the house"; "I'll start studying after dinner."

The challenge for all of us is to integrate our own personal subjective time and our focus on event time with the inexorability of clock time. If we are lucky, we can move among them with relative seamlessness. We can be engrossed in an activity, realize that it's time to leave, and then mobilize ourselves to be on time for an appointment without feeling that we have compromised our integrity. Or we can track the approach of a long-term deadline, and even though it's so far off in time that it doesn't quite feel real, we start on the project anyway.

Many procrastinators live with a profound conflict between subjective time and objective time, unwilling or unable to recognize that their version of time can be very different from clock time. Instead of moving easily and fluidly between subjective and objective time, they struggle. Some reject clock time as irrelevant, as though it were meant for lesser mortals. Some live in an eternal state of time confusion, going along as if they understand clock time and then suddenly feeling walloped by the shock of running out of time, only to repeat this experience again next time. Your subjective sense of time seems so much an integral part of who you are that it may be difficult to accept that it is a personal perspective rooted in your cultural or familial environment, your biological inheritance, and your personal psychology.

Yet personal it is. In fact, your subjective sense of time may be confusing or aggravating to others, who have their own unique, and possibly very different, sense of time. A wife might ask her husband, "Why are you always on time for the softball game but late to the opera?" The husband might respond, "You get to the opera twenty minutes ahead of the curtain and think I'm late when I sit down in time for the overture!" A procrastinator rushing to the post office on the night of April 15 was asked why he was late mailing his taxes; he asserted, "It's five minutes to midnight—I'm not late!"

When two people relate differently to time—and to being "on time"—making plans can be maddening. "When I agree to leave the house at nine, I mean 'nine-ish' (which might mean "by nine-thirty or so"), and after all these years, my wife should understand that," said an architect whose wife fumes at 9:05 when she has been ready and impatiently watching the clock since 8:45. Lenora grew up in Hawaii, where everyone jokes about being on "Hawaiian time," but even there, people tacitly agree that, although being late is often expected, there are some times when it's important to be prompt. Clearly, "on-time" and "late" are open to interpretation.

It is a losing battle to try to get someone else to adopt your subjective sense of time, because everyone's relationship to clock time is idiosyncratic. You might aim instead for a mutual understanding of your subjective differences and the possibility of arriving at compromises.

We are all different in our subjective sense of time because many factors affect it. The biology of our brains influences how we perceive and process the passage of time. Scientists have discovered "clock genes"[4] that operate on a cellular level throughout the body, regulating daily activities like sleeping and waking. The brain has many different clock genes, as well as a master clock that coordinates them.[5] Clock genes lead some people to be effective morning people and others to be active night owls. Generally, our brains are pretty good at estimating the passage of time, but time perception can be distorted by changes in attention, emotional states, expectations, and context.[6] People with ADD are not very good at estimating time intervals.[7] For them, time seems to pass more slowly, so they continually underestimate time intervals, hence their frequent lateness, characteristic impatience, and wish to move fast and faster.

Social psychologist Philip Zimbardo's extensive research on time perception has shown that people have different orientations to time that are based on past, present, or future.[8] If you are locked into one primary time perspective, your view of life is biased and limited. Those who can maintain a balance among these three perspectives are likely to function better and enjoy life more fully.

An example of an unbalanced perspective is de-emphasizing the future, which can create a problem for the present. Behavioral economists as well as social psychologists have observed that when an event or goal is far off in the future (such as funding your kids' college education or creating an adequate retirement account for yourself), it seems almost unreal, and therefore it feels less important than it might actually be. By contrast, goals that are close in time (such as getting a big-screen TV for the weekend playoffs or doing your taxes on April 14) are experienced as more vivid or "salient."[9] So, even if the present goal (getting the TV) is less important than the long-term goal (saving for college or retirement), people are more likely to do what's immediate rather than what's important for the future. This is called "future discounting,"[10] and it is a part of the human experience that makes procrastination so compelling.

The cultural differences in the way people experience and value time can lead to confusion and misunderstanding when it comes to time management and time agreements between people. Some studies suggest that Americans focus on the now, on youth, on doing the most in the least amount of time, and on being prompt. Asian cultures, by contrast, have a much broader time perspective that takes into account history and tradition as well as long-term future planning. In some European countries like France, Spain, and Italy, being "late" is more acceptable and not typically experienced as an offense, the way it is in the United States.[11] In Middle Eastern, African, and Hispanic cultures, people tend to experience time as flexible, fluctuating, and spontaneous. They expect to be involved in multiple activities and transactions at the same time and don't feel a need to keep precise time commitments.[12]

No matter what our culturally influenced experience of time is, we all have to grapple with the interweaving of our private experience of time and the public time that connects us to the rest of the world.

Refusing to accept clock time and insisting on following only your subjective sense of time separates you from everyone else and can lead you to procrastinate or to be late. One function of procrastinating— doing things in your own way on your own schedule, feeling in charge of your own time no matter the consequences—is to create an illusion of omnipotence over time,[13] over others, and over reality. But like it or not, you, too, are subject to the rules of time, to loss and limitations, to transience and mortality.

The fantasy of omnipotence (and it *is* a fantasy) is something that we all hold as very young children and that we all have to deal with in later developmental stages, as we are confronted with evidence of our limited power. If life is kind to us, we are helped gradually and gently to acknowledge and accept our limitations, understanding that our humanity does not diminish our value or make us less lovable.

THE EVOLUTION OF A TIME SENSE

The subjective sense of time develops and changes as we go through life.[14] Let's look at these developments and consider how they might relate to your procrastination. Your relationship to time in the present may be characterized by time perception that was developed at an earlier stage of life.

Infant Time

For infants, life is lived totally in the present moment, and time is purely subjective. It doesn't matter if the clock says 2:00 A.M., "I'm hungry NOW!" To an infant, "time" means the interval between feeling a need and having that need satisfied. Infants can't bear pain for very long, and if satisfaction doesn't come soon enough, they become desperate: survival is at stake.

When fear and anxiety are inevitably encountered in later life, a person responding in infant time will experience these feelings as intolerable and unending, instead of as normal feelings that come and go. Procrastination helps people escape from unbearable discomfort and emotional pain in the moment, such as the humiliation of not being good at something and feeling stupid, the crushing disappointment of a poor first attempt, the empty isolation of working alone at the computer. Instead of sticking it out, you find ways to exercise a level of control that was not available to a dependent infant. Off to the movies! Computer solitaire! Raid the refrigerator! Text message a friend! Plug into your music! Even though procrastination may lead to painful consequences in the future, at these moments, thinking about consequences is about as irrelevant as tomorrow's breakfast is to a hungry baby tonight.

Toddler Time

Children gradually learn the meaning of past, present, and future. Although they're hungry *now*, they will have something good to eat *in a few minutes*. Though toddlers live primarily in subjective time, they begin to bump up against parent time. Parents might insist on immediate cooperation—"Stop that right now and come here this minute!" or they may gently ease the child out of his timeless state with reminders that playtime will end soon. Parents want toddlers to do things all the time, often on parent time; toddlers quickly learn they can wield great power by refusing to cooperate.

The child may view the clock as an enemy trying to control him or as an ally providing reliability and structure. Since the parents' messages about time are embedded within the whole parent-child relationship, it's not really *time* that creates those attitudes; it's the quality of the *relationship* that does so.[15] Later, when procrastination feels like a battle against being controlled by time, it may actually reflect an ongoing struggle against feeling controlled by others. Fighting against objective time may represent an ongoing resistance to parent time.

Child Time

At about age seven, children learn how to "tell time," recognizing that the relationship between the numbers on a clock reflect intervals of time passing. They are also confronted with more rules and expectations from the outside world. Teachers have schedules, schoolwork has deadlines, and parents expect kids to clean their rooms and help with chores before playing with friends. For children who are already sensitive to issues of power and control, time can be an oppressor (when you have to act according to somebody else's schedule) or a liberator (you act on your own schedule). Some children, particularly those with ADD or related issues, do not have a good biological sense of time and have difficulty shifting back and forth between subjective time and objective time as the conditions of life demand. In later life, they may find that their experience of time is not smooth or fluid, and procrastination reflects this disjointed experience of time.

Teen Time

The onset of puberty marks a dramatic shift in one's sense of time. There is undeniable evidence that time is passing, because the adolescent's body is demonstrably different from the child's body, and there's no going back. These adolescent changes push away the childhood past; bodily sensations and passionate ideals reflect the present; and the yet-to-be-lived future offers the grandiose sense that life is limitless. As choices about schooling, work, and relationships become imminent, however, the future comes crashing into the present with deadlines for applications and demands for decisions.

People who are conflicted about this transition out of adolescence into adulthood may reject the dawning awareness that some roads will never be taken and may enlist procrastination in their refusal to grow up. Tenaciously holding onto the adolescent's sense of endless time and limitless possibility, they put off achievements that would move them along the path toward adulthood—finishing school, getting a job and earning their own way, establishing an independent life. In a sense, they are attempting to deny the passage of time, struggling to remain an eternal child.

Young Adult Time

By your mid-to-late twenties, time is more tempered by reality, though it continues to stretch far into the future and feels like an abundant resource. Procrastinators often begin to examine their relationship with time more closely in this phase, as they consider the possibility that there is not enough time for everything, and some opportunities are slipping by. Procrastination is no longer a joke or something you can always make up for later. It begins to have more serious consequences: work deadlines have implications for career and income, and when you establish long-term relationships, procrastination impacts others as well.

When you are single, you're the only one paying a price for your delay. Once you become part of a couple, someone else is directly affected by your delaying, and it can become a contentious issue in the relationship. If you become a parent, you are catapulted from being a member of the younger generation into being a member of the older generation on the day a child enters your life. From then on, "future" is defined in terms of the next generation. And from then on, your procrastination impacts the whole family.

Midlife Time

Thirty is a great divide. After thirty, you're no longer a young person with lots of future potential; you are expected to live up to your potential! The thirties initiate midlife, when delays in career achievements and intimate relationships may become painful signals of being off-track. Since procrastinators have difficulty accepting limitations, they can be shocked in midlife to discover that they may not achieve some of the goals they always thought they would get around to "someday." Some procrastinators struggle with depression in middle age, as it becomes clear, for example, that they will not have children, discover a cure for cancer, create a billion-dollar start-up company, or win a Pulitzer Prize.

Sometime in midlife, if it hasn't sunk in before, we confront the fact that we all are destined to die. On a rational level, we all know that life ends, but at the same time, procrastinators live with the fantasy of the infinite—infinite time, infinite possibilities, infinite achievements, always more time to make up for all that has been put off. Coming to terms with the finiteness of time is a central psychological task of middle age: What have I done with my time so far? How much time do I have left? How do I want to spend that time? It can be difficult to look back and accept what you have chosen to do (or not) with your life and to look forward at the limitations as well as the possibilities for what lies ahead. No wonder people have midlife crises.

Senior Time

As we get older, it becomes even less possible to deny that time is running out. From late adulthood to old age, we are more and more surrounded by the realities of loss and death: physical capacities are lost; diseases develop; loved ones pass away; there is less and less time left to live. The future no longer holds the promise it did in earlier life stages. Clock time may no longer be very important, and subjective time matters much more.

For procrastinators who struggle against the finite, accepting the inevitable end of life can be a significant psychological challenge. At this point, the consequences of lifelong procrastination are undeniable. The money you never got around to saving isn't there. The house remodel never happened. There will be no graduate school education. There is no more "tomorrow" or "someday." Maybe it is possible to accept what you did and what you will never do. Looking back, you had your issues and anxieties; circumstances were what they were; you did what you could with what you had. Acceptance of the past might bring peace instead of despair or self-criticism. It might even be liberating to feel freed from having to chase the unattainable—finally. We certainly hope so.

STUCK IN ANOTHER TIME ZONE

Procrastinators, with their unique relationships to time, may have time perceptions that don't match their current stage of life. For example, many adults who procrastinate still relate to time as they did when they were adolescents, who typically feel invulnerable and indifferent to the passage of time. As adults, they run into trouble because they are stuck in their teenage time perspective, which is out of sync with the adult world of work, family, health, and financial responsibilities.

Some people don't allow themselves to think about the future. Did you expect to live to be the age you are now? If you never thought you would survive, or if you never thought you would age, then you may not have planned for the future or made decisions and choices that would provide opportunities and security. Many procrastinators ignore the possible future repercussions of their delaying in the present, but at some point, the unproductive present becomes the past, and the unexpected future becomes the present.

Almost always, procrastination catches up with us eventually. It's one thing to put off a decision about having children when you are in your twenties and quite another when you are in your late thirties. Avoiding the effort required to research different health insurance plans or retirement options may not have major consequences in your thirties but will have a big impact in your fifties. When your time stage is not in sync with your life stage, you can procrastinate yourself into big trouble.

Lost in Time

A subjective sense of timelessness can lead to both positive and negative experiences.[16] Heather was a single, thirty-two-year-old woman who enjoyed living in the moment. When she was surfing, she felt outside the bounds of clock time,[17] immune from the demands and expectations of work, family, and culture. It was a freedom she found truly exhilarating.

Heather's sense of timelessness, however, extended into her "regular" life and led her to ignore long-range goals—how long it might take to shape herself into a compelling applicant for graduate school, or how she was going to develop a long-term relationship so she could have the family she wanted. Her entry-level job didn't pay well enough for her to buy the latest cell phone or laptop computer without adding to her credit card debt. She saw her friends making progress in their careers, but she hadn't yet chosen hers. Living in the timeless "now" supported Heather's feeling of freedom and separateness, but it did not help her move forward into her future.

You may have noticed that a sense of timelessness occurs with some of your deepest pleasures and most playful moments. Creative experiences feel timeless. When you are doing something that engages you deeply, you can't tell if minutes or hours have passed. Being lost in time for an hour, a day, or a weekend can be profoundly rejuvenating and generative.

But if timelessness becomes your way of living, as it did for Heather, there may be serious consequences. It is essentially disorienting not to be able to tell the difference between the finite and the infinite.[18] As we see with Heather, for whom time felt infinite, timelessness can lead to immobility, being stalled in life instead of developing. You may not even notice how much time has gone by while things apparently stay the same. Even though a sense of timelessness may feel soothing or safe in the present, procrastinators often pay a price for it in the future, when they are suddenly shocked to realize that life has passed them by.

Disconnected in Time

A sense of timelessness makes it hard to recognize the link between past, present, and future not only in time but also in ourselves.[19] Procrastinators desperately want to believe in a future that has nothing to do with past problems. You may not want to recognize that the "you" who procrastinated last time is the very same "you" who has a project deadline this time. You may want to forget the feelings of dread, anxiety, and pressure you felt last time and assume instead that the New You will sail through the current project feeling capable and inspired.

The hope for a New You may be tantalizing, but it can also be problematic. Without accepting the connection between "you" in the past and "you" in the present and future, you lose the feeling of continuity that is part of an integrated self. If you live through time in separate, disconnected moments that are not linked together to form a coherent narrative, then those moments can have no real meaning.

In order to change how things are going, you first have to accept the experiences that make up your life. Then, you have to accept that it's the Same Old You who is in charge of making changes. And, paradoxically, when you accept the Same Old You, you are starting where you truly are, and this makes it more possible to become a New You.

The Good Old Days

Josh reveled in the successes of his past. He had always been a gifted athlete, popular and successful. A college basketball star, he hoped to go all the way to the NBA, but a knee injury ended his basketball career. After that, Josh didn't know what to make of himself. He began working in sales for a software company, where he was affable and likeable but didn't bother to meet deadlines. Habitually late submitting sales reports and travel receipts, disdainful of the administrative aspect of his job, he resented the "nerdy" guys who got promoted or left the company for better jobs. "They've never done anything special in their lives," he complained. "They never had a whole gymnasium chanting their name."

Josh's self-image was locked in the past, when he had been a star. But the present pressed on him whether he liked it or not. He was thirty-eight when his wife got pregnant. Then Josh's father had a heart attack and died within a year. Josh was shocked to find himself in middle age holding a toddler at his father's graveside.

We can see that living in the past might offer some psychological comfort. It seems to provide a safe haven from adult realities, which can feel demanding, overwhelming, and deflating.[20] Memories of past glories or fantasies of future success can function as a soothing buffer against the pain of real life or a stalled life.

It's not just young people who live in the past: the realities of the next stage of life can be avoided at any age. Middle-aged people may put off going for medical checkups, because they don't want to face the beginnings of their biological decline. In middle age, you may expect your body to behave as it did in your twenties, and you don't want to accept that, even if you are active and healthy, body changes are inevitable. Many people in their fifties put off thinking about retirement or planning for their financial security, acting as if they will keep on working at the same pace and with the same abilities for the rest of their lives. Delaying forestalls a confrontation with some of the certainties associated with time: Time is passing; the future is coming; you are getting older; there are limits to what you will accomplish in your lifetime; and most starkly inevitable of all, eventually you will die.

IS THE PAST IN THE PAST?

As you reflect on your unique subjective experience of time, it's helpful to consider the mutual influences of past, present, and future, because they are constantly affecting each other. Although we are accustomed to thinking of past, present, and future as occurring in succession, in linear time, it's not as simple as that. Everything we experience occurs in the present moment.

When you remember a time in the past, you are remembering it in the present, so your present state can color your memories of the past. When you look ahead to the future, the anticipation is happening in the present. The past, present, and future cannot be separated from each other; they are always intertwined.[21]

In the present, you are a product of your past. Margaret Atwood, in her novel *The Blind Assassin*, wrote, "Old, cold time, old sorrow, setting down in layers like silt in a pond."[22] Whatever floats on the surface of the pond is affected by those layers that reach all the way down to the bottom. Similarly, our past is always with us, registered in our brains, in our bodies, in our psyches. People may try to reinvent themselves, cut themselves off from their past relationships and past experiences, but history can't be changed; it can only be reinterpreted and learned from in the present.

Procrastination may be a sign that something from your past is intruding into the present, because hesitation to move forward usually has a lot to do with past experiences. If you grew up with a controlling parent who micromanaged your homework and your social life, you may expect that every teacher, boss, and partner will treat you in the same way. Or, if you grew up with a sibling who won every award and was the star of school and family, you might assume that there's no point in trying your best as an adult because somebody else will always get the glory. In other words, your past relationships are laid down as the blueprint for what you expect relationships to be in the present and future. Turning in an academic paper, applying for a new position, reporting to a new boss, or dating on the Internet may fill you with apprehension that has more to do with significant past relationships than with the reality of the present situation. When we talk about the extra "meaning" that is attached to the tasks you are avoiding, we are referring to this aliveness of the past in the present.

Sometimes the influence of the past on your present behavior is obvious, and sometimes it is buried near the bottom of the pond. Tess didn't like her job in Milwaukee and wanted to move back to her hometown, Dallas, where most of her family still lived. Although she's usually a "get it done" person and was clear about wanting to make this move, she hadn't done anything to make it happen. Tess was perplexed by her uncharacteristic procrastination.

It took several months of counseling for Tess to realize what was interfering with her plans to move. Although she loved visiting her family in Dallas now, she remembered being afraid of the big city when she was young. She had moved from a small town when she was fourteen, feeling awkward and unprepared for the social and academic pressures of a large middle school. In an effort to fit in, Tess had gone out with any boy who asked her, and one night, she endured a terrifying experience of date rape. Her family had been more shaming than supportive, and she had never told anyone else about the experience.

After that, she had "forgotten" about it until she began talking about her adolescence in counseling. Tess gradually realized that she was afraid of moving back home because she might see people who would remember her from school, and she worried that she would re-experience the disgrace and helplessness she'd felt back then. Although Tess was a thirty-five-year-old successful professional woman in the present, the thought of living in Dallas took her back into her past, making her feel like a vulnerable fourteen-year-old who was going to get hurt. Her procrastination was the signal that, beneath the surface of her pond, something old was awry. The past, though buried in the present, was preventing her from claiming her future.

Your past is your past, whether you like it or not, whether you re-member it consciously or not, whether you take responsibility for it or not. Many of the things that happened in the past were not your fault—maybe they weren't anybody's fault, maybe some were your fault—but the events in your life are yours and always will be. You can't go back and change them, even if they feel unfinished and unfair. We each have the task of integrating our past into our present and de-ciding on the paths we want to pursue in the future. Procrastination may be a sign that the past is dragging you back in time instead of the future pulling you forward to new experiences and possibilities.

We hope we have helped you to think about your relationship with time and your experience of yourself in time, both of which are deeply connected to your procrastination. We think this reflection can help move you toward an experience of Mature Time, which in turn will allow you to do, rather than avoid, the things that are im-portant for your life.

What is Mature Time? We see it as the "capacity to assess and accept what is real in both the external and internal worlds,"[23] the acknowl-edgment and acceptance of both clock time and subjective time, and the ability to move flexibly and comfortably between the two. Clock time doesn't have to be your enemy or your boss. Time is neither good nor bad, neither fast nor slow, neither friend nor foe. It just *is*. Your job is to figure out how to work with it and to live as fully as you can within its bounds, rather than spend your life battling against it.

7

Current Neuroscience
The Big Ideas

When we said in the first edition of our book, "There is no such thing as a procrastination gene," we were right according to the current knowledge at that time. But since 1983, there has been an explosion of progress in the field of neuroscience, which enables researchers to study specific parts of the brain and how they function separately and together. While we still don't believe there is a single gene that creates a procrastinator, we now understand enough about the workings of the brain to say with confidence that indeed there *are* biological factors that contribute to procrastination. Some are general factors, integral to how the brain works, develops, and changes over time, which indirectly relate to putting things off. Other factors involve specific functions (or dysfunctions) that lead quite directly to procrastination. For example, if you have some degree of attention deficit disorder, executive dysfunction, seasonal affective disorder, depression, obsessive-compulsive disorder, chronic stress, or sleep deprivation, what's going on in your brain is likely to be closely tied to your procrastinating. We discuss those conditions in the next chapter, but first we want to summarize a few of the "big ideas" from recent developments in neuroscience, so that you better understand how your brain works. All of us can benefit from understanding this complex part of our body, and you can use this knowledge to bolster your efforts at overcoming procrastination.

BIG IDEA #1:
YOUR BRAIN IS CONSTANTLY CHANGING

Scientists used to think our brain develops in a predictable, predetermined way: certain attributes are "hardwired" from birth, then the brain grows through childhood, peaks at about the age of eighteen, and it's all downhill from there. It is now absolutely clear that this is not true. Research has shown that your brain is a dynamic, living system that is constantly changing and being rewired until the day you die.[1] The brain's ability to reorganize, break old neural links, and form new neural connections throughout life is referred to as "neuroplasticity."[2] We now know that your brain changes every day: what you do today, for good or ill, affects the structure and function of your brain tomorrow.[3] How does this happen?

Our lived experience activates our brain cells (neurons), sending electrical impulses from neuron to neuron, releasing biochemical signals and priming them to grow both in number and in connectedness to each other.[4] As hypothesized by Sigmund Freud in 1888 and so aptly expressed by psychologist Donald Hebb in 1949, "Neurons that fire together, wire together."[5] The more you do something, the more your brain responds to support that activity; it learns to do what is asked of it faster and better (whether it's good for you or not).

The brain is always changing. The good news is that it can generate new, flexible behavior. The bad news is that it can also strengthen old, rigid behaviors. This is called the "plastic paradox."[6] The classic metaphor to describe getting stuck in old patterns is the image of sledding down a hill on fresh snow.[7] The first time you sled downhill, there are many routes available. The more you go down your chosen path or one close to it, the more tracks you create and the deeper the tracks will be, until you are going down very quickly—but in a rut. In the brain, repetition means that we lay down "mental tracks," which, once established, "tend to become *self-sustaining*"[8] and increasingly difficult to get out of. It takes a lot of conscious awareness and effort to interfere with old habits, to break recurring neural networks, but it can be done. Our book is intended to help you increase your conscious awareness of what you're doing and why you're doing it when you put things off, so that you can help your brain shift out of its ruts. Thinking about your procrastination in new ways and using the techniques we suggest for taking action can help you break old neural patterns of delay and develop new patterns of getting things done on time.

BIG IDEA # 2: FEELINGS MATTER, EVEN IF THEY ARE UNCONSCIOUS

Your feelings are linked to your unique self—only *you* can experience your feelings, and feelings are an essential part of being conscious.[9] There is great value in being able to use your feelings to guide you and to inform your decision making. As researchers are now learning, there is wisdom in gut reactions and intuition. The capacity to use emotions to make wise decisions can be lost if certain parts of your brain (the frontal lobes) are damaged.[10] If you don't have access to your feelings, you can't use this crucial source of self-knowledge to help you make your way through life. It's important to be able to say, "This *feels* right to me," or, "That just *doesn't feel* right." Without an inner sense of rightness or wrongness that comes from feelings located in your body, you're limited to thinking intellectually about a decision, or obsessing endlessly about a long list of pros and cons. You can look for the "logical" answer or the "right" answer or the "perfect" answer. But basing your decisions on these external factors won't bring you closer to knowing how *you* feel. Instead, you put off making the decision because you can't (or are afraid to) consult the authority that matters most—your inner self.

We can think about procrastination as an attempt not just to avoid particular tasks but to *avoid the feelings* that are somehow associated with those tasks. Recent findings from neuroscience can help us understand more about why feelings are so powerful and how the regulation of feelings plays such an important role in being able to face tasks you'd rather avoid. Sometimes you are well aware of what you feel, and sometimes the clue that you are having feelings comes from signals in your body, because emotions arise from bodily, sensory experiences.[11]

Your feelings may be conscious, such as when you are aware of why a task is aversive: "Balancing my checkbook is boring"; "I hate to spend my time cleaning"; "I don't understand algebra." However, "much of what the brain does during an emotion occurs outside of conscious awareness."[12] It is widely accepted in cognitive neuroscience today that *"consciousness is a very limited part of the mind,"*[13] so it's to be expected that there are a lot of times when you are not consciously aware of the feelings that lead you to avoid a project. Even if you don't know exactly which emotions are happening outside of your conscious awareness, your body is reacting.

In order to stop procrastinating, you will have to tolerate some uncomfortable feelings in your body, such as fear and anxiety. Going ahead in spite of fear takes deliberate effort, because fear is triggered instantaneously, once registered in the body it lasts forever, and it sends very strong signals in the brain that are hard to override.[14] Fear is triggered so rapidly, it's incredible. If you touch your arm, it takes your brain 400–500 milliseconds to register the sensation. But fear is registered in a mere 14 milliseconds![15] Before it's even possible to know it, your body has registered fear and started responding. By the time you think about doing a task you've been avoiding, like making a dreaded phone call or adding up your income from last year, your body has already reacted with fear. No wonder you put it off.

In addition, your body holds onto fear. Once your brain makes a connection between a stimulus (for example, a snake, a term paper, a presentation to your executive team) and a feeling of danger or fear, that connection cannot be extinguished.[16] After just a single exposure to a threatening stimulus, fear can be reactivated whenever that stimulus is encountered again, even if you don't remember it.[17] A famous case in neuroscience illustrates how fear can be experienced unconsciously without being understood by the conscious mind. In 1911, a patient with brain damage couldn't remember her past. Every day when she met her doctor, she had no memory of ever having seen him before. One day he concealed a pin in his hand, and when they shook hands on greeting, he pricked her outstretched hand. Subsequently, every time he attempted to shake hands, she refused, even though she could not explain her aversion. The traces of the past painful experience remained in her brain and exerted a powerful unconscious influence on her behavior.[18] You may recognize yourself in this example—you don't know why you avoid a particular task, but you avoid it every time. The link between the original stimulus and your fear is now unconscious.

Another reason fear is so difficult to manage is that the brain pathways that carry fear messages are so strong. The messages from the fear center (amygdala) to the thinking center (cortex) are stronger than the messages going back from the thinking center to the fear center.[19] This means that fear invades our consciousness more easily than our thoughts can control our emotions, so we have to do extra work to manage our fears and our impulses.

People develop different solutions to the problem of managing fears and impulses. Freud was one of the first to observe that people develop an array of defense mechanisms that keep unbearably painful ideas, feelings, and memories from conscious awareness.[20] Defensive patterns develop in childhood and then are repeated many times into adulthood, laying down deep neuronal tracks, becoming ingrained.[21] For example, if you tell yourself that you don't have to study calculus because you'll never need to use it in real life, you're using the defensive system of "intellectualization" (rationalizing, making excuses), perhaps developed over time to protect you from the pain of feeling stupid and hating yourself when you struggle to understand complex concepts.

Another defense against unwanted feelings is suppression, actively trying to push them away. ("I'm just not going to think about that.") But trying to ignore feelings will keep you tangled up in a knot. Paradoxically, people who suppress their feelings are more likely to remain vulnerable to negative emotion and to experience higher levels of stress.[22] For procrastinators, avoidance is the king of defenses, because when you avoid the task, you are also avoiding the many thoughts, feelings, and memories associated with it.

How can we respond to danger without relying on self-defeating psychological defenses? We can work on developing a capacity for emotional regulation, so that we can live comfortably in our own skins. With emotional regulation, the thinking parts of your brain (the frontal cortex) calm down the activity in the emotional part of your brain (the amygdala), enabling you to soothe yourself when necessary or to think through the consequences of your impulse to scream at your boss, throw your computer out the window, or have sex with that attractive stranger you see on the street.

Managing your procrastination is going to require a lot of help from the thinking parts of your brain, as you confront situations that stimulate the emotional parts of your brain and generate so much anxiety that you want to avoid at all cost. Ideally, the capacity for emotional regulation is developed through interactions with responsive caregivers beginning in infancy, when an attuned caregiver recognizes the baby's anxiety, understands it, is not afraid of it, and responds by taking care of the baby's needs in a reassuring way.[23] If a caregiver can hold onto the ability to think in the presence of intense anxiety, the baby develops this ability, too.[24] Even if you have not had the benefit of learning how to regulate your emotions through these early interactions, you can learn to do it later in life. You can respond to that feeling of danger by thinking things through ("I'll practice my talk so I'll be less anxious"), considering what the realistic dangers are ("Will I really get fired if it's not perfect?"), considering the context of the danger ("My new boss is scary because he reminds me of my father, but he's not my father"), reminding yourself about your competency and resilience, or giving yourself encouragement. This process of cognitive reappraisal[25] is an essential part of being able to soothe yourself.

Jane has a vivid memory of a time when she stumbled upon cognitive reappraisal to calm herself in the face of disaster. When she was in graduate school, she had a very upsetting meeting with a statistician who questioned whether her dissertation data were reliable. Having struggled for years even to get to the point of having data to analyze, she was extremely distressed and raced to call her husband for reassurance, but he was not home. Standing alone in a phone booth, she talked out loud as if he were there, and then she answered herself as she knew he would, with calming reassurance and reasonable suggestions. Eventually, this kind of dialogue can take place more automatically, internally, silently, as you help yourself stay calm enough to think in the presence of anxiety.

In addition to allowing you to proceed with your work, there are health benefits to emotional regulation. Recent neurological research has shown that people who respond with cognitive reappraisal to an emotionally negative experience reduce their levels of stress[26] and are more successful in freeing themselves from the well-worn grooves of maladaptive thoughts and urges.[27]

By consciously modulating our emotional responses to feared situations, we can avoid the full-blown anxiety attacks that we might have experienced in the past.[28] When we can regulate our feelings, we become free to decide how to respond. In the end, being able to tolerate the entire spectrum of feelings within you will enable you to face those tasks you put off. When you can stand how you feel, you can stand taking action.

BIG IDEA #3:
THE INFLUENCE OF IMPLICIT MEMORY

You may realize that your procrastination is driven by some of the fears we have explored, such as fear of success or fear of feeling controlled, and you may find it easy to accept what we've just described: feelings, especially fear, are fast, powerful, and not easy to change. Even so, you might find that your fear doesn't make sense to you. However, fears that don't make sense at face value are not necessarily "irrational"; they make their own kind of sense. If you procrastinate on a task but can't pinpoint exactly what makes you fearful or uncomfortable, chances are an "implicit" memory has been activated. What this means is that you may not remember the experience itself, but your brain and body respond to it nonetheless, generating a cascade[29] of emotional distress that leads you to avoid the task. A British psychoanalyst, Donald Winnicott, expressed this idea when he said: "The things we are afraid of are the things that have already happened."[30]

Implicit memories are sometimes referred to as "early" memories because they tend to be laid down before the age of three[31] when a part of the brain central to memory storage, the hippocampus, becomes more fully developed.[32] From birth to eighteen months of age, the right hemisphere of our brain is dominant,[33] undergoing rapid growth and absorbing the world in an intuitive way. The right hemisphere responds to the music of language—the nonverbal aspects of speech, such as tone and rhythm, not the content, which is why lullabies are so soothing to infants. From eighteen months to three years, coinciding with the magic of language acquisition, there is a growth spurt in the left hemisphere of the brain, which is more logical, analytical, and linear, and which processes speech as words and thoughts.[34] During this time, however, the hippocampus has not yet developed, so all the experiences of these early years remain in your implicit memory and are activated throughout your life without conscious memory or cognitive understanding.

It's important to note that the hippocampus is very vulnerable to stress: the chronic elevation of the stress hormone cortisol damages the hippocampus.[35] As hippocampal cells die, the structure literally shrinks, so it's no surprise that chronic stress makes it harder to remember and harder to think clearly. (But don't despair, hippocampal cells can grow back. See Chapter 15.) This is why people who were traumatized as children often don't remember even the later years of childhood, yet their implicit memories remain stored in body and brain and leave them immobilized without knowing why.

Implicit memory can't be seen directly, but it can be inferred from our expectations of ourselves and others. These memories shape our perceptions, which are based on the early experiences of how we were cared for—the unique feelings we have about the world and about ourselves in that world, the assumptions about what we can expect (or not), experiences that seem so natural that we assume everyone feels the way we do. When Jamar fell behind on his work, asking for help was unthinkable: "Of course I should do everything myself. If I ask for help, I would be a failure. It would be too shameful. Doesn't everyone feel that way?" (Well, no . . .)

Implicit memories cannot be accessed consciously no matter how much time we spend or how much effort we make, because they are memories of experiences that occurred before we had words and the capacity to think about what we experienced.[36] In contrast, explicit memories, sometimes called "late" memories, are more familiar to us, coming after we have developed language and consciousness. They include "autobiographical" memories that hold the stories and narrative of our lives, as well as memories that hold our knowledge of social norms, our recognition of people's faces, and the intellectual knowledge we acquire during our years in school and in the work world.[37]

Even if you don't remember the parts of your history that lead you to get stuck in avoidance, it's important to honor and accept the response your brain is generating. *Something* from your past has been triggered; it can help a great deal to understand what that something is, but even if you can't ever identify it, you can still take action. You can remind yourself that you are here now, in this present moment, and that your memories, remembered or not, are from the past. Terror, shame, guilt, disgust, and self-hate are often by-products of old memories. With the help of the thinking parts of your brain, you can "override" the activation of your implicit memories, creating alternative neural circuits and changing your brain, allowing you to act instead of procrastinating, paralyzed by fear.

BIG IDEA #4: WIRED TO RELATE

When you are putting off something you feel you can't handle or that makes you uncomfortable, you are experiencing not only the activation of implicit memories and the powerful feelings evoked by them. You are also involved in a struggle about how to view yourself: Are you capable? Are you permitted to have your own thoughts? Are you worthy of being loved and respected?

Research confirms that low self-esteem contributes to procrastination.[38] Your self-image—whether you have confidence in your ability to succeed and can value who you are—is being shaped from the earliest days of life. We know now that the brain is wired to be "ultrasocial":[39] it literally grows and develops in response to the way we are responded to by the people who care for us. We are born to seek connection with others: when a baby sees the mother's face, brain chemicals are released that make the baby feel good and stimulate further growth of the brain.[40] The discovery of "mirror neurons" suggests that watching how other people behave and feel activates the same neurons in *our* brains that are active *their* brains.[41] More and more, it is becoming clear that the state of one person's brain affects what happens in another's. And that means caretakers do much more than change diapers and provide food: "*They activate the growth of the brain through emotional availability and reciprocal interactions.*"[42]

As an infant you looked to others to find yourself, and the emotional experiences (conscious and unconscious) of your caretakers helped shape your brain and began to influence your sense of yourself. What did you see when you gazed into their eyes? Was there a gleam of pleasure because you exist? What image did you see in the mirror they reflected back to you? Someone who is a joy and a delight? A mother who is relatively free of anxiety, able to enjoy and be attuned to the changing needs of her baby, will help her child become a person who can regulate emotions, trust others, think well of himself, and maintain positive expectations.[43] These capacities are the foundation for confidence and healthy self-esteem.

Children of parents who are depressed, angry, preoccupied, or disinterested for other reasons can't find what they're looking for in the parents' response. Rather than seeing themselves as lovable and welcomed, they may see a reflection of themselves as an imposition, a disappointment, a source of trouble, or an ornament for display. These damaging emotional connections have profound consequences, shutting down brain centers involved with feelings of security, well-being, and openness to the world and activating parts of the brain that resonate with the parents' distressed emotional state.[44] The child's developing self-image incorporates this parental state. If a parent cannot respond with appropriate emotion to the child, the child may begin to feel uninteresting or empty, unable to succeed at the most important thing in a baby's life: connecting with his caretakers. These early misattuned interactions affect the child's brain, self-concept, and confidence, setting the stage for procrastination in later life. Keep in mind that misattunements are inevitable in all relationships and are not necessarily problematic. Every parent has a bad day. It's when these misattunements occur regularly and often that the child is left with a legacy of inadequacy.

Maria's mother suffered from a postpartum depression when Maria was born and continued to struggle with depression for many years. When parents are emotionally unresponsive, children (even babies) will try all kinds of things to evoke an emotional response from them. The infant Maria had the feeling that, hard as she tried, nothing she did could engage her mother, who remained emotionally flat and unresponsive. Later in school, Maria felt tremendous pressure to be first in her class and to excel in sports, yet she put off homework and was often late to practice. Without realizing it, she viewed every grade and every activity as an attempt to prove she was worth her mother's attention, something she'd sought since birth. With this emotional pressure on each and every endeavor, she felt that only a perfect performance would be enough to delight her mother. It's no wonder that Maria often found herself procrastinating: there was too much at stake.

BIG IDEA #5: THE LEFT SHIFT

There is growing evidence that certain parts of the left hemisphere (the left frontal cortex) are associated with feelings of caretaking, empathy, and compassion.[45] When activated, they allow us to be relaxed and open to world, in contrast to being in a state of withdrawal based on uncomfortable, negatively charged emotions, which appear to be encoded in the right hemisphere.[46] Treating yourself with kindness will stimulate this part of your brain (the "left shift"), creating a state that is correlated with feelings of resilience and well-being. This left shift is also correlated with better functioning of your immune system[47] and with the health of the vagus nerve that wanders from your brain stem all throughout your body.[48] The vagus nerve makes an essential contribution to your capacity for emotional regulation and comfortable social engagement[49] and is associated with an increase in the amount of the hormone oxytocin in your body.[50] Oxytocin helps regulate social bonding and emotional attachment to other people. Some studies suggest that oxytocin can be increased by touch (massage is a good thing) and certain foods, such as chocolate (which is a *very* good thing!).[51] In Chapter 15, we will describe the practice of "mindfulness," which can activate this left shift in your brain.

What do oxytocin, the vagus nerve, compassion, and kindness have to do with procrastination? Being able to calm yourself and treat yourself with compassion and kindness has everything to do with your being able to face tasks or situations that frighten, anger, threaten, or bore you. Unless you break the patterns of negativity that produce procrastination and replace them with something positive, you are likely to stay stuck in that old rut, like a river running through the mountains in the same channel, carving out a canyon that gets deeper and wider, until you can't see the sun and you can't climb your way out.

When you do something that is hard for you, your brain will still show the neural signature for fear, and you will feel that instant shot of anxiety. This is when you can respond to yourself in a new way, with encouragement rather than criticism, with compassion rather than attack. A voice of kindness can help you feel secure enough to venture into uncomfortable emotional territory. Over time, with practice (and perhaps a few pieces of good chocolate), you can develop a different relationship to yourself. When your thoughts are compassionate, your body responds well and your whole self can function in a more harmonious and integrated way.[52] Well-integrated systems are "flexible, adaptive, coherent, energized, and stable,"[53] and we believe that the more you can create an integrated state within yourself, the less you'll be a prisoner of procrastination.

8

Procrastination and Your Brain

In this chapter we examine several biologically based conditions that often go hand in hand with procrastination: executive dysfunction, attention deficit disorder, depression, anxiety disorders, stress, and sleep problems. If you have or think you might have any of these conditions, they could be making a significant contribution to your procrastination. Don't despair, and don't ignore them. Consider getting a medical evaluation; medication may be helpful in treating the condition and may help reduce your procrastination.

EXECUTIVE FUNCTION

When we talk about executive function, we're not talking about the performance of CEOs in large corporations. We are talking about the performance of the CEO of your brain.[1] Just as the CEO of a business is responsible for the performance of the overall company, the executive part of your brain coordinates, regulates, and integrates the different structures and systems of your brain to give you a smooth, ongoing sense of yourself with your personality, goals, values, and skills. Your inner executive takes in information from your senses, your history, your thoughts, and uses this information in a goal-directed way to enable you to accomplish what is important to you.

Just as it is possible for a company to have well-functioning departments led by an incompetent CEO, it is possible for a person to have a brain that functions well in many ways, yet lacks overall leadership.[2] A person with poor executive function may struggle with important life skills in spite of possessing many mental strengths. Perhaps you know someone (maybe even yourself?) who is smart and has good ideas, but who is "terminally disorganized"[3] and never seems to have the right papers or materials, can't remember what was planned or decided, and loses track of the steps necessary for the completion of a task. Sound familiar? This kind of disorganization easily leads to procrastination, because you lose track of timelines and deadlines, and because it can become so frustrating to locate what is needed to complete the project that you just give up.

A person who has difficulties with executive function often has problems with procrastination; however, not all procrastinators have executive dysfunction, so this is an issue that you must consider in figuring out what your own procrastination is all about. Almost all people who have attention deficit disorder (which we discuss in the next section) have executive function difficulties, but executive dysfunction does not necessarily imply ADD.[4]

There are different opinions about which capacities are involved in executive function, but there is general agreement that there are several basic factors: attentional control, cognitive flexibility, goal setting, and information processing.[5] These can be further divided into the following specific functions:[6]

1. Initiate tasks (get started, generate ideas for action)
2. Sustain attention (follow through, stick with an activity)
3. Inhibit impulses (think before acting, not respond immediately)
4. Shift attention (change focus, move from task to task, respond flexibly)
5. Working memory (remember plans, instructions, and past learning for use with new learning and situations)
6. Emotional control (regulate and manage feelings)
7. Organize material (obtain needed materials and create order)

8. Self-monitor (verbal capacity to review one's performance, to talk oneself through difficult tasks or experiences as needed)
9. Time management (be aware of and realistic about time)
10. Planning (prioritize, identify steps toward a goal, anticipate future needs and events)

As you read through this list, do any of these issues sound familiar? Are you constantly late because you don't have the things you need? Do you dash around madly trying to locate them? Are you lost in time? Do you forget what you planned to do, even though it was only five minutes ago that you decided to do it? Are you at a loss when someone asks you, "What were you thinking?"

If you have problems with executive function, we're sorry to tell you that there is no magic cure. Some issues, such as attention focus, and working memory may be helped by medications that are used to treat ADD. However, problems with organization are usually not helped by medications,[7] so the suggestions we offer in Part Two are especially important. You don't have to feel ashamed, but you do have to figure out how to work with what you've got. Many of the techniques we suggest for managing procrastination are techniques that also help with executive function problems: identifying a goal and breaking it down into small steps, taking a small first step, learning how to tell time, and optimizing the environmental conditions to support success. Our suggestion to "get a buddy" may be the most important step of all, because it is difficult to teach executive functions to yourself. It can really help to team up with someone who is kind and who has strong executive functioning. Perhaps this is one reason why a huge new service industry has developed over the last ten years: the personal organizer and clutter management expert!

ATTENTION DEFICIT DISORDER

Attention deficit disorder and its variations, attention deficit hyperactivity disorder (ADHD) and ADD of the inattentive type, have received a great deal of scientific and clinical attention over the past twenty-five years.[8] Although for centuries, some children across all cultures have been recognized as "fidgety," "ill-mannered," "wild," "erratic," "motor-mouthed," or "excessively passionate," "dreamy," or "lost in thought," it is only relatively recently that we have come to understand that there is, in fact, a biological basis for such behavior, and only more recently still that science has begun to identify some of the biological substrates involved.

Here are the basics: ADD is characterized by three core symptoms of distractibility, impulsivity, and restlessness.[9] This does not refer to the garden-variety distractibility that all of us experience from time to time,[10] but rather to the experience of not being *able* to focus, attend, or remember, even though one wants (often very badly) to do so. About 30–40 percent of children with ADD experience a diminishing of symptoms as they move through adolescence.[11] For the rest, symptoms can persist throughout adulthood, leaving in their wake unfulfilled dreams, unfinished projects, and countless missed deadlines.

But what does it actually mean to say that someone is distractible, impulsive, or restless? Russell Barkley, a scientist who has researched ADD since the 1970s, believes that the fundamental problem lies in the inability to *inhibit* oneself. That is, people with ADD cannot "inhibit immediate reactions to the moment so as to use self-control with regard to time and the future."[12] Instead of thinking, "I want an A in my history class, so I've got to finish this homework and turn it in tomorrow," the student with ADD feels, "This is boring! I don't want to do it!"—and then finds something much more fun and interesting to do. Procrastination in action.

Inhibition is a crucial activity of the brain, and a brain that does not inhibit itself effectively leaves its owner at the mercy of impulse.[13] It is because we can inhibit our instant reactions that we can think through a problem, delay gratification (how else would anyone graduate from high school or college?), and keep sexual and aggressive impulses under control. It is this capacity for inhibition that gives us the feeling that we are free to decide—we don't *have* to respond to the immediate stimulus; we can wait a moment, think and reflect, and then *choose* whether and how to respond. As Barkley says, waiting is not a passive act. Inhibition takes effort.[14]

Inhibition is also closely linked to having a sense of time. When you can remember that something is important to you in the future and that what happens in the future is linked to what you do in the present, you are more able to inhibit your urges to respond to immediate desires. Research has demonstrated that people with ADD are not able to sense time as accurately as people who don't have ADD.[15] Subjectively, time passes more slowly for them than for others; things seem to take longer than expected, and they quickly feel frustrated and impatient. Not knowing where they are located in time, they focus on what is immediately at hand, with no sense of what lies ahead. Being "blind to time," they do not see events approaching and end up careening from crisis to crisis.[16] This focus on immediate satisfaction instead of long-term benefit underlies the observation that many people with ADD have trouble pursuing educational goals, saving money, or engaging in behaviors that support long-term health (such as diet and exercise). If you can't grasp that you exist in time, preparing for and taking care of yourself in relation to the future seems irrelevant.

Barkley notes that people with ADD are hyper-responsive to environmental stimuli. Everyone has trouble sustaining attention; after a few seconds *all* of us look away from what we're doing, adjust our bodies, have another thought, or notice a sound or sensation. It has been estimated that our minds wander 15–20 percent of the time without our even realizing it,[17] and that the tendency to get distracted increases with age.[18] But people without ADD can return to the task easily and seamlessly, whereas people with ADD take longer and struggle harder to return to the task. It is more difficult for people with ADD to sustain attention, for sustained attention is also sustained inhibition.[19]

Recent findings in brain research support Barkley's view. Some parts of the brain (in the frontal cortex) appear to be smaller or less active in people with ADD compared to those without the disorder; these are precisely the structures that are central to sustaining attention, regulating impulses, planning for the future, and employing self-control.[20] And in some children who have ADD, parts of the frontal cortex develop about three years later than in children who don't have ADD, so the parts of the brain most closely involved with the regulation of attention and motor activity are most delayed in developing.[21] This finding helps explain why some children outgrow their symptoms by their late teens.

It has also been observed that people with ADD often have low levels of the neurotransmitter dopamine in their brains; since dopamine is a substance that helps us experience pleasure, one speculation is that people with ADD must do more and risk more in order to experience the well-being that people without ADD experience at ordinary levels of intensity. Psychiatrists Ned Hallowell and John Ratey describe the feeling as an "itch,"[22] a need for an intense, high level of stimulation that becomes a biological necessity—the person feels she or he *must* do something to alter an unbearable inner state. When people with ADD take stimulant medication (such as Ritalin, Adderal, or Concerta), the amount of dopamine in the brain is increased and brain activity increases to near normal levels.[23]

Most researchers have come to view ADD as an extreme variation of a normal trait, like height or weight, that has a strong genetic and biological component.[24] Others believe that "culturally induced ADD" is developing as well.[25] We are faced with so many distractions, so many competing demands for our attention, that ADD may be "the official brain syndrome of the information age."[26] To be successful in today's society, you have to be able to function in an ADD-like way: shifting attention rapidly and constantly, tracking multiple projects simultaneously, and operating in sound bites.[27] So, as you watch a favorite program on TV, station logos flash at you, news crawlers move across the bottom of the screen, and reminders about upcoming programs pop up every few minutes, and on top of all that, you're simultaneously checking your e-mail, the weather report, and sports scores on your Blackberry.

Thus, rather than seeing ADD as brain damage, a moral failing, or a character flaw, we can look at it as a condition caused by a host of complex genetic, biological, and environmental factors. If you have ADD, you have a brain that really does work differently, and you are much more likely to procrastinate. It really *is* harder to keep your focus on a task, to return to it after each one of the numerous, inevitable distractions that claim your attention. If you find yourself "addicted" to the frenzy of last-minute action, you may be medicating yourself with adrenaline, your own naturally produced stimulant, which increases your ability to focus. Consider whether this ad hoc self-medicating, with all the drama surrounding it, is worth it—or whether you could use prescribed medication to achieve better focus without last-minute panic or find work that provides the fast pace and intensity you need for your mind to feel fully engaged.

DEPRESSION: THEME AND VARIATIONS

There are many different variations on the theme of depression, some having to do with the severity (for example, major depression versus its milder, chronic form, dysthymia), others having to do with cyclical patterns (for example, bipolar illness, seasonal disorders, hormonal changes). What these conditions have in common is that you feel less energized, engaged, or connected to life than you'd like, less interested, motivated, or optimistic than usual. If you're consumed by sadness, feel hopeless, or don't care about life, you're probably not going to care about doing a good job at work, doing well in school, getting together with friends, doing your taxes, or taking care of your body. If you're depressed, you're probably procrastinating on something (maybe a lot of things) important to you. It feels impossible to drag yourself out for a walk; it's overwhelming to sort through boxes when you barely have the energy to brush your teeth. It seems pointless to work hard for a promotion if the future looks bleak and empty. And why would you even think about calling a friend if you're convinced nobody cares about you?

We now know there are strong biological underpinnings for depression, especially if it is the downward swing of bipolar disorder. While there is no single approach that works for everyone, treating this life-draining experience is not only possible but critically important. Although most episodes of depression will get better over time, being depressed leaves you at greater risk for more depression in the future.[28] And depression can be very costly indeed: depression, along with the procrastination that may accompany it, affects not only your feelings about yourself but your job or school performance, your physical health, your financial well-being, and your relationships.

Depression has biological, psychological, and environmental facets. There may be situational triggers to depression—for example, a significant loss, difficulties in a relationship, or a major life change, such as moving, children leaving home, or retirement. It is normal to grieve losses, feeling sad or empty for a time. But normal grief doesn't bring the self-hatred or the pessimism about self, world, and future that come with depression.

With symptoms of depression, people often have a chemical imbalance in the brain of the neurotransmitters serotonin or dopamine, and medication can be useful in restoring the balance. If depression is one side of bipolar disorder, mood stabilizing medications are essential. Beyond the issue of a potential chemical imbalance, however, is the more disturbing evidence that depression can permanently alter some structures of the brain, such as the hippocampus, and that the longer and more severe the depression, the greater the damage to individual neurons as well as larger structures.[29]

Many studies have shown that the best treatment for chronic depression is a combination of medication and talk therapy, and the more chronic the depression, the more important it is to continue both medication and therapy.[30] Regular, moderate aerobic exercise has been shown to reduce depression,[31] but it's hard to get yourself moving when all you want to do is sleep. You may have to treat your depression in order to have the energy and the hopefulness to take the steps necessary to end procrastination.

If your procrastination takes the form of feeling sluggish, lethargic, and unable to motivate yourself to get going during winter months, you may suffer from seasonal affective disorder (SAD).[32] People with SAD typically describe feelings of wanting to go into hibernation as the days shorten and darkness surrounds them. Rather than feeling sad, they feel fatigued. They lose energy, have trouble waking up in the morning, and want to withdraw from the world. They cancel social activities and hide out in their offices so they don't have to talk to anyone. They often crave carbohydrates, yet have trouble getting themselves to exercise, and so gain weight each winter. They have trouble thinking or being creative. Endeavors that seem easy in the summer seem impossible during the winter, so the list of undone tasks can spiral out of control. Then spring comes along—moods lighten, motivation and energy return, engagement with friends resumes, creativity comes alive, and procrastination is a distant memory—at least until the following fall.

Students, even in primary grades, can suffer from SAD. They may start the school year full of energy, enthusiasm, and motivation, but by December, to the puzzlement of everyone, they have trouble just getting out of bed in the morning and their performance plunges. Students who procrastinate should take a close look at any seasonal variations in their performance. Typically, more than a dozen winter depressions have come and gone before a patient is correctly diagnosed with seasonal affective disorder.[33]

The reduction of environmental light as the days shorten is a primary factor in SAD; the duration of symptoms tends to vary with geographic latitude with people farther away from the equator experiencing longer periods of fatigue than those who live at lower latitudes. Blood serotonin levels have been found to vary with the amount of sunlight on the day the blood sample was taken,[34] supporting the observation that medications that increase serotonin often improve the symptoms of SAD. Researchers have also found that SAD tends to run in families, so there appears to be a significant genetic component to the condition.[35]

ANXIETY DISORDERS

Obsessive Compulsive Disorder

Obsessive compulsive disorder (OCD) can contribute to procrastination: while people with OCD are making lists of pros and cons or checking that the stove is turned off, nothing else is getting accomplished. They repeat thoughts and behaviors because their brains are stuck in a process it can't stop. Normally, one part of the brain worries about mistakes (orbital frontal cortex), one part responds with heightened anxiety that something bad is going to happen unless they do something to prevent it (cingulate gyrus), and one part shifts gears when the crisis is over (caudate nucleus).[36] In people with OCD, the signal that the crisis is over doesn't happen, leading to a state Dr. Jeffrey Schwartz at UCLA calls "brain lock."[37] The brain does not change gears automatically, so the gears must be changed consciously to break the loop of endless thoughts or behaviors. For example, one could break the anxious thoughts by instead thinking: "The stove is off; the real problem is that I'm having an OCD attack." Engaging in a pleasurable activity (but not for too long!) or taking a step toward your goal can interrupt brain lock.

You don't have to have OCD to experience brain lock. Procrastinators can be so anxious about making mistakes that they become paralyzed. When we were writing the first edition of this book, Jane was stuck right at the beginning. She could not make progress with the first chapter she tackled, "Fear of Success." (Irony noted. . . .) She devised an outline, but when she tried to write, she could not get past the first paragraph. Overwhelmed and frustrated, she lamented to Lenora, "How am I going to explain fear of success to America?" Lenora had the brilliant idea (which Jane strongly resisted at first) of beginning with a chapter that would be easier to write, one that would not have the emotional charge carried by "Fear of Success." So Jane began working on the chapter dealing with setting behavioral goals and found that she could think clearly and write more easily.

Clutter and Hoarding

While most of us probably have more clutter than we would like, some people procrastinate so much on clearing it out that their quality of life is compromised significantly. During one of our first radio talk shows in New York City, a caller asked for help: he couldn't bring himself to throw out even a single issue of the six years' worth of the *New York Times* that was stacked floor to ceiling in his apartment. He and other clutter procrastinators often harp on themselves for not getting rid of things that have accumulated for years; they may be hounded by spouses who are tired of being surrounded by mountains of stuff; they may be isolated because they wouldn't dream of allowing visitors into their homes. Because it is so difficult to make decisions about what to keep and what to discard, they put off cleaning out. Everything must be kept "just in case."[38] As Neziroglu and her colleagues note:

Indecisiveness + Fear of Making a Mistake = Clutter[39]

Even though it may be embarrassing or feel overwhelming to live with so much "stuff," the anxiety and discomfort of dealing with it feels worse—hence, "I'll do it later."

When clutter expands to fill every nook and cranny so that you can't walk across the room in a (mostly) straight line, and you still can't bring yourself to throw things away, you may have graduated from clutter to hoarding. If so, you're not alone; there are an estimated one million compulsive hoarders in the United States[40] and many millions more who have hoarding tendencies. Hoarding and saving are known to run in families (a chromosomal marker has been found), and there appears to be a "different pattern of cerebral glucose metabolism" in hoarders than in people in general who don't hoard or in OCD patients who do not hoard.[41]

So, if you save, accumulate, hoard, and put off throwing things away, know that you will need to work hard to create new brain pathways to compete with these powerfully entrenched circuits. If you even *think* about sorting or throwing things out, the familiar circuits will warn you: "Don't do it! You might need it. . . . You may never find another one. . . . It could be worth a lot of money someday. . . . It belonged to my grandmother!" Remember that the reasons you give yourself for holding onto your stuff are a form of brain lock and that it's important for you to find a way to shift your mental gears—get a fun friend to sort through things with you, put on your favorite music and dance your way to the wastebasket, or remind yourself that you can find any information you really want on the Internet, so you don't need to hold onto those old magazines or newspapers for those articles you hope to read "someday."

THE EFFECTS OF STRESS

Most procrastinators know that putting things off can be very stressful: you worry about what there is to do, yet don't do it; when you finally gear up to meet a deadline, the intensity of the last-minute push stresses you out even more. Chronic procrastination can mean chronic stress, which is not good for your brain or your body.

The stress response, known as the "fight-or-flight" response, is an important biological mechanism designed to protect us from danger; it mobilizes us to react quickly when our survival is threatened, just as the zebra runs to safety when a lion approaches on the savannah.[42] One part of the brain, the hypothalamus, triggers an alarm system, increasing heart rate, raising blood pressure, providing energy, and shooting the hormones adrenaline and cortisol throughout the body. Our bodies need time to recover from the intensity of this self-protective spurt of energy; we all need a chance to return to a state of rest, in much the same way that a good night's sleep helps us recover from the activity of one day and prepares us for the next.

All too often, however, we do not allow ourselves that time to rest. After meeting one deadline we worry about the next. We stress about tomorrow's test, the mortgage, a fight with a friend, next week's performance review, the nagging pain that doesn't go away. We live in an age of fast-paced competitiveness, of crowded urban landscapes and rush-hour traffic jams. Even in small towns and on isolated islands, we check e-mail and text messages feeling pressed to respond instantly. Unfortunately, when we live in a chronically stressed way, our bodies are constantly producing stress hormones, which over time, damage important brain structures.[43] The more these structures are damaged, the less effective our cells are at repairing damage and stimulating new neuronal growth.[44]

Stress is magnified when we procrastinate. We anticipate being criticized not only for our work but for turning it in late; we tempt fate by pushing limits; we expect the worst to be waiting right around the corner; we feel guilty for disappointing, inconveniencing, or irritating others. It's a vicious circle: procrastination produces stress, and stress can produce procrastination. When your body is bearing the effects of a stressful life, you have less creative energy available for things that need to be done or things you would enjoy doing.

BIOLOGICAL RHYTHMS

The natural rhythms of your biology can significantly impact your performance. We discussed an example of an annual rhythm when we described seasonal affective disorder. Other examples of biological rhythms are circadian rhythms (some people are most alert and productive in the early morning, while others can't get going until noon), hormonal rhythms, such as menstrual rhythms in women, and testosterone changes in men as they approach midlife.[45] Another example of a biological rhythm is the need for quiet time versus social time. Some people feel overwhelmed by too much activity or social interaction and need to create quiet, alone time to soothe themselves and recharge their batteries. Knowing the ebbs and flows of your own biological states will help you act in harmony with your body rather than constantly fight against what is natural for you. If you push yourself to work in the morning when you're really best at night, for example, you're setting yourself up to procrastinate. Wouldn't it be more effective to work in a way that's easiest for you?

SLEEP: SLEEP DEBT AND SLEEP APNEA

Dr. William Dement, head of the Sleep Disorders Clinic at Stanford University, almost single-handedly created the field of sleep medicine.

Thanks to Dr. Dement, we now know how essential good sleep is for good functioning.[46] When you're not sleeping well, your brain can't work well, and you're likely to experience the typical problems of insufficient sleep: low frustration tolerance, inability to concentrate, low energy, irritability—and procrastination. "The impact of sleep deprivation on executive functioning is direct, since the pre-frontal cortex helps regulate sleep, arousal, and attention. Youngsters who are sleep-deprived have been shown to have difficulty initiating and persisting at tasks, especially those viewed as tedious or 'boring.' They also have difficulty with complex tasks that require planning or goal-directed persistence, particularly when the goals are abstract and the rewards are delayed."[47]

Although you may do all-nighters and seem to pull through unscathed for a night or two or three, especially when you're young, we now know that when you don't get enough sleep, you accumulate "sleep debt."[48] When your body is deprived of sleep, you can't be at the top of your game, and your tendency to procrastinate will be greater. So, if you're not getting enough sleep, take short naps (less than fifteen minutes; napping for a longer period allows you to move into deeper stages of sleep, and you're likely to feel groggy when you wake), and try to go to bed earlier (yes, we know, you can't go to bed early when you're far behind and have to work through the night; that's why we recommend starting sooner!). If you are sleeping enough hours but are still waking up tired, check with your doctor. You might be depressed or have another medical condition. You could have a serious life-threatening condition called sleep apnea, a disruption of sleep that deprives you of oxygen and leaves you feeling fatigued.[49]

OTHER MEDICAL CONDITIONS

There are other medical issues that could play a role in procrastination. For example, some thyroid disorders can cause the low energy and fatigue that make it impossible to get going or take action, and anemia can cause depression.[50] It has been suggested that some cases of writer's block may be connected to problems in the temporal or frontal lobe.[50] It's important to get a thorough physical to make sure there isn't an underlying biological issue that is contributing to your procrastination. If you're someone who's been putting off health checkups for years, we encourage you to make an appointment to see your doctor—or to find a doctor if you don't have one.

A FINAL THOUGHT

Whatever your struggles with procrastination, there is always a biological component to what you experience. Somewhere in the process of delaying, your brain perceives danger, and procrastination is your response and your protection. Perhaps your brain has particular challenges that lead you to put things off, such as those of executive function or ADD. Perhaps your procrastination reflects ways in which your brain has shut down, as in depression. Whatever your situation, we hope that understanding more about what happens in your brain will help you treat your brain and your body with care and respect. In Part Two we offer some suggestions for doing just that.

9

How You Came to Be a Procrastinator

You were born into the world straight from the environment of your mother's womb with your unique DNA, your particular brain, and your innate temperament. You were born into a particular family at a particular time. The combination of how you came into the world (nature) and how your family responded to you (nurture) set in motion a series of complex interactions that have led you to become the person and the procrastinator you are now. Some parent-child pairings are an easy fit, and some are not. When there is not a good fit, children can end up feeling defective in some way, not entitled to claim and pursue their own interests and goals, paving the way for procrastination.

Adam has ADHD. As a toddler, he was constantly on the go, climbing up the bookshelves, imitating police car sirens, and taking things apart. Although his energy was delightful in many ways, it was exhausting for his family. They often became irritated and scolded him for not playing quietly. In school, Adam had difficulty sitting still and talked out of turn so that teachers complained to his parents about conduct problems. Later, he forgot his homework assignments and lost track of test dates. He and his parents engaged in homework wars, nightly battles over sitting down to study. Adam's parents became aware that he had ADHD but were not sympathetic. They wanted him to snap out of it—just focus and do it. Procrastination became a bigger

117

and bigger problem. Adam put off anything he considered boring in favor of his passion for skateboarding.

Adam now says, "I wish my parents had understood how hard it was for me to focus. They knew I had ADHD, but they couldn't handle it. They said I was lazy and unreliable. They blamed me, but they didn't help me." Adam contrasts this with his parents' response to his sister's food allergies. "They accepted that this was how her body worked. They bent over backward to find the right foods for her, and they helped her learn to manage her condition. I wish they could have done that for me."

Perhaps like Adam, you had ADHD and felt blamed. Or you might have had a temperament that was different from others in your family—like being an introvert in a family of extroverts—and you felt out of sync with the other members of your family. How parents respond to their children's biological givens affects the course of those traits in later life. For example, Jerome Kagan, a child development researcher, studied shy children over time.[1] Shyness is a temperamental trait that is associated with fear and withdrawal from novelty. Kagan observed that if parents were emotionally attuned to their children, giving them a secure base and loving support for exploration, these children could, over time, outgrow their shy tendencies and engage the world with enthusiasm and resilience. Children who did not have attuned parenting maintained their anxiety into later life. If there isn't a good fit between what you were born with and how you are responded to, it's hard to develop solid confidence in yourself,[2] and lacking confidence is one of the main factors that contribute to procrastination.[3]

Not only did you have to mesh with your family environment, but your family also had its own place in a cultural environment, which might or might not have been an easy fit. If your family was not part of the dominant culture—either because of homeland, language, skin color, education, religion, or economic status—you faced special pressures that may have contributed to problems with procrastination.

We offer suggestions to address the special pressures of immigrants and first-generation college students in Chapter 17, but for now, we ask you to think about whether there were cultural issues in your family background that might be involved in your procrastination. Was there a shift that required you and your family to make cultural adjustments? For example, if your family came from a culture in which individual achievements were not as important as looking out for the community, the Western emphasis on individualism and competition may feel wrong and confusing.[4] If English is not your first language, or if you grew up in a family that did not speak English at home, perhaps you delay writing papers, reports, or business correspondence because it is so frustrating not to be able to express yourself as articulately in English as in your native tongue. If you were the first person in your family to attend college, you may have felt unprepared for the academic, financial, social, and bureaucratic demands of school,[5] and procrastinated rather than asking for help. If you come from a background of financial struggle and you are now in a more privileged setting, you may feel out of place, insecure, or even fraudulent, and procrastination may be a way to avoid testing whether you really belong. New cultural situations are stressful; often they pose a conflict between assimilating into the new culture and holding onto family and friends from the old culture. Procrastination helps you avoid making difficult choices and facing the potential loss of important attachments.

MODELS OF SUCCESS AND FAILURE

Parents, siblings, teachers, coaches, neighbors, and even people you've read or heard about become models for how to live. Sometimes they are models of the kind of person you would like to be—for example, the young boy who wants to be just like his dad, or the student who decides she wants to grow up to be like her favorite teacher. There are also people who may be models of what you do *not* want to be. A parent may be disorganized or inefficient, leading a child to decide that he will never be like *that!* Or a parent may be so extremely efficient, giving top priority to work over everything else—including the family—that the child vows never to put work ahead of people.

Who were your models for "success"? What about them made you think they were successful? What were they like? How did others view them? How did they treat you? How did they treat themselves? How did you internalize them?

Now, think of the people who may have been models of "failure." What was it about them that made you think they were failures? How did they behave toward others and treat themselves? How did they impact you?

And of course, who were the procrastinators?

Consider how these models have affected you and your procrastination. For example, you may have tried hard to be just like the most successful of them. Did that create impossible standards? Or you may have assumed that you could never be as successful as they were, so you gave up. Or you may have decided that, at all costs, you must *not* emulate one of your models, and so you tried to be everything he or she wasn't, but then lost a sense of who you really wanted to be. If it's helpful, you may want to list your early models, writing down your ideas about them and how you think they may have influenced your procrastination.

Here are a few examples of models that some procrastinators have described to us as having had an effect on their procrastination. One man remembered being intimidated by his successful father, a hard-driving man who had pulled himself out of poverty and become an award-winning scientist. He worked constantly at his computer, kept a yellow pad on the nightstand next to his bed, and used his time on the toilet to read scientific journals. "If you aren't doing something important," the father would say, "you're wasting the space you're standing in!" The young boy drove himself relentlessly to emulate his father. Doing anything for the sheer pleasure of it was perceived as a waste of precious time. Not surprisingly, the pressure weighed him down—he was often inhibited and unable to produce.

Another procrastinator, a restaurant manager whose delaying kept her business in constant jeopardy, viewed the women in her extended family as "just housewives who didn't have to work," content to spend their years living for their husbands and through their children. To her feminist mind, they were failures. She was determined to have a busy career. Yet she was afraid of losing her family's support as she developed her profession and her life path diverged from theirs. Her procrastination kept her from going too far in her work and feeling like an outsider in her own family.

We heard about conflicting models from a procrastinating college student who was strongly influenced by two of her elementary school teachers. One teacher was the picture of efficiency, but the student experienced her as humorless and unavailable and remembers her with little warmth or affection. The other teacher was constantly disorganized and running late, yet she really enjoyed life and was playful with her students. For that young child, liveliness went with disorganization and delay, whereas coldness was linked to efficiency.

You may have thought the only way to be successful was to be *exactly* like your model of success, with no deviations, identifying with the whole and not allowing for your distinct parts. You might admire one trait in a parent or friend and overvalue or idealize it, so that you don't see the person very clearly, and you diminish yourself in comparison. An idealized model of success is impossible to live up to! We would like to suggest that the person you admire also had traits and qualities you might not admire; your idealization keeps you blind to their limitations and stuck in a one-down position. Perhaps you use procrastination to stay one down.

FAMILY ATTITUDES:
THE MAKING OF A PROCRASTINATOR

Like all families, your family transmitted values, attitudes, beliefs, and expectations to you from a very early age, even starting before you were born, as your parents imagined what they wanted their child to be. These family messages let you know how the world worked and what your place in it was supposed to be. You were undoubtedly taught some basic ideas or rules about how people treat each other, about what is right and what is unacceptable, about what is safe and what is dangerous, about how to deal with conflict, negotiation, and decision making. You also learned quickly about how you were valued and how you fit into the family system—or didn't. You got messages about who you were, what you were capable of, and what the future held for you. You may have accepted these notions without question, assuming they were true and anyone would agree, or you may have rebelled against the rules and values your family espoused.

The influences of our families run deep, and even as adults we are affected by them, often without being aware of it. Some aspects of your early family relationships actually become hardwired in your brain, as these interactions create neural pathways that become established. Neuroscientists have suggested, "The brain uses past learning as the guide for what to expect in the future."[6] You anticipate what you have experienced in the past.

Robin was startled when her boss approached a coworker and said, "Hannah, you've made a mistake on the spreadsheet that throws all the numbers off." Robin braced for a tearful response to this harsh judgment, but Hannah's reaction was news to Robin: "Oh good, show me," she said. Robin had expected Hannah to react as she would have, with either defensive self-justification or tearful hysterics, but Hannah did neither. Later, after talking with Hannah, Robin understood that her friend didn't think their boss had been harsh, and she actually views mistakes as learning opportunities! It had never occurred to Robin that a mistake could be anything but an invitation for criticism, because that's what her mistakes had always generated, first criticism from her parents and now her own internal criticism.

When the assumptions and rules we learned in our families *automatically* govern our thoughts, feelings, and behavior, without our evaluating or challenging them, we can be headed for trouble, particularly if the rule is a very rigid one that inhibits our development as capable, creative individuals. It's like eating everything that is put on your plate without ever considering whether you like it, whether it's good for you, or even whether you're hungry! You just open your mouth and swallow, causing psychic indigestion.

Sometimes what you have come to expect does actually happen, and the brain's prediction is accurate. Other times things turn out differently. It takes active thinking and conscious awareness to evaluate whether your hardwired expectations are true. This is why it's so important to pay attention to the messages you received in the past. Maybe they once held a kernel of truth but now no longer fit. When you think carefully about these messages, you'll see that some of what you learned is invaluable, but some of it gets in your way.

Whose Version of You Are You?

Recall the messages you got from people in your early life—family, teachers, coaches, and other significant people. Originally, these messages came from the outside, but over time they become our inner voices.

Consider several types of messages: those that you experienced as pressures to succeed, those that communicated doubts, and finally, those that came through as basic support regardless of your success or failure. Jane, the younger sister of a brilliant older brother, never forgot the day she came home from school carrying a sixth-grade report card with all As, and her mother exclaimed with surprise, "Wouldn't it be funny if *you* turned out to be the smart one?" Sometimes the pressuring or doubting messages are communicated without words through body language, tone of voice, or facial expressions, like a mother's raised eyebrow when you announced you had landed a part in the school play, or the ugly family fights that erupted every time you had a special occasion to celebrate.

You might find it helpful to write down each message you can remember in these categories and identify the person it came from. If the message was an indirect one, what was communicated between the lines? Someone may have given you contradictory messages and may appear in more than one category.

Below are a few examples of remembered messages we've culled from our Procrastination Workshops.

Pressures to Succeed

Mother: I know you'll be a success! You can do anything!
Father: If it's not done right, it's not worth doing.
Grandfather: Coming in first is all that counts.

Father: A mistake is an indication of a disorganized mind.

Mother: You have to make a lot of money to help support this family.

Mother: You're such a good kid. What would I do without you?

Sister: You're so pretty; you'll never spend a Saturday night alone.

Teacher: You're the smartest student I've ever had.

Doubts about Your Success

Father: I'll help you with your math homework, because you'll never get it.

Mother: You're just a good-for-nothing loafer!

Father: What do you want to go to college for?

Mother: If you'd listened to me in the first place, you wouldn't be in this mess.

Father: I was expecting too much from you. I should have known better.

Father: I'm your father. I know what's best for you.

Mother: Well, at least you're cute.

Coach: This kid is nothing but a whiner.

Basic Support

Grandfather: Whatever happens, we're always behind you.

Grandmother: I love you no matter what you do.

Father: That's not what I would do, but I hope it works out for you.

Mother: You should live your life the way you want to.

Father: Don't worry, everybody makes mistakes. It's only human.

Aunt: You really tried your best. Good for you!

Brother: No matter what, I've got your back.

Neighbor: I love being with you. Come visit me anytime.

Look at your list. Think about how these messages have affected your life. Is this how you talk to yourself now? Have these outer voices become your inner voices? How do they contribute to your procrastination? How can you respond to unhelpful messages? See if you can answer with something positive or hopeful. For example, when that inner voice says, "If it's not done right, it's not worth doing!" you might respond, "That's not true. It's worth getting started." Or if that inner voice says, "Be careful! You're not ready!" you might stand up for yourself by saying, "It's all right if I don't know exactly what I'm doing. I can give it a try anyway." This new conversation has both psychological and biological benefits. When you consciously shift from a negative to a more positive emotional focus, you are disrupting ingrained brain patterns and creating new ones.[7]

FAMILY THEMES

Over the years, we have heard procrastinators describe five primary family themes that go along with the fears that underlie procrastination: pressuring, doubting, controlling, clinging, and distancing. All five themes exist to some degree in every family. In your family, the one that somehow bred a procrastinator, what was the particular mixture of these themes? One theme may stand out as primary, or you may have received a confusing array of mixed messages. Some families, for example, hold all their members up against a high standard of achievement, while other families are primarily concerned with demonstrations of family loyalty. By contemplating the interplay of these five themes in your own family, you may see a fuller picture of the development of your self-esteem and of your tendency to procrastinate.

The Pressuring Theme

The pressuring theme is apparent in families that are highly achievement-oriented. There may be a long lineage of accomplishment, or perhaps the parents are unsatisfied with their own lives and place their hopes for great achievement onto the children. In pressuring families, top-notch performance is the only thing that's appreciated. Strengths don't matter unless they're perfect; limitations are viewed as unacceptable. Mistakes are evidence of failure and therefore a source of shame: "You're either first or you're nothing!" The pressure can be a heavy burden that can lead to maladaptive perfectionism and procrastination, if you're not supposed to be anything less than #1. In a study of college students, maladaptive perfectionism was associated with high parental expectations and parental criticism, and the students were overly concerned with living up to the expectations of others.[8]

Being average is not tolerated, although this message can be conveyed in the guise of support: "You're so smart. You can do anything you want!" Hearing inordinate and indiscriminate praise can leave a child feeling fraudulent, confused, and ultimately inadequate. Or, an average performance may be blamed on external factors, not on you, conveying the idea that if not for outside interferences, your performance would have been top-notch. It's as if your true ability can't stand on its own but must be falsely embellished to be good enough.

Siblings play a role in pressuring families, too. Having a "perfect" sibling can drive you to try to be even more perfect (what's more perfect than perfect?), or maybe you were the one the family counted on to make up for the failings of the other kids. A transfer student from junior college who was in danger of flunking out of the university tearfully insisted that he *couldn't* fail, because his other siblings were a mess, and he was the only child left in the family who could make his parents proud.

Pressures to succeed can extend well beyond the immediate family. Rico, an intelligent Chicano man, was the first person from his small California farming community to graduate from college. Everyone in the town proudly followed his academic progress through graduate school. When Rico went home for vacations, he felt that many people expected him to represent not only their community but all Chicanos. Rico experienced their praise as an honor but also as a responsibility— one he was not sure he could live up to. He procrastinated for years on his doctoral thesis, feeling it was never good enough.

However the pressure was conveyed in your family, the focus was probably on what you *did* rather than on who you *were*. If your acceptance in your family has been tied to achieving greatness, it may seem safer to procrastinate and never risk falling short after you've done your best. You may not realize that most people will accept your normal human limitations more than you are accustomed to expect.

The Doubting Theme

When the doubting theme is prominent in a family, the communication is, "You don't have what it takes." Doubts may be conveyed directly—"What are you so proud of? It's only a baseball game"—or indirectly, through lack of interest. Encouragement may come only when the child does things that interest the parent, so that the child doesn't develop confidence in his own passions. Parents who have unsuccessful or chaotic lives may convey the idea that their children should not expect their own lives to be any better. When parents feel threatened by their child's progress, they may express criticisms that make the child doubt not his parents but himself.

Children may be given the message that there are some things they just can't do. Perhaps you are compared to a sibling who performs well, implying that you can't measure up. An older brother or sister may resent being shown up by a younger sibling who is in fact better at some things, and the younger one defers by lacking confidence, procrastinating, and limiting achievement. Or you might get the message that because of your gender some things are off-limits to you ("Girls aren't good at math"), so you just don't try.

Children who are heavily exposed to these doubting messages are likely to believe them and act accordingly, retreating from new challenges or anything that feels like a test, whether it's batting practice or homework. Their automatic reaction is to feel apprehensive and think, "I can't do this." Even when they do take the initiative, they may give up as soon as the least difficulty is encountered, reinforcing those old doubts.

Another way procrastinators respond to their doubting families is by rebelling, taking on the attitude, "I'll show them how wrong they are!" They push themselves hard, determined to succeed in spite of the doubts, but this determination can lead them straight into the trap of perfectionism, which as we've seen can lead to procrastination.

Whether you have retreated or taken a defiant stance, if you have internalized self-doubt, you may lose heart when you are faced with a challenge. Procrastination appears to be a safe course of action, because it protects you from testing what you fear to be the awful truth: you can't do it.

Procrastinators who come from families that continually expressed doubt tend to assume that any failure, big or small, means that *all* those doubts are true. What they have lost sight of is that one failure, or two, or even a hundred for that matter, does not make a person bad, unlovable, or incapable forever.

The Controlling Theme

The controlling theme comes through in efforts to take over and direct a child's life. A parent may make all decisions for the child—what to do, what to wear, how to act, whom to befriend—and give "advice" that the child is expected to follow without question. Parents are often unaware of being controlling, feeling instead that they are protecting their children or using their wisdom to prevent a child from making mistakes. Some parents feel they have the right to be in control. They set the rules, call the shots, and are clear about the "shoulds" in life. You should always eat everything on your plate, whether you like it or not. You should want to visit your grandparents every week. Every child should learn to play the piano. A child on the receiving end of unending advice and directives develops the feeling that he or she has no right to an independent self. Sometimes the control is harsh. A parent may explode with anger, and while the anger may have little to do with the child's actions and more to do with what kind of day the parent is having, the child absorbs the anger just the same. Verbal or physical expressions of anger undermine a child's confidence in himself and in others. When the world has in fact been a dangerous place, direct rebellion is too risky, and procrastination can be a way to rebel while staying under the radar.

If rules are changed capriciously, or if rewards and punishments are doled out inconsistently, the child gets the idea that parents can change the rules whenever they want. Too frightened to protest directly, confused by inconsistencies, the child may slow down and do chores or homework at a snail's pace and become skeptical that consistent effort will reap steady rewards.

When someone else is always directing your life, you may find relief in procrastination. By delaying and refusing to do things, you can exasperate a controlling or demanding parent and attempt to weaken their hold over you. Although in the long run procrastination may not have been in your best interests, this passive resistance was a relatively safe way to fight back at a time when direct, open rebellion was too dangerous. Procrastination may even have helped you preserve some sense of independence, which was more important than grades or praise. Sometimes procrastination is a strategy for psychic survival.

The Clinging Theme

Clinging families discourage family members from creating lives of their own and instead promote dependency and enmeshment. Parents become not just a source of support and encouragement for their children but a lifeline assumed to be necessary for the child's survival, as if the children need to be helped, protected, and taken care of into adulthood. Children who receive so much help may never discover what they can do for themselves or develop faith in their own capacities. So they put off not only challenges but also activities that would require them to be on their own, like getting a driver's license, leaving a relationship, experimenting with some new activity that is not of interest to others in the family, perhaps even voicing a differing opinion. Some families operate like a single organism with many heads, everyone connected and interdependent. Having interests that don't involve the family may be seen as betrayal. Making independent judgments, moving away, having different religious or political views—these steps toward separateness are not encouraged. The message is: you can't think on your own, and you can't survive without us.

A clinging theme may also be manifested in the expectation that a child take care of other family members. Explicitly or implicitly, the message is, "I need you; don't leave me." A parent may be ill, depressed, or emotionally needy and turns to the child for support and reassurance. Of course we all want to help family members in need. The problem occurs when the child takes over as the adult in a role reversal with the parent, managing the household, looking after siblings, mediating disagreements, or functioning as a quasi spouse. The child feels so responsible for the family that her own interests are sacrificed. She might not go out with friends or join after-school activities; she might postpone doing homework in order to attend to family matters. Children from clinging families may feel too needed to be able to leave the family, and if they do manage to separate, they continue to have deep feelings of guilt.

Procrastination may be used to keep you clinging to your family, as you avoid activities that could create a wedge. Or you may use procrastination to aid in the struggle for some sense of autonomy, an attempt to create distance between yourself and other people, avoiding entanglements. If the experience of being close has meant being smothered, leaned on, or isolated from the rest of the world, you may rely on procrastination to avoid attachments.

The Distancing Theme

The distancing theme is evident in families in which the members are unable to develop emotional closeness, physical affection, attentive interest, or protective comfort. Whether or not they give the appearance of being a "close" family, each person lives within a separate world. Feelings are rarely expressed or even alluded to; upsets are played down, if acknowledged at all. They don't know much about each other's emotional lives, and they don't ask for or offer help.

Parents may go on with their adult lives almost as if they have no children, sending the message, "Go away, don't bother me," sometimes in words, sometimes in behavior. Think of a father who works all the time or one who watches TV every night, ignoring everyone else in the house.

Some emotionally distant parents are not able to empathize with a child's experience, so that the child can feel isolated even in the company of the family. The child is expected to solve problems alone; no one is there to offer help with homework, to demonstrate how to approach writing a term paper, or prepare for a sports tournament. When in trouble, the child is expected to manage frustrations and disappointments by himself. Sometimes this training lays the groundwork for procrastination. In later life, the painful feeling of loneliness may interfere with a person's effectiveness, as working alone can elicit a feeling of emptiness. If no one has expressed interest in a child's thoughts and opinions, he may be reluctant in later life to express his ideas—who will care? So writing projects and other independent projects may be avoided through procrastination.

In an attempt to spark a connection with a distant parent, some children try to make themselves so delightful, interesting, and appealing that their parents can't resist being drawn to them. "If I just make myself *better*, then they're bound to be interested in me." "Better" can mean anything: more intelligent, more attractive, more self-reliant, more athletic, more dignified. "Better" is defined by the child's understanding of what the family values. But we've seen the relationship between perfectionism and procrastination: the more you expect of yourself, the more frightening it is to discover whether you can actually get what you want. When the purpose of being perfect is to make yourself appealing enough to be worth someone's interest, the gamble is especially risky. With a background of distancing, people can seek out the intimate connections they've missed, or they can perpetuate the distance in relationships, using procrastination to keep people at bay.

THE FAMILY'S INFLUENCE ON SELF-ESTEEM

Perhaps the most profound impact, and the one that is most directly linked to the fears we've discussed, is the inhibition of the development of a child's self-esteem. Self-esteem represents your assessment of your own worth. If your general self-esteem is too low, you feel worthless. If your self-esteem is inflated, you feel all-powerful. One of the tasks of growing up is to develop a realistic sense of your capabilities and to accept your limitations, while maintaining positive feelings of self-worth. This task can be supported by a family that embraces you as you are and helps you develop a sense of yourself that does not fluctuate wildly under different circumstances.

A fundamental lack of support for a child's developing sense of self is common to the family themes we have mentioned. Overcontrol undermines a child's sense that he or she has what it takes to survive independently, make good choices, and chart a self-determined course. A family that focuses so much attention on achievement puts a child in a precarious position, because the child is defined by performance. The overly praised child is left with an unrealistic sense of omnipotence—"I can do anything!"—because the parents did not help the child to tolerate failure and accept realistic limits. On the other hand, the child who received too little praise or too much criticism may continue to believe that he or she can never be anything but a disappointment—"I am nothing!" When personality dimensions other than achievement are ignored, a child cannot develop a broad-based self-image. A sense of humor, the capacity to make and keep friends, having passionate interests or creative talents, a willingness to put forth great effort, the ability to empathize—these are only a few of the human qualities that are ignored or undervalued in many procrastinators' families.

Some of you may find that thinking about your family history brings up painful memories, because in some families, there is trauma—high conflict, multiple moves, immigration, divorce, illness, and death. Parents may be emotionally unstable or may abuse substances, resulting in neglect of their children or in physical, emotional, or sexual abuse. A series of repeated smaller traumas can add up to "cumulative trauma,"[9] which can have a significant impact even though it may be harder to identify. If you came home with a good report card, and your father was busy on his computer and didn't seem interested, that's one experience. In the context of a responsive and supportive relationship, it's no big deal. But if your father was consistently unable to respond to your pleasure and pride, all of those moments can add up to your feeling invisible.

These traumas stay with us, leaving us feeling fundamentally vulnerable and unsafe. Tasks that might otherwise have a neutral valence may feel risky simply because day-to-day existence feels threatening. Unfortunately, when you respond to risks by procrastinating, you actually increase the possibility of being in danger.

Rupture and Repair

Just as we are not perfect, parents are not perfect either. Everyone makes mistakes. All parents have bad days, bad moods, and bad behavior. At these times, parents can't recognize the needs of the child. Fortunately, parents don't need to be perfectly attuned to be "good enough" parents.[10] Researchers who studied parent-child attachment patterns found that parents who were attuned to their children as little as 30 percent of the time were able to foster secure emotional attachments in their children.[11]

Ruptures, large or small, are an ordinary part of being in any relationship. One critical factor is how people handle ruptures when they occur. If a parent behaves badly or ignores the needs of a child, the parent can initiate a process of repair: "I'm sorry I got so angry"; "I didn't realize how upset you were and that you needed to talk to me." It's helpful when parents can acknowledge their faults and take responsibility for their actions. Making the child a partner in reconnecting communicates respect, value, and esteem. A child who is treated with esteem develops self-esteem.

An Unremembered Legacy

When you procrastinate on a task, all of your history is alive in you at that moment. You might consciously know what makes you so fearful or uncomfortable. But even if you don't, you can bet that an old memory related to your self-esteem has been activated.[12] Our earliest experiences have a profound and lasting influence on our developing self-esteem. They function as a mirror that reveals who we are, and that reflection forms a background tone and texture for the rest of our lives.

Writing about these earliest life experiences, the psychologist Louis Cozolino asks,

> Did our parents seem to cherish, love, and value us, or did they find us annoying, disgusting, or uninteresting? When we were with them did we feel safe and protected or worthy of rejection and abandonment? Were we loved for who we were or for what we did that pleased them? When we gazed into their eyes, did they reflect back our love or did they appear irritated, indifferent, or unhappy? . . . Our only access to these primitive experiences is what we see reflected in our self-esteem, the way we treat ourselves, and how we allow others to treat us. Do we take care of ourselves, nurture ourselves, and feel we have value? Do we live under the scrutiny of an internal jury, second-guessing and criticizing our every thought and deed? How do we treat ourselves when we make a mistake? When we fail, can we face the disappointment, learn from the experience, and move on?[13]

An attuned parent provides a secure base,[14] which is the foundation for us to feel accepted, whole, and loved and to have confidence in ourselves. The secure base is also the foundation for healthy exploration of the world and for the pursuit of interests, opportunities, and new learning. Fortunately, children who did not have a strong sense of security growing up can acquire it in later life, if they are able to choose safe, reliable, loving people for their significant relationships.[15]

It's All about Love

All family experiences leave children with certain ideas about how to be loved. In some families, love is unconditional, and people are accepted as they are. In other families, love is more conditional. What is acceptable in one family may not be acceptable in another. For example, in some families, love and affection depend on being interested in every detail of each other's lives. In other families, that same behavior would be considered intrusive or insulting; love is given instead to those who take care of themselves and do not make demands on others.

A child may come to believe that it is possible to be loved only when he or she fulfills certain special roles within the family. For example, the child may assume that I will be loved only if:

- I am the perfect child
- I can do what comes easily to everybody else
- I don't threaten you with my success
- I follow your rules
- I always put you first
- I don't demand too much from you
- I can become a different person

These conditions represent the child's hope for being loved. But is that hope likely to be fulfilled? Even if a child molds himself to be just what he thinks he's supposed to be, there's no guarantee he'll be received with love. And if he is loved under these narrow conditions, only certain parts of him are being welcomed. Procrastination serves to maintain assumptions about what's permissible or possible by keeping parts of the self under wraps. A child may feel that this is the only way to be loved.

Suppose a child holds the idea that in order to be loved, he must always believe his father is right about everything. The child's self-esteem is compromised because the father is the "one who knows" and the child must remain the "one who does not know." When the child chooses to write papers at the last minute, he is handicapping himself, refusing to use his full talents and abilities. This keeps him in the position of being one who does not know. If the child did not procrastinate and allowed himself to explore and express his own ideas, he would be taking the position of one who knows, which would be a direct challenge to his assumption about where he is permitted to stand in relation to his father.

Confronting and changing long-held assumptions about you and your family can be unnerving and disorienting. This is why procrastination is so hard to overcome. It's not simply a matter of changing a habit; it requires changing your inner world. However, as you access capacities and parts of yourself that have been held back by procrastination, you can derive great pleasure in claiming your whole self. This integration is the true basis for self-esteem.

10

Looking Ahead to Success

So, procrastination isn't so simple, is it? We've come a long way from attributing it to laziness, lack of discipline, and moral decay. And yet, your procrastination is understandable—it is not a plague that descends upon you by chance; it is a behavior you engage in for particular reasons. Procrastination represents a complex interweaving of psychological roots, biological factors, and a lifetime of experiences.

In one sense, procrastination has served you well. It has protected you from what may be some unpleasant realizations about yourself. It has helped you avoid uncomfortable and perhaps frightening feelings. It has provided you with a convenient excuse for not taking action in a direction that is upsetting in some way. But, regardless of the reasons for your procrastination, and in spite of whatever "comfort" it has given you, you have also paid a price for it.

Let's look at the costs. You've inhibited your efforts at work or school; you've held yourself back from taking risks and exploring new possibilities; you've put a lid on the natural and spontaneous expression of your ideas and emotions; you've been acting in accord with a limited view of who you think you must be. You've disappointed people you love and let down or irritated others. On top of all this, you've been paying the emotional price of anxiety, resentment, fraudulence, or despair, and—most expensive of all—diminished self-confidence.

If you are going to let go of procrastination and face your fears head-on, what do you think might happen? What if you're not perfect? What's dangerous about being successful or realizing your limits?

137

Would you really be trapped if you made a commitment? If you stated your own opinion? Who says you can't be an individual if you do things according to someone else's timetable? You can begin to do something about your procrastination in spite of the fact that you are afraid. As Mark Twain said, "Courage is resistance to fear, mastery of fear—not absence of fear." It will take courage to give up the familiarity and the usefulness of procrastination. In this section, we offer a number of ideas to help you get started.

THE DANGERS OF IMPROVEMENT[1]

If you have felt frustrated and thwarted by procrastination, the prospect of delaying less and accomplishing more may be very appealing. In fact, you might think life will improve 100 percent. Many people assume that after conquering procrastination they'll be happy, successful, and relaxed. But they don't realize that making progress also means confronting the fears they've been avoiding.

For example, if you become noticeably more productive at work, you could be promoted to a new position with even more demands and greater responsibilities. You might worry that you'd be in over your head or that you would travel more and have to spend time away from your family. Or, if you finally file your long-overdue taxes, not only will you face what you owe, but you will have to acknowledge that you, too, must play by the rules.

We would like you to consider the "dangers of improvement," the troublesome consequences that might result if you were to give up procrastination. The potential dangers may not necessarily be reasonable or logical. We're not asking you to predict the reality of what would happen if you stopped procrastinating, but rather to play with ideas about how things might change and how that might feel.

If you stop procrastinating, what new problems or situations would you have to face that you don't have to contend with now?

Take a few minutes to think over this question. Try to come up with at least five dangers that you might face if you stop putting things off. Let your imagination go. Below are some of the dangers of improvement identified by procrastinators in our Procrastination Workshops. We have grouped them according to several common themes.

My illusions could be shattered . . .

What if I finally do my best, but I'm mediocre?
I might not be able to achieve what I always thought I could.
I couldn't feel superior if I found I was in the same boat as others.

There's always more to do . . .

I'll turn into a workaholic.
I'll take on more and more responsibilities and put my own needs last.
I'll find there's even more to do than I thought. It will never end.

My relationships would change and not for the better . . .

It's lonely at the top; I'd lose my friends.
People will compete with me and try to cut me down.
My flaws will be obvious and no one will like me.
Everyone will be envious of me.
I'll be too different from my family.

I'd lose control over my life . . .

I'd have to accept a lot of other people's routines and expectations.
I'd have to learn new things and be a novice again. I'd rather be the expert.
I'll be taken over by this new culture.
People will demand more and more of me—and I can't say "No."

Life would seem boring . . .

I would miss the excitement and challenge of "cutting it close."

I wouldn't be inspired and I'd be less creative.
Things done early will seem too easy. That's no fun!

I'd be completely responsible for myself ...

I couldn't blame other people or circumstances for what I do or don't do.
What would it be like to be completely on my own without getting everyone to help me at the last minute?
I'd have to make a lot of difficult decisions about how to spend my time.

I wouldn't be a nice person anymore ...

If I'm successful, I might turn into a pompous ass.
I'd become self-righteous and disdainful of those who still procrastinate.
I might be dull, less fun, no longer a unique person.
I'd start to feel competitive with everyone else.

Maybe I don't deserve this ...

I'd have to acknowledge that I'm worth something.
I haven't punished myself enough for procrastinating.
I'd be even more disappointed in myself if I started to procrastinate again.

These dangers of improvement provide more clues about why the cycle of procrastination is so hard to break. If you stop procrastinating, things *will* change. Even though they change for the better, you may feel you're on unfamiliar and dangerous ground. Until now, procrastination has seemed the lesser of many evils by offering refuge in spite of its costs and restrictions. Your new, un-procrastinating self is unknown and therefore represents a risk. One of the greatest dangers of improvement will be finding a new way to define yourself.

PROCRASTINATION AS IDENTITY

People vary greatly with respect to how much of their identity is wrapped up in being a procrastinator. Before you make a move to reduce the extent of procrastination in your life, we'd like you to consider some of the ways putting things off may give you a particular kind of personality or image that could be difficult to relinquish.

The Lovable Clown

One way people deal with procrastination is to treat it as a joke—and then build an identity around it. They may use their experiences with procrastination as comic material: entertaining friends with tales of their latest close call, making jokes as they arrive hours late for dinner, or laughing all the way to the post office at midnight on April 15. Making procrastination such an important part of their repertoire, they may worry that giving it up will somehow diminish their personality and cramp their style.

Sergio regaled people with his procrastination stories. He told everyone he knew about the time he had to tape the unfinished hem of his pants cuffs in a department store bathroom, because he bought a new suit thirty minutes before meeting the executive director of his company. In his college fraternity, he'd been voted "Most Likely to Rush." Sergio's procrastination gave him a way to entertain people. If he gave up the comic role, he wasn't sure exactly who he would be or whether people would still find him funny.

The Saint

Some people add purpose and direction to their lives by taking care of others' needs while procrastinating on their own. Of course, there will be times when you want to help your family and friends, but constant caretaking can distract you from the fact that, in your own life, you may be quite stuck. You may make yourself so available to others that you never have time to take care of your own priorities.

Even though you've planned to spend the evening on work, when a friend calls in tears, you're on the phone for two hours. When the PTA asks you to be chairperson of the spring festival, you agree, even though it means that you must give up all your free time. All because you are *needed*.

Because it seems so justified, being overly available to other people is a deceptive kind of procrastination. When you choose to do for someone else instead of doing for yourself, you seem to be making an unselfish, generous, praiseworthy decision. But helping others to the exclusion of taking care of yourself makes it difficult to develop a sense of what's best for you. Your own identity and your own goals never have a chance to emerge as long as you're using all your time to take care of someone else. We're not advocating that you lead a completely selfish life, intent only on pursuing your own goals. But if taking care of others has allowed you to avoid knowing yourself, then you're not a saint; you're a martyr.

The Renaissance Man

Some procrastinators create an identity based on knowing something about everything. They want their lives to encompass every dimension of human interest, from politics, philosophy, and technology to exercise physiology and basket weaving. Needing to know everything takes up a lot of time! Instead of doing their work, they spend hours online following the multiple threads of their latest interest, downloading books, and reading newspapers from all over the world.

Often, these people are unable to use their considerable talents to their own benefit. The need to be well versed in *everything* prevents them from pursuing *anything*. They refuse to be limited to one field of study, one special interest, one predictable career. Believing they can embody the Renaissance ideal, they end up spreading themselves in so many directions that they can't move forward.

The Miracle Worker

Procrastination can produce last-minute chaos and disaster, and some people thrive on making a heroic effort to save the day. They meet a deadline by working frantically for thirty-six straight hours or come up with an ingenious plan to buy more time. They use their creativity not to produce but to find an imaginative, brilliant solution to the crisis. They are seen as miracle workers.

Often, the crises these people are heralded for resolving are of their own making. Disaster is imminent only because they've procrastinated themselves into a corner. Without their delay, they would have no problem to solve, no miracle to work in the first place. They need the miracle solution to feel special, and procrastinating provides the need for their magic touch.

The Blank Slate

Procrastination can camouflage the fact that you may not be very clear about who you are and what you want for yourself. It may look as if you haven't achieved your goals because of your problem with procrastination, but perhaps you haven't come to grips with what your priorities are in the first place: What *are* your interests, preferences, values, needs, and goals? Without more self-knowledge, even if you were to stop procrastinating, you might not know what to do with your newfound ability to make progress.

If you haven't asked yourself questions about what you really want out of life, or if you've asked and not been able to find authentic answers, you may be left with a sense that your life doesn't have enough direction or purpose. This lack of direction can set the stage for procrastination. People who can't clearly discern what really matters to them may be equally interested in each new opportunity that comes along. Incomplete work may pile up, as they abandon one activity after the other. If you are up to your eyeballs with half-finished projects, lists of things to do, anxiety about deadlines upcoming and deadlines missed, you may be filling yourself up with worries because you need to fill up with *something*.

The Person beneath the Procrastinator

Procrastination gets in the way of knowing yourself. When you are preoccupied with procrastination, you can't really think clearly about important issues. You're busy presenting an image to the world, maybe even lying about how you spend your time, hiding the truth of what you go through. Procrastination breeds feelings of fraudulence, a precarious way to live. We encourage you to reduce your reliance on procrastination, so that you can lead a more authentic life.

It's important to know yourself apart from your procrastination. Then you can begin to accept yourself as you are, not as you wish you were or think you should be. This is by no means easy to do. It involves knowing yourself honestly, evaluating yourself realistically, and ultimately, accepting what you find. The psychoanalyst Carl Jung said, "The most terrifying thing is to accept oneself completely."[2] Yet this "terrifying" process of accepting oneself—warts, scars, scabs, and all—can also bring relief.

GETTING REAL

We all have aspects of ourselves that we wish we could change, but they are intrinsic to who we are. As long as we avoid or deny them, they can't be understood or integrated, nor can they be the basis for change.

Biological Realities

We are each born with a unique temperament. You may be someone whose temperament makes you shrink from loud noise and boisterous activity, or someone who needs constant action and lots of company. Maybe you thrive on novelty or need time to get comfortable in new situations. If you need quiet time to think, then working in a café may be fine for your friends, but it isn't productive for you. If you think you should be able to stay up all night, but your body never makes it past midnight, maybe your body is telling you something you should listen to. There isn't a good or bad temperament; there is only your temperament. And that's where you have to start. It's important to accept your biological reality and deal with it, not procrastinate because of it.

Every brain has strengths and weaknesses. Some functions come easily, and some are a struggle. Jane, for example, can do a lot of things well, but when it comes to spatial relations, she is in the bottom .03 percent! She used to get mad at herself for always getting lost, and her struggles with solid geometry were a stain on her high school transcript. So it was tempting to put off things that involve her weakest skill, like any kind of repair project or packing the trunk of the car, because it was so frustrating and made her feel stupid. But if you accept the reality that you have weak brain functions in some areas, then you can make compensations. Jane now has a GPS system, checks Mapquest before she sets out, and tells people she needs explicit directions. Fortunately, as a psychoanalyst, she has little need for solid geometry. You can help yourself and your brain if you pay respectful attention to your weaker areas, treat yourself with compassion, and practice your weaker skills or arrange for compensations that will help.

Our areas of brain weakness can get us into trouble if we deny them or if we hate ourselves for having them, but accepting them has important advantages. You can work on improving those areas with focused attention and sustained practice, so that, over time, your brain will make new connections, and the weaker areas will become stronger.[3] Even so, with some things, there's only so much you can do to compensate. Therefore, accepting that your brain is what it is can help you live life without hating yourself and wishing you were someone else.

Emotional Realities

Accepting yourself completely involves knowing and living with your emotions—all of them—the good, the bad, and the ugly. Love and excitement, hatred and self-hatred, envy and gratitude, desires and regrets, all are part of the spectrum of human emotions.

Knowing your feelings, whatever they are, will help develop what author Daniel Goleman calls emotional intelligence, "the capacity for recognizing our own feelings and those of others, for motivating ourselves, for managing emotions well in ourselves and in our relationships."[4] Emotional intelligence is not about being book smart or fact smart, but being people smart, starting with knowing your own feelings. Not only is it important for successful relationships, but research has also suggested that emotional intelligence is more important than the traditional measures of IQ in determining career success.[5]

Procrastination may trigger emotional reactions, like self-criticism and disgust. But, as we have suggested, it may also be helping you avoid other, more anxious, feelings. When you spend a lot of time and energy avoiding tasks and projects, you are also probably avoiding the uncomfortable feelings associated with those tasks. For example, people may put off doing taxes because they feel bad about not earning enough money in the past year, or because they are so disorganized that they can't find what they need and will have an attack of self-hatred as they rummage through piles of papers, or because they feel anxious about doing the math. The feeling of anxiety associated with doing a task is usually a signal that there are other feelings involved as well, which ultimately lead you to avoid the task.

Feelings don't have to be mysterious enemies that keep you from getting what you want. When you notice feelings of hesitation, discomfort, or anxiety that usually lead to procrastination, you have an opportunity to get to know yourself better, to discover more about your procrastination, and to take steps that will help you feel better.

Many people believe that feeling uncomfortable is a good reason to procrastinate. But the assumption that you can take action only if you are comfortable is very limiting. It's a version of perfectionism to believe that your emotional state has to be "just so" in order for you to take action. If everyone waited to feel comfortable before taking action, there would be no risk-taking (because there is some anxiety associated with the unknown), and there would be no learning (because some anxiety motivates learning, though too much anxiety interferes with learning).

Even if your anxiety about a task feels overwhelming, we encourage you to pay close attention to it rather than wish it away. Notice your feelings; observe them with a compassionate attitude. Try to understand them, and try to act anyway, so that anxiety and procrastination no longer dominate your life. Psychologists George Eifert and John Forsyth observed that "clients have spent their energy trying to manage their anxiety, almost as if anxiety management were their occupation."[6] We would say that the same holds true for many procrastinators, and we respectfully suggest that if this is the case for you, perhaps it's time to make something other than managing procrastination the central focus of your life.

If you allow, accept, explore, and try to manage your feelings, they don't have to stop you from taking action. When you are anxious about confronting a dreaded task, try to calm yourself down. This may require a conscious effort to breathe deeply, to reassure yourself that you are not, in reality, facing total disaster and ruin at this moment, and to regain a more balanced state in which you can actually think again. Remember that the signals from the fear center of the brain to the thinking part of the brain move very rapidly, whereas the pathways from the thinking part to the fear center are much slower, so don't expect to calm yourself as quickly or as thoroughly as you became overwhelmed.

The Reality of Your Values

Accepting yourself as you are also means getting real about your values. Values represent the attitudes that are most important in your life. "A goal is a destination. A value is a direction for living."[7] Knowing your values helps you connect to your core self. It is not possible to see values directly, but they are reflected in your actions. Whether you aim to make a lot of money or to donate most of what you have to charity, to work for yourself or to work for your community, to wield power or to avoid power struggles, these goals express your values. If you are putting off things that would move you along your chosen direction for living, then procrastination is interfering with the fullest expression of who you are. If you value achievement, for example, then putting off your work is interfering with your living according to that value. If you value relationships, then procrastinating at work may be a sacrifice you're willing to make in order to spend more time with your family. Some other examples of values are helping others, living according to spiritual or religious beliefs, maintaining physical well-being, and developing personal insight. Values—like biology and feelings—are idiosyncratically yours.

Identifying your own values and priorities may require you to separate yourself from some of the ideas and roles you have incorporated over the course of your lifetime. If you come from a different culture than the one you're in now, there may be a conflict between the values of your original culture and the values that are prominent in the new country. We encourage you to identify what's important for you and whether or not it matches what's important to other significant people in your life. Sometimes delaying behavior reflects the discrepancy between what you think is expected of you and what you really want to do.

Your procrastination may be warning you that you are trying to pursue a course that raises some moral or ethical questions for you. For example, a carpenter berated himself for always arriving late to the construction site on his new job. When he thought it through, he realized that he questioned his boss's business practices. The contractor who hired him was involved in several shady business deals, including using illicit monies to build houses. The carpenter's tardiness was a sign that he was compromising his values.

At times, you may find that your values and priorities are congruent with those other people have transmitted to you. You may want for yourself exactly what someone else wants for you, yet you procrastinate as a way of resisting the influence of others, giving up what you value in the process. Is it really more important to rebel by deny-ing your values than to pursue what matters to you?

If your procrastination in one area is helping you express your val-ues in another area, then it's communicating something important that you should try to translate. But if procrastination is interfering with your being able to live according to your values, then you are depriving yourself of the solid feeling that comes from living in har-mony with your core self.

Integration

This feeling of harmony reflects the functioning of a healthy system. A healthy system is one that is coherent and integrated, neither too rigid nor too chaotic.[8] The coherence of a system can be observed in any type of organization, whether a business, a family, a body, or a self. When your self-system is too rigid, you hold yourself fast to the perfectionist demands that lead to procrastination; you keep doing the same thing over and over, whether it's working or not; your ex-pectations of others are unyielding; and you experience inner tur-moil when you assume life will be a certain way, and it just isn't. At the other extreme, a chaotic self-system reflects disorganization. When you're confused about who you are and what you want, torn by distress and conflict, or lost in the last-minute frenzy of procrasti-nation, you are not functioning in an integrated way. If you're being either too rigid or chaotic, you lose genuine freedom and spontane-ity. Either way, you compromise your vitality; it's deadening.

If instead, you aim for a coherent self-system, you move toward an experience of aliveness, of harmony and balance. That will help you develop the resilience to experiment and explore, with the belief that you can handle what comes, whatever that might be. A belief in your resilience will help you be more confident, and that confidence be-comes the cornerstone of your self-image. When you define yourself as someone who is resilient rather than someone who must perform, you are breaking the self-worth equation we presented in earlier chapters, so that neither performance nor ability defines your value as a person.

THE INNER PROSECUTOR
AND THE DEFENSE ATTORNEY

Getting to a state of resilience is not easy. Procrastinators tend to judge their feelings and actions harshly and rigidly. They constantly compare themselves with some standard that seems to reflect the *right* way of being a person and the *right* way of doing things—as if there were in reality one (and only one) right way. Procrastinators are very hard on themselves. In fact, for some, their own "internal judge" is often so critical, so biased, and so impossible to please, that it is more appropriately called a "prosecutor" than a judge. A judge hears evidence from all sides and tries to make a fair decision. A prosecutor wants to prove guilt and only produces evidence that will help fix blame. An inner prosecutor has free rein to make vicious personal attacks whenever it likes. It acts as no friend would, hitting hard in the aftermath of disappointment, pouncing on weaknesses, predicting failure while offering no consolation or encouragement for the future.

The inner prosecutor's specific criticisms vary, depending on the issues most sensitive to the procrastinator. Someone who is afraid of being too successful might hear his inner prosecutor saying, "Who do you think you are, anyway? What makes you think you can take the pressure of having your own company? Who are you to take business away from people who have been your friends?" Someone who resists feeling controlled might hear, "Only a weakling would go along with that order. Next thing you know they'll be walking all over you." Unfortunately, for many people, the critical voice of the inner prosecutor dominates their lives and goes unchallenged.

To counter the allegations of their inner prosecutor, procrastinators can develop another inner voice, that of a "defense attorney," to speak on their behalf when the prosecutor starts in. David, the lawyer who wanted to prepare every case brilliantly, wrote down a conversation between his inner prosecutor and his newly hired "defense attorney." You could try the same exercise, mentally or in writing.

> **Prosecutor:** You stupid idiot! You screwed up again. You're not smart enough to be working for this firm, and sooner or later they'll find you out.
>
> **Defense:** I would have done a better job if I'd started sooner.
>
> **P:** You should have known better than to wait so long.
>
> **D:** I had a lot of other things to deal with.
>
> **P:** You're always making excuses. If it's not one thing, it's another.
>
> **D:** If you would lay off, it would be easier for me to get back on track.
>
> **P:** I'm only demanding for your own good. Without me, you'd have no drive, no motivation.
>
> **D:** That's not true. I could do more if you didn't constantly attack me.
>
> **P:** But then you'll never amount to anything.
>
> **D:** Don't predict the future for me. I've learned a lot, and every experience makes me better. I can only go on from here.

The challenge is learning to come to your own defense, to allow your values and actions to emerge as much as possible, in a judgment-free response. There is no absolute right or wrong answer to the question, What do I want for myself? This means that you have to separate yourself not only from the influence of others but also from your over-developed critical perspective. You have to get out of your own way.

The voice of the defense attorney creates fresh positive thoughts, which, as we have seen, helps to build new neural connections and weaken old ones. The more you practice defending yourself, the more automatic it becomes, the more it helps your brain stay in balance, and the more you develop confidence in yourself.

Perhaps you can now consider an alternative to the Procrastinator's Code:

THE FREEDOM FROM PROCRASTINATION CODE

It is not possible to be perfect.

Making an effort is a good thing. It is not a sign of stupidity or weakness.

Failure is not dangerous. Failure is an ordinary part of every life.

The real failure is not living.

Everyone has limitations, including me.

If it's worth doing, it's worth making mistakes along the way.

Challenge will help me grow.

I'm entitled to succeed, and I can deal with other people's reactions to my success.

If I do well this time, I still have a choice about next time.

Following someone else's rules does not mean I have absolutely no power.

If I show my real self, I can have real relationships with people who like the real me.

There are many possible answers, and I need to find what I feel is right.

As you read this list, how you do feel? These ideas may be shocking at first, but if you let them percolate they may sink in gradually. They offer you a new attitude toward living, and can become a foundation for a more confident you. This will allow you to explore and take risks without relying on procrastination for protection.

PART TWO

OVERCOMING
PROCRASTINATION

TAKING STEPS

In the following chapters, we have brought together a smorgasbord of techniques to help you begin to manage and eventually overcome procrastination. These techniques have been designed with procrastinators in mind, and they work, *if you use them.*

When you try to practice these suggestions, you will probably have a push/pull relationship with them; you'll encounter resistance and make excuses, just as you have with other tasks. We encourage you to pay close attention to how you approach these reasonable, effective approaches to change, because resistance does not have to be your enemy; it can be transformed into an ally. If you find yourself putting off experimenting with these techniques, you can learn a lot by asking: What specifically do I feel uncomfortable about? Is this touching on something from my past? Am I confronting something I usually try to push out of my mind? What makes me think I can't do this now?

When people observe their behavior and clarify what's behind their resistance, they may realize they are automatically reacting with old patterns and fears from the past, rather than responding to circumstances in the present situation. In addition, once people identify the issues involved in resistance, they often feel less overwhelmed or frightened and are more able to proceed.

CHANGE IS A PROCESS

Making a change and learning new behavior happens gradually over time. There are many different models of how change occurs. James Prochaska and his colleagues have researched the change process in health habits and substance abuse and have identified a predictable sequence they call the Stages of Change.[1] The first stage is "Precontemplation," when you're not ready to change and not even thinking about it. "Procrastination? What procrastination?" By reading this book, you have already moved beyond this first stage, at least to the second stage, "Contemplation." This is a time of thinking through whether you're ready to take action and deal with the repercussions, positive and negative. "I know I procrastinate, but I'll think about it tomorrow." Prochaska's third stage is "Preparation," when you're testing the waters, not fully committed but willing to try something new. "OK, I'll finally start exercising." Then comes stage four, "Action." "I went to the gym today; it wasn't so bad."[2] We think it's interesting that you have to go through the first three stages before you even begin to do things differently. This is one reason why it's hard to "just do it."

Michael Hargrove, a success coach and workshop leader, also uses a four-step model that emphasizes people's experience at each stage of change.[3] Hargrove's first stage is "Unconscious Incompetence or pre-change," a time of ignorance or denial, when we don't let ourselves notice how much it is hurting us not to do the things we think we should be doing. The second stage is "Conscious Incompetence or waking up," when we realize the price we are paying for not doing what we know we are supposed to do. Hargrove considers this the "single most important step to change," because it means we are becoming aware that we need to be different.

Third is "Conscious Competence or choosing change," the stage in which we work to accomplish what we now realize we should be doing. This can be an awkward stage in the change process, because learning new behavior takes effort, practice, and repetition, and there are many frustrations along the way. The fourth stage is "Unconscious Competence," when the things we know we should do become such a habit that we can do them without having to struggle or even think about it.

From a neurobiological perspective, by the time you get to the fourth stage, your old brain pathways are being disconnected, and new pathways are in use (new neurons are "firing together"). At some point, doing things on time can become the natural thing to do, although you still have to be on the lookout for the tendency to fall back into old habits, especially when you are stressed. Effort, practice, and repetition are important in maintaining change, and over time, you may even lose that temptation to put things off and find it easier to "do it now."

You are likely to make small improvements or changes at first, rather than experience a sudden, grand transformation. In the Fixed Mindset, every step taken is a measure of success, and every step not taken is a measure of failure. In the Growth Mindset, any step— forward or backward—is an opportunity to learn from your experience.[4]

ADDRESSING THE FACTORS THAT LEAD TO PROCRASTINATION

The techniques we offer in this section address the four main factors that research has shown produce procrastination.[5] (For a summary of the research on procrastination, see Appendix A.) The four factors that make procrastination more likely consist are:

1. Low Confidence in Your Ability to Succeed

In order to build up your confidence that you can succeed, we suggest you pick a goal that is realistic, achievable, and easily measured. Then break it down into small, manageable chunks and begin with something you can accomplish in a short amount of time, because nothing succeeds like success. We offer specific techniques to increase the confidence for people with ADD and executive function problems, and for people who are managing cultural changes.

2. Task Aversiveness: Expecting That the Process Will Be Difficult or the Outcome Will Be Unpleasant

We hope the first half of this book helped you understand that finding a task difficult or unpleasant may have little to do with the task itself. A task is uncomfortable because it's related to an underlying fear or anxiety, and it is this discomfort that makes a task so aversive that you avoid it. As you understand your fears and develop self-acceptance, you may be surprised to find that tasks may actually become less aversive. Some tasks may become neutral (yes, even taxes), and some may even become fun!

In Part Two we offer suggestions to make the process or outcome more pleasant, like enlisting support from a friendly ally, rewarding yourself with social experiences, delegating to reduce your to-do list, setting limits so that you are less overwhelmed, and letting go of what you don't need. We also offer suggestions that will help you manage uncomfortable feelings, so you don't have to come to a halt just because you're uneasy.

3. The Goal or Reward Is Too Far Away to Feel Real or Meaningful

To help make a faraway goal or reward feel more real and salient, we encourage you to work in short intervals and reward yourself frequently. We also offer techniques to improve your relationship with time, so that the future seems less vague and more tied to the present. And we encourage you to pay attention to your values, so that you can remind yourself how a long-term goal is important to who you are and what you want.

4. Difficulties in Self-regulation, Such as Being Impulsive and Distractible

For self-regulation, we offer techniques that help your body and mind relax, so that you can manage your emotions and interrupt the path to distraction. We also include some suggestions specifically for people with attention deficit disorder and executive dysfunction.

HOW TO APPROACH THESE TECHNIQUES

Try One New Thing at a Time

We suggest that you experiment with one technique at a time. Trying to put them *all* into practice immediately may make you feel overwhelmed, overworked, or discouraged. The result is likely to be that you give up before you achieve any real progress.

Go Slowly

Many of you will be tempted to begin by throwing yourselves wholeheartedly into this project. Yet, as we have already said, trying to do too much is part of the problem—so slow down. You won't stop procrastinating altogether tomorrow, or next week, or next month, no matter how much you want to or how hard you try.

Watch for Resistance

As you use the techniques we present, we suggest that you keep an eye out for resistance. For example, even though you may begin to make progress in handling your procrastination, you may feel disappointed or angry with yourself for not trying hard enough, not making progress fast enough, or not accomplishing all that you set out to do. Or you may feel we are demanding too much of you, that these techniques require too much effort. Whatever form it takes, resistance can keep you stuck in one place as if your feet were planted in cement.

People usually resist when something feels uncomfortable. These techniques may appear simple, but their appearance is deceptive. The techniques work, but only if you take action and use them. This, of course, is exactly what procrastinators have the greatest difficulty doing: putting into action things they know in their heads! When you get stuck, think back over the issues we raised in Part One. How are your fears getting in your way? Are you stopping because you are on the threshold of possible failure or success? Are you determined not to give in? Are you apprehensive about getting too close or being on your own? Are you playing a familiar role from your family dynamics or a role you took with friends or at school? In spite of your fears, there are steps you can take. Remember, it's *your* procrastination. Nobody else can make you change it or change it for you.

Use a Notebook or Journal

One way to track your experience is by keeping a journal. We strongly urge you to get a notebook you can use for working on the exercises that follow and for jotting down thoughts or reactions you have along the way. Some people like to record specific incidents as they occur. Patterns and themes not easily identified at first often become apparent when you review a series of events. You can also observe patterns in your thinking and emotional responses if you include some notes about them, in addition to describing the event itself. Monitoring your attempts and reactions can give you valuable information that won't get lost or distorted in memory.

Free Writing

You can use your journal for "free writing." Free writing is the process of writing down whatever is on your mind for a limited period of time *without stopping, without judging, and without editing.* Writers use this technique as a way to get themselves started or as a means to discover ideas that are not in the forefront of their minds.

During ten to twenty minutes of free writing, you just keep going, even if what you write down is, "I have nothing to say," or, "I don't know what to write next." Don't even pick up your pen or stop typing; just write down your thoughts as they come to you. Don't worry about punctuation, spelling, grammar, or whether what you are saying makes sense or is accurate. Don't erase, cross out, or delete. The purpose of free writing is not to produce a gem but to explore your thoughts and feelings without judgment.

You can use free writing in any way you find helpful in your quest to overcome procrastination: to explore your fears, understand your resistance, identify your values, examine your reactions to our suggestions, or to monitor your response to change. The reason free writing is effective is that it helps you bypass the inner prosecutor who judges your ideas. It also allows your brain to follow a chain of associations that are linked together,[6] often without your being aware of it until you begin writing nonstop. (Remember, 80 percent of brain activity occurs outside of awareness.) The great novelist and short story writer Flannery O'Connor said, "I don't know so well what I think until I see what I say."[7]

Consider Psychotherapy

If you are able to put our suggestions to work, and they help you overcome procrastination, we congratulate you. However, if you find that you put off trying these new approaches, you may feel stymied. If you can't make use of our suggestions and procrastination continues to hurt your work, your relationships, and your self-esteem, then it might be helpful to talk to a therapist. In therapy, you can explore the worries that underlie procrastination, closely examine what happens at those moments when you choose avoidance instead of progress, and benefit from the supportive, respectful, and confidential relationship therapy offers.

Many non-Western cultures disapprove of taking problems outside the family or the church, and there is shame attached to seeking counseling. African Americans, Asian Americans, Hispanic Americans, and immigrants generally do not look for help from mental health services, but prefer to get help from family, friends, spiritual leaders, traditional healers, and finally, if all else fails, a primary care doctor.[8] Even when they attend college and begin to trust mental health services, they aren't likely to use them.[9]

Mental health agencies and college counseling centers usually have bilingual counselors from diverse backgrounds. It can be difficult to disavow cultural values in order to get help, but as you see from Part One of this book, procrastination has complicated roots that make it difficult to fix by yourself. A psychological perspective can be very helpful.

Some people are skeptical about whether therapy can help them. A landmark study conducted by *Consumer Reports* showed that therapy is effective.[10] Most of the people who had been in therapy reported that they improved significantly. The type of therapy and the credentials of the therapist are not as important as finding a therapist with whom you're comfortable. Give therapy a chance to work; long-term therapy produced more improvement than short-term therapy. If you're taking medication for anxiety or depression, therapy is a good addition, since the combination is more effective than medication alone.[11]

It turns out that therapy is even good for your brain. Nobel Prize-winning psychologist Eric Kandel stated, "There is no longer any doubt that psychotherapy can result in detectable changes in the brain."[12] During therapy, the plasticity of the brain allows it to reorganize itself as a result of talking with the therapist and thinking and feeling in new ways. The more successful the treatment, the greater the change.[13]

————

Now you're ready to move to the next step in the change process, learning and practicing techniques that can actually end procrastination. Whether you are able to use these techniques immediately or you struggle to implement them, you are engaging in a process of understanding more about your procrastination and getting to a place where procrastination doesn't run your life. Remember, repetition is important, and every step matters in changing your brain. So hang in there. Don't give up!

11

Taking Stock
A Procrastination Inventory

An essential step toward managing procrastination is taking stock of your own personal way of postponing. Although most procrastinators are used to living with delay, they usually don't think much about it except to wish it would go away! It helps to look at your procrastination as if you were an objective observer: you're not judging. You're just taking inventory, trying to become more aware of your own experience with procrastination.

EXAMINE YOUR WAR STORIES

Think back to times when you put something off. The incidents may have happened two hours ago or two years ago; they may have been catastrophic, or perhaps they wouldn't seem significant to someone else. Sometimes a situation that appears innocuous on the surface can have great emotional impact. Here are a couple of our stories.

Two years after the original deadline, the first edition of *Procrastination* was finally completed and ready to deliver to the publisher. Our editor came to Berkeley from Boston, and we went out to lunch to celebrate. After lunch, she took a cab to the airport, and we walked to Jane's car—but it wasn't there. First, Jane had the horrible thought that her car had been stolen. Then, with sickening awareness, she realized that it had most likely been towed. Jane sank down on the curb in a daze. Not only had her car been towed, but she realized there were *two* possible reasons: she had a pile of unpaid parking tickets, *and* her annual car registration was overdue. The irony was overwhelming: this occurred on the day we had toasted our book on procrastination! So much for celebration. All the excitement, pleasure, and relief were wiped out and immediately replaced by feelings of self-hate and humiliation.

As a graduate student, Lenora, on impulse, bought a tape deck for her tiny San Francisco apartment. Just after bringing it home, her friend Rickie called to say that she could get a great deal on a tape deck, one of better quality for less money. Who could resist an offer like that? So Rickie brought the better tape deck over, helped Lenora set it up, and all was well—except the tape deck Lenora bought remained in an unopened box on the floor just inside the door. Lenora planned to return it, of course, but the seven-day return period came and went; then the fourteen-day exchange period passed. She never had enough time; before she could return the tape deck, she needed to go to the library (remember, no computers, no Internet!) to research (thoroughly) *Consumer Reports* to figure out what to exchange it for. Then she needed *all day* to take the box back to the store. Who has that kind of time?

Soon it had been a month, then two, then three. Every time Lenora entered or left her apartment, there was the unopened box, waiting by the door. As the weeks and months passed, going in and out of the apartment became more and more of an ordeal. Lenora heard an increasingly harsh refrain, "What's wrong with you? Why can't you do this one simple thing?" On the surface, returning the tape deck seemed a small thing. Inside, Lenora was haunted by feelings of guilt, dread, anxiety, and total incompetence every time she walked into and out of her apartment.

Write down two or three of the experiences you remember best. What happened? Who was involved in the incident? What led up to your procrastinating? How did you feel? What was the eventual outcome? Was anyone else hurt or inconvenienced? Now ask yourself if there are any common themes or patterns among them. What might you have been afraid of?

When Lenora was finally able to calm herself down enough to think through her situation objectively, she decided to take the tape deck back to the store when she had a free *hour*, even though she hadn't touched a single issue of *Consumer Reports*. Heart pounding, mind rehearsing dramatic excuses for being six months past the return date, she walked up to the door and was met by the same forceful, intimidating saleswoman who had sold her the tape deck in the first place. "Would you like to return that?" the woman asked. "Yes," said Lenora. "OK, I'll write a return slip for you." It was only at this unexpected, anticlimactic moment that Lenora realized that she had been terrified of facing this woman again, imagining the woman's contempt: "You're so capricious! Don't you ever think before you act?" Though she hadn't thought about it consciously for years, this was a refrain she'd heard in her childhood that made her feel stupid and ashamed. No wonder she had put off going back to the store! And this realization also helped Lenora understand why, when she later faced the prospect of writing this book, her first reaction was, "How could I possibly write a book? I can't think!"

EXTERNAL AND INTERNAL CONSEQUENCES

Procrastination has consequences. Sometimes the consequences are obvious to you and everyone else: the car that runs out of gas in the middle of the freeway, the woman who is fired because of chronic lateness, the garage filled with half-completed projects, the boxes still unpacked from the move ten years ago, and Jane's car being towed. These are examples of *external* consequences.

There are *internal* consequences as well. These can include feelings of inadequacy, sadness, guilt, fraudulence, panic, and a sense of never really being free to enjoy the pleasures of living. Lenora suffered great angst every time she saw the unopened box beside her apartment door. A procrastinator may appear to be successful, competent, talented, intelligent, and generous, but the internal consequences of procrastination place a tremendous strain on any life and undermine feelings of confidence and satisfaction.

Consider the following list. Which consequences apply to you? Are there others?

CONSEQUENCES

External
monetary loss
losing a job
lowered grades
incomplete academic or
    training program
lost opportunities
conflict with manager, co-workers
decreased job responsibilities
lowered credit rating
tension with family or friends
accidents or physical injury
loss of friendships
marital separation or divorce
governmental penalties
    (e.g., tax fines, parking tickets)
avoiding romantic relationships
calls from creditors
excess use of substances
    (alcohol, prescription and non-
    prescription drugs, illegal drugs)

Internal
self-criticism
embarrassment or shame
anxiety, dread
lack of concentration
guilt
inability to enjoy other
    activities
feeling of fraudulence
tension, physical pain
panic
depression
sense of excitement or thrill
physical exhaustion, stress
physical illness
insomnia, other sleep
    problems
denial
feeling incompetent
feeling constantly hounded
    by your "to do" list
last-minute "brain lock"
feeling isolated, alienated

Now that you have reviewed your procrastinating behavior and its consequences, notice how you feel. Sad? Angry? Relieved? Sobered? If you are caught up in berating yourself for your stupidity, moral weakness, or lack of character, try to step back and quiet your internal critic. Use your defense attorney to find a compassionate voice. Try to consider what you can learn from your experience.

YOUR PROCRASTINATION TODAY

Areas of Procrastination

Some people procrastinate in only one specific area of their lives and in every other area do just fine. A woman who was married, had two children, and a full-time job was very efficient at work and in organizing the household, but she could not keep up with her e-mail. She felt so overwhelmed whenever she saw how many messages were waiting that she avoided opening her inbox. Other people procrastinate in almost every aspect of their lives. An airline pilot in his forties didn't pay his taxes for years, put off necessary home and car repairs, didn't make minimum credit card payments, never developed a lasting relationship with a woman, and planned for years to stop smoking.

It is rare to find a procrastinator who puts things off in every area of his life. Even the pilot was always on time for work, and he did make it through flight school. It's important to remember that no procrastinator is hopeless, including you. However pervasive your procrastination is, it doesn't affect every aspect of your life.

To help distinguish between those areas in which you procrastinate and those in which you don't, we've compiled a checklist of activities grouped into six categories: household, work, school, personal care, social relationships, and finances. We bet you'll find that no matter how extensive your procrastination is, when you take a closer look, you'll see that you procrastinate selectively.

Household
__ day-to-day chores (e.g., dishes, cleaning, recycling, laundry, changing the cat box, garden or yard maintenance)
__ minor home projects or repairs
__ calling a repairman, contractor, landscaper, housecleaner
__ returning defective or unwanted merchandise
__ large home or yard projects
__ car maintenance and repairs
__ opening mail or filing papers

__shopping for groceries or supplies
__making decisions
__throwing out newspapers, magazines, and other stuff
__unpacking
__upgrading computer security or software
__Other _____

Work (Paid or Volunteer)

__being on time for work or for meetings
__handling business phone calls, e-mails, and text messages
__learning new skills
__implementing new ideas
__making decisions
__doing administrative and bookkeeping chores
__writing reports or spreadsheets, designing a presentation
__confronting someone about a problem
__complimenting someone
__billing clients or submitting receipts for reimbursement
__asking for a raise or promotion
__doing research, strategic planning, or work-related reading
__arranging a meeting with your manager
__looking for a job, planning a career direction, networking
__Other_____

School

__attending classes
__doing homework assignments, studying for tests, writing papers
__talking with a teacher or advisor
__applying to college or for financial aid
__doing bureaucratic tasks (paying fees, buying textbooks, etc.)
__completing degree requirements
__choosing a major
__studying for entrance exams
__reading the syllabus to find out when assignments are due
__getting together with other students

__ calling, writing, or visiting home
__ looking for employment or internship opportunities
__ applying for special programs
__ Other _____

Personal Care
__ getting physical exercise
__ losing weight
__ stopping smoking or use of alcohol or drugs
__ making (and keeping) medical or dental appointments
__ personal hygiene (brushing your teeth, getting haircuts)
__ filling prescriptions
__ shopping for new clothes
__ cleaning out your closet
__ taking clothes to cleaners or to be altered
__ pursuing hobbies or doing personal reading
__ pursuing meaningful activities—service projects, helping others, spiritual growth, adult education courses
__ planning for and taking vacations
__ making long-term life decisions
__ setting up your will or medical power of attorney
__ Other _____

Social Relationships
__ staying in touch with friends, personal correspondence
__ asking someone for a date
__ inviting people to your home
__ visiting, calling, or writing relatives
__ planning recreational activities with other people
__ expressing appreciation or giving gifts to others
__ being on time for social events or meetings with friends
__ asking for help or support
__ confronting someone about a problem
__ ending an unsatisfying relationship
__ Other _____

Finances
__filing taxes on time
__organizing receipts and tax records
__finding an accountant
__making a budget, tracking expenditures
__making financial investments
__contacting the bank or credit card company about a problem
__paying rent or mortgage
__paying bills, credit card debt, insurance premiums
__paying parking ticket fines
__paying back institutional or personal loans
__collecting debts owed to you
__submitting insurance claims for reimbursement
__balancing your checkbook or monitoring online bank
    statements
__opening mail from your bank, mortgage, or investment company,
__checking your credit rating
__Other_____

In each area, consider how much your delaying bothers you. The areas in which you procrastinate most extensively may or may not be causing you the most trouble. For instance, you may be in the habit of leaving dirty dishes for several days in a row, but a sink full of dishes may not bother you. However, even though the problem arises only periodically, you may be very upset about your tendency to put off buying cards and gifts for friends and relatives and not acknowledging them on special occasions.

Think about what differentiates the things you put off from the things you do on time. What themes or patterns do you observe? What do they tell you about your procrastination? Do you put off minor chores, or do you postpone the most important things? Do you put off doing things for yourself, but not for others? Are the activities you put off in areas where you're expected to excel or areas where you have little experience? Are you aware of any fears or anxieties about the things you postpone?

Your Style of Procrastinating

People procrastinate in very different ways. One person may spend a lot of time on the telephone and never get around to cleaning the house, while someone else may vacuum twice a day instead of returning phone calls. A woman goes sailing for the weekend, whereas a young man sits indoors at his computer fantasizing about being a successful professional, a talented athlete, or a Don Juan. There are thousands of things people do when they procrastinate: procrastinators are very creative. Here are a few examples:

I raid the refrigerator.
I read mystery novels and science fiction.
I start calling my friends.
I read my e-mail, surf the Web, blog, or text my friends.
I work on something that's less important.
I become obsessed with cleaning my desk.
I go to the gym.
I sit and stare.
I keep doing research.
I watch TV, download music, watch movies, read the news.
I go to sleep.
I go shopping.
I go to a café with my computer, but I end up talking to people.
I drink or do drugs.
I think about sex, have sex, look at Internet porn.
I spend time with my pets.
I read cookbooks.

What do you do when you procrastinate? Notice as many things as you can think of, including both your typical patterns and your most unusual delaying tactics.

At times it can be tricky to distinguish between procrastinating and not procrastinating. For example, when is working out an avoidance tactic, and when is it clearing your head or taking care of your body? Or when is housecleaning a task that needs to be done and not procrastination? Is reading the newspaper delaying, or is it relaxation? If you are someone who constantly gets angry at yourself for putting things off, it is important to learn the difference between goofing off and relaxing. Even procrastinators deserve to have fun.

Most people experience some clues that indicate they are procrastinating. Often it's a nagging internal voice that says, "You know you shouldn't be doing this now." They may have a visual image of what they are avoiding or of the consequences that might follow. One procrastinator said, "When I procrastinate, I see a vivid picture of my boss scowling and shaking his finger at me." Some people feel a physical cue, such as tightness in the stomach, headache, or tension in the shoulders, neck, or back. Or they may be unable to concentrate or to enjoy what they are doing. What are the specific cues that tell you that you are procrastinating?

Your Excuses for Procrastinating

Think about that moment in time when you could get started on a project or put it off. Here you are, faced with the possibility of making the phone call, writing the first sentence, or unpacking the first box. What do you say to yourself at this moment that somehow justifies *not* doing it?

Make a list of your excuses. Some people have trouble thinking of their excuses at first. These thoughts may be so automatic and familiar that they don't seem to be excuses at all. But you can discover your excuses if you pay attention at the moment you avoid taking action. Here are some common excuses for procrastinating:

> I've got to get organized first; I don't have everything I need.
> I don't have time to do it all now, so there's no point in starting.
> It's too nice a day to spend on this.
> I've been working so hard—I deserve a break.
> It might not be good enough.
> If I wait, I can do a really first-class job.

I'll wait until I'm inspired.

I don't feel well; I'm too tired right now; I'm not in the mood.

It won't take very long, and there's still plenty of time.

I'm having so much fun I'll just do this a little longer.

I need exercise (sleep, food, etc.) first.

It's important to keep up with what's going on in the world, so I'd better read the news.

It's too late in the week to start.

Why send it Friday? No one will look at it until Monday anyway.

I'll have more time on the weekend.

If I wait long enough, they'll forget about it.

Why bother to ask? The answer will be "no" anyway.

I've done the worst part of it; the final step will be a breeze.

Two hundred years from now, will this really matter?

Keep track of your excuses over the period of a week. Pay attention to your thoughts at those very moments when you put off something you want or need to do, the thoughts that provide you with a justification for waiting. It's a good way to become more aware of what goes on inside your mind and to observe how your thoughts affect your behavior.

See if you can identify what happened *just before* you came up with a reason to procrastinate. What were you thinking, feeling, or doing at that earlier moment? What were the circumstances, and what was evoked in you? For example, one man promised to build a table for his girlfriend. Instead of heading into his workroom, he found himself thinking, "It's too nice a day to be cooped up inside." What led him to this excuse? That morning his girlfriend had called to discuss the table. "You're such a craftsman," she said. "Everything you build is a work of art." He envisioned the look of disappointment on her face when his table was just a table and not a work of art. He thought about how much he wanted to please her, and he started to brood about where the relationship was going. Feeling defeated, he wanted to escape.

Many excuses have a kernel of truth. You probably do need exercise, and you might be tired, bored, uninspired, hungry, or sick. The house could stand to be cleaner, and your workspace could be a lot more organized. The point is that, even if there is some truth to your excuse, the function of the excuse is to avoid discomfort. You are using the kernel of truth to arrive at the procrastinator's conclusion: "Therefore I'll do it later." For example, "It might not be good enough, so I'll do it later." "I'm tired, so I'll do it later." "There's an interesting program on TV, so I'll do this later."

Everybody feels tired, bored, uninspired, or too busy from time to time. But whatever your excuse, no matter how tired, uninspired, or busy you are, you can always spend just fifteen minutes working toward your goal. Keep in mind that people who don't procrastinate experience these difficulties, too, but they consider what they *can* do and get started. Overcoming your aversion to starting a task is not about proving yourself, which could be risky; rather, it is a way to stretch yourself. When you notice an excuse, you have an opportunity to think about the issues below the surface of your procrastination. You can reach a better understanding of yourself. With a different perspective in mind, you might come to a different conclusion:

It might not be good enough, but I'll give it a try anyway.
I'm tired. I'll just work for fifteen minutes and then I'll go to bed.
This may not turn out perfectly, but I'll learn a lot from doing it.
I don't have the proper equipment, but is there something I can do anyway?
I don't have enough time to finish now—but I'll spend fifteen minutes on it.
This is going to be hard, so I'd better leave enough time to work out the problems.

With a Fixed Mindset, you retreat from risk and from taking action; when you use an excuse, you are retreating. With a Growth Mindset, you take action even when things are hard or you don't feel like it. Rather than being derailed by believing your excuses, you take action in spite of them.

12

Setting and Achieving Goals

By definition, procrastinators have difficulty achieving goals. Procrastination can interfere to such an extent that you rarely accomplish the goals you've set. Or you may ultimately attain your goals, but only after you've been through agonizing fits and starts.

It may not be as obvious that procrastinators also have difficulty *setting* goals, since they are busy setting (and resetting) goals all the time. But they almost always set ambiguous goals, such as, "I've got to get some work done today," or overly ambitious goals, such as, "I want to be number one in my field." Goals framed in this way are elusive and actually invite procrastination.

When we started out to write the first edition of our book, we thought our goal was clear enough: we wanted to write a book on procrastination. We developed an outline and declared that we would begin. Then it was time to write. Whenever we thought about getting down to work, we'd say to ourselves, "I have to write the book." An invitation to socialize, the opportunity to do other kinds of work, the need for recreation—all these were weighed against the injunction, "I have to write the book." But we didn't get very far with the actual writing. Eventually, we realized that we felt intimidated by our goal to "write the book." Each page seemed like a tiny drop in a huge bucket. Would our little pages ever fit together into a cohesive form? We were taking such a broad view of our purpose that it was antithetical to making progress. We were setting ourselves up for trouble by the way we thought about our goal.

Finally, we started to take our own advice. Instead of thinking about having to "write a book," we focused on only one part of a single chapter at a time, trying to put the rest of it out of our minds. In the process, we began to say something different to ourselves when we anticipated our writing sessions: "I have to spend two hours this afternoon working on the introduction to the goal-setting chapter." It was a more reasonable, reachable goal, and it helped us to get to work.

THE BEHAVIORAL GOAL

It is most helpful to define your goals in behavioral terms. Focusing on what you will be doing when you accomplish your objective helps you recognize where you're aiming to go. A behavioral goal has the following characteristics:

- it is observable by you and others;
- it is specific and concrete;
- it can be broken down into small steps;
- the first step can be accomplished in just five minutes.

"I want to stop procrastinating" is a noble goal, but it is *not* a behavioral goal. You can't actually see yourself stop procrastinating—what would you look for? It is not concrete—stop procrastinating on what? It is difficult to break down into steps—how do you start to stop procrastinating?

Let's look more closely at the elements of a behavioral goal.

Observable.　People can't see how you are feeling or know what you are thinking, but they can see what you do. For your goal to be observable by you and others, it must be defined as an action. Imagine a movie camera filming you as you finish your goal. What action will you be taking when the camera records your accomplishment? If your goal is truly a behavioral one, you should be able to take a picture of yourself doing it.

For example, procrastinators often propose, "I'd like to feel less overwhelmed by all the work I have to do." It's an understandable desire, but it's not a behavioral goal. No one can observe you feeling less overwhelmed. And it's not a helpful statement, either. How would you know when you feel "less overwhelmed"? How much "less overwhelmed" would you have to feel to be relieved? To restate it as a behavioral goal, we suggest that you select one project you've been putting off and define its completion in behavioral terms. You may decide, "I'll update my résumé and post it on the Internet," or, "I'll read one chapter in the book on procrastination," or, "I'll make an appointment with the dentist." A camera could see you pushing the send button on your computer, closing the book at the end of the chapter, or hanging up the phone after your conversation with the dentist's office. If you achieved any of these goals, you'd probably feel less overwhelmed, and you could identify exactly what helped you feel better.

Specific and Concrete.   Procrastinators are prone to thinking in such vague terms that they find it very difficult to be specific. What exactly will you be doing when you accomplish your goal? When specifically will you do it? Who else in particular will be there?

We've often heard people state as a goal, "I'm going to reorganize my life." With a vague objective like this, a procrastinator is stymied. However, if you translate your goal into specific, concrete terms, you will have some clues about where to start to get better organized. You may decide to go through your piles, keeping important papers and throwing out the rest. "Getting organized" might mean cleaning out a closet or hiring a clutter expert. Being specific about where you want to end up will facilitate your getting there.

Small Steps.   The only way to achieve any goal, no matter how large or small, is step by step. As the old saying goes, "Life by the yard is very hard; life by the inch is a cinch."

A behavioral goal can be broken down into small, observable steps, and like the final goal, each of these steps should be observable and specific. You will end up with a series of minigoals that you can work on one by one. The advantage of aiming toward interim minigoals instead of the ultimate final goal is that each minigoal is more vivid than a distant goal and therefore more likely to be achieved. A goal such as "I have to prepare next year's budget for the annual meeting next month" can feel overwhelming, and next month may seem far off. This makes the task both aversive and less salient, even though it's very important. Instead, the project could be divided into its component parts: locate last year's budget; update budget categories; estimate expenditures in each category; estimate income for each category; confer with your assistant during Friday's meeting. As a series of short-term steps, "preparing the annual budget" will be much more manageable.

Sometimes as you break down a goal, you discover it's more complicated than you thought. Breanna chose as her one-week goal the completion of her quarterly report on the use of services in her information technology department. The report was already late, as she had missed the deadline at the end of the quarter. The steps she anticipated were (1) ask all the IT technicians to send her their work reports for the quarter; (2) review and integrate their reports into one spreadsheet; and (3) send the compiled spreadsheet to her manager with a note listing the most frequent reasons departments asked for IT help.

Breanna had indeed created a behavioral goal, as she could see herself sending the report to her manager. But as she was about to take her first step, composing an e-mail to send to the IT technicians, she realized that, during the quarter, one had left and a new person had been hired. Did she have the data she needed from the person who'd left the company? Had she explained well enough to the new hire just how he was supposed to keep track of his service contacts? She would need to spend more time with the new technician to make sure he understood how to organize the data she needed. Breanna also remembered that when she had filed her previous quarterly report, she had made notes about how to improve the presentation. Where were those notes? Should she spend time looking for them, or should she just follow the old template? When Breanna avoided even thinking about the task, she certainly wasn't thinking about how to get it done. Now, as she reviewed her behavioral goal, she realized that there were some steps she had not considered, and she was no longer certain that one week was a realistic time period for finishing the report. Breanna was upset that she had underestimated the time needed to complete her goal, but reassessing your time frame as you work with your goal is frequently part of the process. Breaking your goal down into smaller steps can help you clarify—for better or worse—the reality of the task you face.

Focusing on the steps you need to take will also serve as a reminder that you have to travel down the road in order to reach your destination. Most procrastinators think only about "being there" and have a hard time thinking about "getting there." Many are surprised to find that the process of getting there—accomplishing each step along the way—can be challenging and rewarding in its own right.

Minimal Acceptable Goal.   Procrastinators tend to be unrealistic about their goals because they often think in terms of an ideal situation, as if there were no limitations on their time or energy. As a way of establishing a more realistic goal, we ask procrastinators to consider what their *minimal* goal might be. What is the smallest goal you could set that would give you some sense of progress and accomplishment? Is there part of a larger goal you could choose to work toward over a limited period of time? For example, your ideal goal may be to redecorate your house, but a minimal goal might be to reupholster the sofa.

Some of you may be reluctant to lower your sights even the least bit. This is your perfectionism in action! You devalue anything that is short of your ideal goal. Although it may feel like a blow to your pride to choose a minimal goal, thinking small could ultimately be more rewarding. You can build on real accomplishment by achieving your goal, minimal step by minimal step, rather than insisting on setting lofty goals and doing nothing.

A ONE-WEEK EXPERIMENT

Selecting a Goal

We suggest that you choose one goal to work toward during the next week, and we'd like you to try to approach this goal with a Growth Mindset—a desire to learn from both success and failure, an openness to challenge, and an understanding that effort is not a sign of weakness but is necessary for growth.[1] See what you can learn about your procrastination as you approach or avoid your goal. Pay attention to how you set up goals and how you handle them, when you make progress and when you procrastinate. It is important to examine both your successes and your setbacks. Think of this week as a time for self-observation and learning. It is not an evaluation of how smart, responsible, or talented you are. Try to take the perspective of a researcher gathering data, not the role of a critic passing judgment. Use the following steps as a guide to accomplishing your goal.

Choose Just One Goal. What are some things you would like to accomplish in the next week? What would be your target date for each goal? Remember that a behavioral goal should be observable, specific, and able to be completed in steps. Write down three possible goals and when you'd like to finish them.

Of the possible goals you've considered, select one—and only one—to use as your behavioral goal for your one-week experiment. Choosing one and only one goal should make this experiment less aversive and therefore more approachable. It doesn't have to be the most important goal in your life or the most challenging task you face. Which goal you select is not as crucial as the process of defining and working toward one goal of your own choosing.

We realize that asking a procrastinator to select only one goal is like asking a dieter to eat only one potato chip. It's hard to limit yourself to just one, but having more than one is dangerous. For most procrastinators, trying to do everything is part of the problem.

List the Steps. Break your behavioral goal down into its component parts. Each part is one step, a minigoal. Start with the first step and work forward, or start with your last step and work backward. An example of how one procrastinator broke his one-week goal down into small steps is shown below.

Write down your one behavioral goal, the steps involved to achieve it, and when during the next week you plan to take each step. Don't forget to consider other time commitments and obligations you have in the coming week.

Goal: Spend two hours on Saturday and two hours on Sunday reorganizing and cleaning my home office (total of four hours)

STEPS:
A. ORGANIZE PAPERS AND PRINTOUTS

1) Sort through piles on the desk and the floor; throw away nonessentials without reading them!
2) Move clothes and shoes to closet, cups and glasses to kitchen, books to the bookcase, magazines to the recycle bin.
3) Put all bills to be paid in a box. (Do I have a box?)
4) Put receipts in another box. (Do I have enough boxes?)
5) Buy file folders.
6) Sort through articles, photos, and clippings.
7) Make files for items I want to save, and throw the rest away.

B. CLEAN THE ROOM

1) Clean computer screen and keyboard.
2) Dust file and bookcase.
3) Empty wastebasket.
4) Vacuum.

Reality check: Can all this be done in four hours?
Don't forget to buy file folders on Friday.

Your First Step.   Now that you've identified a behavioral goal (and perhaps revised it to be more realistic) and the steps you'll take toward achieving it during the next week, how do you get started? What is the very *first* step you will take? It should be something very small and easy, like finding last year's tax return, buying a notebook, or finding some empty boxes. Exactly where and when will you begin? No matter how small an effort it is, you are moving in the right direction. "The journey of a thousand miles begins with a single step," as the saying goes.

Get Feedback.   Your one-week behavioral goal may seem clear and realistic to you. We suggest, however, that you ask someone else for feedback. You may find that what seemed clear may be too vague; what seemed realistic may still be too much; what seemed broken down into steps may still be too broad. In particular, ask your partner to help you consider whether the goal you've selected is really your minimally acceptable goal. In our example, maybe it would be better to start with one hour on Saturday or Sunday than to aim for two hours on each day.

The Start-Up

Now you have a project you want to work on, and you've defined it so that it is clear and realistic. It's actually possible that you *can* get this done in the next week. How does this prospect make you feel? What thoughts are going through your mind? Here are a few of the reactions we've heard from procrastinators as they've looked ahead to the prospect of an accomplishable goal: "I feel a sense of relief, because I finally have a way to start." "I'm very anxious. What if I fail again?" "I feel like I'm in prison. I want to run away!" Notice your reactions as you anticipate your experiment. The thought of getting started is a trigger, a stimulus that sets off a whole chain of internal reactions—images, feelings, thoughts, expectations, and memories of past experiences.

Visualize Your Progress.　It may be helpful to visualize the specific steps and the exact circumstances of progress made toward your goal. Imagery is used to reduce stress and increase relaxation, to practice assertive behavior, to cope with anxiety, to aid physical healing, and to improve performance in academics and sports.

Imagine yourself taking your very first step, going through the motions you would actually make. Then see yourself continuing through each of the steps toward your goal. If your pessimism intrudes and you anticipate a snag, try to imagine yourself finding a way to cope with the problem. Eventually you'll watch yourself coming to the end of the process and accomplishing your goal. Imagery of this sort— best done when you are comfortable, alone, and relaxed—can prepare you for the real moment of action and make it easier for you to cross the threshold between thinking and doing.

Optimize Your Chances.　Even if you have a well-delineated behavioral goal and a manageable first step, where and when you plan to begin can be crucial. The circumstances you set up can either greatly increase or significantly decrease the probability of success. Trevor, a twenty-year-old undergraduate student, decided to complete a term paper on Middle Eastern politics as his behavioral goal. His first step was to spend from 9:00 to 10:00 P.M. the next evening reading one book. So far so good. He planned to read the book in his room at the fraternity house. Not so good. The fraternity was an extremely social, distracting environment, and as 9:00 P.M. approached, Trevor was having too good a time hanging out with the guys to go into his room alone to read. He put it off until nine-thirty, then ten, and at ten-thirty, he gave up because "it was too late by that time." Trevor made his first step more difficult by trying to achieve it under less than optimal circumstances. He thought he would—and should—be able to overcome the social temptations, but he just made things harder for himself.

The next day, Trevor revised his plan and decided to read the book in a campus library. In order to increase his chances of actually getting to the library, he arranged to go with Peter, a studious fraternity brother. Instead of going to the undergraduate library where he might run into friends and yield to social pressure again, he chose the law school library, where "people are really serious." Trevor didn't change his first step, but he did alter the circumstances to maximize the chances that he would actually take it.

Stick to a Time Limit. Another way to make getting started less aversive is to set a limited period of time to work toward your behavioral goal and stick to it. Don't go over the time limit. If you decide to spend thirty minutes on your project, and you stay with it for that length of time, you've been successful, regardless of how much you accomplished or how well you think it turned out. Your success is based on following through with your intentions and honoring an agreement you made with yourself. This builds trust and confidence in yourself, valuable feelings that many procrastinators have lost.

The shorter the time frame you set, the easier it is to begin. Most procrastinators find that an initial period of fifteen minutes to a half-hour works best. And if fifteen minutes feels like more than you can stand, set a limit of ten minutes, five minutes, or even one minute!

It is absolutely necessary at first to stop when you reach the end of your time limit. It's tempting to think, "If I'm doing well, I should capitalize on it and keep up the momentum." But if you get carried away and work for two hours the first time, going well beyond your set limit, next time you'll expect that you should again work for two hours. That's a set-up for discouragement and avoidance.

Don't Wait Until You Feel Like It. If you wait until you feel like starting, you may never get started. Many procrastinators expect to feel unafraid, totally confident, completely prepared, or inspired at the moment they take their first step. Kelly, a thirty-three-year-old nurse said, "I keep thinking I should really be ready before I apply to go back to school. I should feel calm and completely together, not have any doubts about myself. Once I stop feeling anxious, school should be no problem." Kelly has been waiting for three years to feel "completely together." But she's been out of school for a long time—how could she not feel anxious about going back? Waiting until she's anxiety-free may mean she'll never do it.

Others expect they should want to start, so they wait for desire to develop. There are some things, however, that are inherently unpleasant, tedious, or boring. Take taxes, for instance. We don't know anyone who looks forward to doing his or her taxes. If you wait until you *want* to do something, you can wait forever.

However, you *can* start, even if you're not in the ideal mood or frame of mind.

The Follow-Through

Once you do get started, how can you follow through beyond the first step to give yourself a chance to complete your goal? Procrastinators are all too familiar with the cycle of making early efforts and then slowing down or giving up altogether. They are typically suffused with optimism at the beginning and then, at some point, they get stuck and stay stuck.

How can you keep from being disappointed by yet another incomplete project? Here are some guidelines for following through instead of giving up.

Watch Out for Your Excuses.   Inevitably, many of the excuses you've identified in Chapter 11 will come up during your one-week experiment. Remember that an excuse means you're at a choice point: you can procrastinate or you can act. Instead of delaying automatically, you can transform your excuse—change your conclusion of "So I'll do it later" to "So I'll just spend fifteen minutes on it now." You can always use your excuse as a reward *after* you've taken some steps toward your goal. "It's a beautiful day, and I'll go for a walk after I spend a half hour paying bills." Keep in mind that an excuse is also an invitation to explore your feelings about the goal—are you ambivalent, afraid, rebellious, angry? Taking a few minutes to pay thoughtful attention to what is going on in your thoughts and feelings when you start making excuses can help you learn something important about yourself.

Focus on One Step at a Time.   In the process of writing this book, there were many times when we felt depressed by thoughts such as, "There's so much left to do," or, "We'll never finish on time," or, "What if it doesn't turn out well?" The task seemed enormous, and we felt overwhelmed. At these moments, one of us would say to the other, "Don't think so far ahead. Just take one step at a time." It diverted us from our fears of a disastrous future and brought us back to making a plan of action for the immediate present. If you focus on one step at a time, you are shortening the length of time before reaching your interim goal, which is one of the important factors in reducing procrastination.

Work Around Obstacles.   Even if things go smoothly at the beginning, at some point you will certainly encounter a bump in the road. Maybe the person you want to talk to is not available, or you can't figure out how to solve a logistical problem, or it rains on the first day of your new jogging program, or you just don't feel like it. At that point, you have reached a critical moment: the first obstacle, the first of many. Procrastinators are likely to come to a halt when an obstacle can't be easily removed or overcome. Any snag, large or small, can become a source of frustration and humiliation if you take it as proof of your inadequacy and evidence of your failure. If you feel defeated by an obstacle, you will have trouble returning to the problem and grappling with it again. It is easier to work around an obstacle if you view it as an interesting puzzle to be solved or something that takes more effort, a reflection of the task—not of you. An obstacle is *just an obstacle*: it is not an indictment that you are completely stupid, incompetent, or unwanted.

Sometimes when you face an obstacle, it might be in your best interests to take a break. At the end of a long day of writing together, we sometimes found ourselves getting irritable with each other and arguing about wording to such an extent that we could not agree. After a few fights, we learned that our irritability was a signal that it was time to stop for the day and didn't mean that the other person was stupid or incorrigible. Miraculously, the next day, finding the right words and reaching agreement came easily.

If you decide to take a break, set a specific time and place to approach the situation again. Identify as concretely as you can what action you will take at that time. If you are in the midst of a writing project, jot down a sentence or a few thoughts or phrases before you take your break. That way you'll have a place to start when you come back. If you temporarily retreat from an obstacle, consider whether there is any other part of your goal that you can work on. If it's raining outside, can you do indoor exercises? If someone you need is out of the office, can you make other calls? Although you might stop momentarily in one area, you don't have to stop completely. The danger for procrastinators is not in withdrawing temporarily; the danger lies in giving up altogether.

Reward Yourself After You've Made Some Progress. The notion of giving yourself a reward may be foreign, because procrastinators are much more likely to punish themselves than to praise themselves. It's very sad to see that, in almost every case, procrastinators are highly skilled at beating themselves over the head but are not very good at being kind to themselves when they deserve it.

Scott, for example, was mad at himself at the end of his one-week experiment. He'd selected the goal of paying three long-overdue bills that had been plaguing him for months. He reported with regret that he'd only taken care of one of them—he'd covered his unpaid parking tickets, so that now he could reregister his car—but he castigated himself for not also paying off his dentist and the credit card company. Scott was unable to appreciate the benefits of what he had accomplished. By paying his tickets and registering his car, he stopped the penalties from accruing, and he could now drive without having an anxiety attack every time he saw a police car. But, as is the case with most procrastinators, it never occurred to Scott to feel good about what he had done, because he continued to focus only on what he had not accomplished.

When you do make progress, even if you don't accomplish as much as you'd ideally like or don't do it as you had imagined, give yourself some reinforcement. A reward can be anything that you enjoy or that makes you feel good: dinner at a favorite restaurant, watching a movie, a weekend trip to the mountains, a game of racquetball, talking to a friend, or reading a book. A reward could also be praise from other people or private acknowledgment that you give to yourself. Try to make the reward commensurate with the accomplishment. After you do an hour of work toward your behavioral goal, take a walk, not a two-week vacation.

Rewards are most effective when they occur just after the desired behavior. "I'll go to a movie and then settle down to work" is not as effective as doing some work first and going to the movie afterward. Rewards work as positive reinforcement, increasing the likelihood that the behavior will be repeated. Your brain also helps you repeat successful behavior. When you achieve a goal, there is a release of dopamine, the feel-good neurotransmitter. Dopamine connects the neuronal networks responsible for those behaviors that led to your accomplishment, making it more likely you will repeat those behaviors in the future.[2] Success generates more success.

Be Flexible about Your Goal. As you progress toward your goal, you may discover that your initial reality checks weren't realistic enough. Perhaps you forgot to allot time for important commitments, like the theater director who set up an ambitious one-week goal but forgot that her college roommate was coming for a visit. Or you may find that things take longer or are more complicated than you'd anticipated. You may be disrupted by circumstances beyond your control: your child becomes ill or your car breaks down. (Of course, if you've been putting off long-overdue car maintenance . . .) In some situations, it may be necessary to alter your goal.

Revising your goal is not necessarily a sign of failure. In fact, it may be a sign that you are being flexible rather than rigid, an important characteristic of healthy, integrated functioning. Revising a goal can be a response to realistic constraints, indicating that you are able to evaluate what is actually possible and adjust to it, instead of holding onto an impossible ideal.

It Doesn't Have to Be Perfect.   If you are a perfectionist, you may get caught up in a struggle to do all things absolutely right, even when there is no real need for such a high standard. It's more important that your holiday cards be sent than that each person receives a unique, well-written personal note about how you are, what you've been doing all year, your current philosophy of life, and a photo that makes you look younger and thinner. With that ideal as your goal, those cards may sit untouched until next year's holidays roll around.

If you can let go of your need for perfection at each step along the way, you'll probably be able to accomplish a lot more in the long run. As you're waiting for the perfect time, hoping for the perfect outcome, remind yourself, "It doesn't have to be perfect. It just has to be done!"

Looking Back

At the end of your one-week experiment, look back over what happened. This may be difficult for procrastinators who hate to be reminded of what they did—or didn't do. Some people feel it's a waste of time to look backward. "What's done is done. It's over, and I can't change it, so why should I spend my time thinking about it?" But a thoughtful looking back is an important form of self-monitoring— how else can you learn from your experience?

Assess Your Progress (or Lack Thereof).   If you actually finished your goal, you may be reluctant to look carefully at how you got there. Some people are almost superstitious about it, worrying that if they examine a good thing too closely, they'll see the hidden flaws and then won't feel good about it anymore. "Even though I finished my project," said an accountant, "there were a lot of times along the way when I goofed off. I'd rather just hold onto my pride and not remember those bad times." She sounds ready to let her regret over her struggles outweigh the satisfaction of her success.

Many procrastinators tend to underestimate how much they've done. Perhaps you took some steps that weren't part of your original plans, but they moved you along. These steps count. Perhaps you aren't giving yourself credit for some steps because they seem so small. These steps count, too. You may feel like you didn't do enough, but if you recount exactly what you have done, you may be pleasantly surprised.

It's also possible that as you review your steps you'll be unpleasantly surprised to find that you have fooled yourself into thinking you did more than you actually accomplished. That's important to discover as well. If you didn't accomplish your goal, you may be even more resistant to examining what happened. If you are already critical of yourself for not finishing what you started, you may not want to add to your self-recrimination.

Whether you completed your goal is less important than how you think about what happened. If you have begun to understand your successes and your setbacks, you are helping prepare yourself to procrastinate less next time. Keep in mind that self-monitoring is a valuable executive function, and with practice, you can get better at it.

Examine Your Feelings. We've heard a wide range of reactions from procrastinators at the end of their experiments: "I feel relieved because I got somewhere, but I'm disappointed that I didn't go all the way." "I did a heck of a lot more than I thought I'd do." "I was sneaky. I took short cuts. I don't feel good about it because I didn't stick to the plan." "I've failed again." "I was really off base in my planning." "I did what I said I would do—finally!"

How are you feeling as you look back on your own experience? Are you disappointed because you didn't do anything, or are you disappointed because you didn't do everything? Are you wounded because you didn't accomplish a project that was really too big in the first place? Or are you relieved because you learned how to live with progress one step at a time? Whatever your feelings are, try to observe them without judgment. Feelings—even powerful ones—come and go, so you won't feel this way forever.

Review Your Choice Points. In the past, you may have made the choice to procrastinate automatically, without even realizing it. Perhaps you accepted your excuses unquestioningly or ran away from your goal on impulse. If you accomplished nothing else during your one-week experiment, we hope that you procrastinated more consciously. Undoubtedly, there were times when you were tempted to put something off and wavered on the brink, debating whether to take the next step or avoid it, times when you could either move toward your goal or away from it. These choice points are important moments. The decisions we make at such times affect not only our performance but also the way we feel about ourselves.

Try to recall one of those choice points from your week. If you can remember a time when you wavered but decided to move toward your goal, what helped you to take the plunge? What did you do or say to yourself that helped you to make progress? Raj, a systems engineer, was a science-fiction fan. Just at the time he'd planned to begin organizing the tools in his workshop, he started instead to read a terrific sci-fi book. Although tempted by the world of the future, he was also nagged by his guilt. "Finally, I saw that I wasn't enjoying the book because I was so conflicted. So I decided to spend ten minutes in my workshop and then return to my book. I was surprised that I actually rather liked straightening out the workshop. When I went back to reading, I felt I'd earned it." Two things helped Raj move forward. First, he decided to take a small first step so that he wouldn't feel imprisoned in his workshop; second, he rewarded his progress by really enjoying his book.

Perhaps you can remember a time when you weren't so fortunate, a choice point when you decided to move away from your goal. What were the circumstances? What thoughts, feelings, or images made it difficult for you to move ahead? Abby, a freelance writer, went folk dancing instead of working on the article her editor was expecting. She explained, "I just felt restless and at loose ends and had to get out of the house." With some further thought, Abby realized, "I was feeling sort of lonely. I didn't want to stay home by myself. When I was folk dancing, I was with a lot of other people, and that made me feel better." What was making her feel lonely on that particular day? She remembered that she was scheduled to have lunch with a friend who'd called and canceled. "I'd been looking forward to seeing him, and when he canceled I felt rejected." It took a lot of hard thinking, but Abby was able to see how procrastinating was her attempt to replace the social contact she'd missed. Had she realized that what she really needed was companionship, perhaps Abby could have called another friend either to join her for lunch or to spend the evening working together.

What Have You Learned? Think back on how you handled the process of approaching your project, from defining your behavioral goal to getting started and following through. What one thing would you do differently next time? Like Trevor, who discovered that the fraternity house was not conducive to studying and decided to work in the library instead, what one change do you want to make that will increase your chances for success next time?

We hope you have also learned things about yourself this week. What one thing do you know now that you didn't know before? Whatever you have learned should help prepare you for the next round of your battle with procrastination. So don't devalue any aspect of your one-week experiment, because no matter what you did or didn't do, you can learn from it.

13

Learning How to Tell Time

On the surface, procrastination appears to be a rather straightforward problem of poor time management. If you organized your time better and used it more efficiently, you wouldn't be procrastinating. Right? With this in mind, many procrastinators turn to experts in time management for advice. You may have already read some of the extensive literature that exists in this area and checked the Web sites of authors, experts, and coaches who are part of the enormous time management industry. You can probably see the wisdom in their recommendations about adopting calendar systems, using to-do lists, setting priorities, and making good decisions. Most time management experts include a brief exhortation to stop procrastinating. But if you're reading this book on procrastination, you've probably found it difficult to put these reasonable recommendations into practice. If you *could*, you *would*. Why can't you?

As we noted in Chapter 6, time is one of the great challenges for procrastinators. They are preoccupied with time, counting the hours and minutes or pretending that time doesn't matter at all. A procrastinator plays games with time, trying to outsmart it: "I'll watch a movie tonight and still have my report ready tomorrow morning." "There's always more time; time is no object."

Yet for all their experience at playing with its constraints, procrastinators' views of time are quite unrealistic. They have a relationship more akin to "wishful thinking" when it comes to time; they hope to find more of it than there really is, almost as if time were a quantity that could be extended instead of being one that is limited.

Perhaps it is this aspect of time—that it is fixed, measurable, and finite—that is so difficult for procrastinators to accept. Procrastinators, as we have observed, prefer to remain in the vague realms of potential and possibility and do not like to be concrete, measured, or limited. When they are ultimately caught short of time, they are surprised, disappointed, and even offended. In order to implement the time management techniques in this and other books, you may have to confront your own wishful-thinking approach to time.

TIME TO THINK ABOUT TIME

If you have chosen a behavioral goal for the next week, have you thought about when you are going to work on it? In order to think more realistically about using your time to achieve a goal, it helps to plan ahead. We know that many procrastinators resist this idea. We are not suggesting that you give up your spontaneity and become an on-time machine. Nor are we encouraging you to spend so much time planning that it becomes another means of procrastination, because at some point, you have to shift out of planning and into working on your goal. But we are suggesting that you take some time to think about time.

We know that planning may be particularly difficult for people with ADD or executive function problems. For you, planning should be approached with extra care and attention, taking into account the challenges of your particular brain. For techniques tailored specifically to those with ADD and executive dysfunction, see Chapter 16. The ideas in that chapter may help you implement the suggestions that follow.

When you plan ahead, you have the opportunity to use your brain in relative calm, before the panic of meeting an approaching deadline takes over. Compare how well you plan when you are relaxed to the frantic thinking that gets you into trouble at the last minute. As we have seen, increased stress interferes with the cognitive functions that are essential for planning, so you are more likely to plan effectively if you start before you are stressed out. Conversely, lack of planning increases the chances that you will become more agitated as you run out of time. As Alan Lakein, the original time management expert, said, "Failing to plan is planning to fail."[1]

People may resist planning because it seems to be about the future, and they want to live now, in the present. They can feel trapped by committing themselves to an activity in the future, as if their freedom is being constrained. Planning does not necessarily mean committing to use every hour of every day; you have to expect the unexpected, and you also want to have time for spontaneous fun and rejuvenating relaxation. Procrastinators may feel so guilty for lost time that they pressure themselves to use every minute productively, only to find that they have set up impossible expectations. It's not the plan that's the problem, it's the pressure.

However, a time plan can be your best friend, a link to your future. To quote Alan Lakein once again, "Planning is bringing the future into the present so that you can do something about it now."[2] In order to be your friend, a time plan should be realistic and compassionate. Planning your time hinges on getting real about what you actually do, not just programming what you should do.

As you plan to work toward the behavioral goal you have chosen, let's look at how you're going to make the time to take those incremental steps. When you think about the coming week, do you know how much time is available for you to use? Are you aware of the commitments you have already made? Have you planned for activities you usually spend time on, like watching the news or blogging? Is something unusual happening this week, such as houseguests visiting, a weekend seminar, or a sports tournament?

THE UN-SCHEDULE

Psychologist Neil Fiore was our colleague on the staff of the Counseling Center at UC-Berkeley when we were designing our Procrastination

Workshops. He understood that many people set up schedules for themselves that they never fulfill, then become disappointed, and eventually give up. So Dr. Fiore developed a method of keeping track of time that is not based on what people *should* do. Instead he created the un-schedule."[3] We have found the un-schedule to be very helpful to our clients and to participants in our Procrastination Workshops.

The un-schedule is a weekly calendar of all your committed activities. It can help you accomplish your goal in two ways. First, in looking ahead to see how much of your time is already committed, you will see the maximum amount of time you have left over to work toward your goal. Second, it helps you at the end of your week to look back and see where your time has actually gone, another example of self-monitoring.

"I Don't Know Where My Time Goes."   Think about the next seven days, starting with tomorrow. Using the blank un-schedule on pages 198–199 as a model, write down all of the activities you can predict you will do in the coming week, however trivial they may seem. Mark on your un-schedule the hours when you most probably will be doing things you already know will occur in the next week. If you know exactly when you will be doing something, write it down in the appropriate box—for example, a lunch meeting, Tuesday, 12:00–1:30 P.M. If you don't know exactly when you will do something, estimate the amount of time it will take and then mark it down on a day when you might do it. Include any special commitments you have scheduled for this week, like an evening meeting or a social date. In addition, mark off time for routine activities, such as grocery shopping or filling the gas tank of your car, that happen each week.

Consider the whole variety of activities in your life: work hours; scheduled meetings and appointments; classes and social events; time for exercise; time for meals, including preparation and cleanup; time given to household chores such as cleaning, laundry, and shopping; time set aside to spend with your friends, spouse, or children; time that you spend sleeping. If you always watch the evening news, Monday

Night Football, or other favorite television programs, put them down as well. Anticipate the extra time you spend reading the newspaper on Sundays. Don't forget to include your commuting and travel time, too. Use a calendar to remind yourself of your commitments, because it's easy to forget something. It's hubris to think you can keep track of everything in your head. On pages 200–201 is the un-schedule for Sonya, a high school history teacher who is behind on grading midterm papers for her students.

Remember, we are not asking you to write down what you *should* be doing. Don't put down when you hope you'll get around to starting on your behavioral goal or when you think you'll send an e-mail to your old friend. If you are a student, don't put down the times when you hope you'll be doing your homework. We are not asking you to promise yourself to try to do anything extra; we are only asking you to acknowledge what times are already spoken for in the coming week.

When you have finished filling out the un-schedule, look it over. This page represents your life for the next week. When you project yourself into the next seven days, how do you feel? Are you overwhelmed by all you are going to do? Anxious about how you are going to fill your uncommitted time? Depressed because you have so little free time? Examine how you feel as you visualize yourself going through this week, and consider what it is about your schedule that leads you to feel that way.

What can you learn about how much time you have available to work on your project? The un-schedule shows you the maximum amount of time you could use; the blank spaces reflect all of your uncommitted hours. Of course, no one will use all of the uncommitted hours to work on a project, but the un-schedule shows you how much time is potentially available.

A design engineer selected delivering a design to his client as his one-week behavioral goal, and he planned to spend three hours a day working on his project. When he filled out his un-schedule, he saw that he didn't even have three uncommitted hours a day! Given his

WEEKLY UN-SCHEDULE

Week of: _____

	Monday	Tuesday	Wednesday	Thursday	Friday	Saturday	Sunday
6 am							
7							
8							
9							
10							
11							
12 noon							
1							
2							

3							
4							
5							
6							
7							
8							
9							
10							
11							
Hours:							

Total Hours Worked Toward Goal: _____

WEEKLY UN-SCHEDULE

Week of: _Nov. 17_

	Monday	Tuesday	Wednesday	Thursday	Friday	Saturday	Sunday
6 am	wake up, jog, shower	wake up, jog, shower	wake up, shower	wake up, jog, shower	wake up, shower	sleep in	sleep in
7	Breakfast, kids to school	Breakfast, kids to school	Breakfast, kids to school	Breakfast, kids to school	Breakfast, kids to school	walk with Jen	call mom
8	AT	AT	AT	AT	AT	Breakfast w/ family	Breakfast w/ family
9	SCHOOL	SCHOOL	SCHOOL	SCHOOL	SCHOOL	clean House	
10	→	→	→	→	→	↓	work in garden
11						LUNCH	↓
12 noon						kids' soccer game	LUNCH
1						↓	take kids to b'day
2	→	→	→	→	→	↓	Party

3	PICK UP KIDS	Orthodontist Appt.	PICK UP KIDS / Soccer Practice	Teachers' meeting	PICK UP KIDS, Soccer Practice		
4	Help kids w/ homework		Soccer Practice	↓	Errands: Bank,		Make DINNER
5	Make Dinner	Make Dinner	PIZZA DINNER	PICK UP KIDS, DINNER	PICK UP KIDS, cleaners, groceries ↓	PICK UP Babysitter	DINNER
6	Dinner w/ Family	Dinner w/ Family	Supervise homework	BOOK	Take-out dinner	Kids' Dinner	Dinner with grandparents
7		Supervise homework, Bedtime		CLUB	Family Movie	Dinner and movie with	Read for
8	KIDS' Bedtime		KIDS' Bedtime		Night at home	Katie and Jack	BOOK CLUB
9							
10	TV NEWS						
11							
Hours:							

Total Hours Worked Toward Goal: _____

WEEKLY UN-SCHEDULE

Week of: ___ Nov. 17

	Monday	Tuesday	Wednesday	Thursday	Friday	Saturday	Sunday
6 am	Wake up, jog, shower	Wake up, jog, shower	Wake up, shower	Wake up, jog, shower	Wake up, shower	Sleep in	SLeep IN
7	Breakfast, kids to school	Breakfast, kids to school	Breakfast, kids to school	Breakfast, kids to school	Breakfast, kids to school	walk with Jen	Call mom
8	AT	AT	AT	AT	AT	Breakfast w/ Family	Breakfast w/ Family
9	SCHOOL	SCHOOL	SCHOOL	SCHOOL	SCHOOL	Clean House	/////////
10						↓	Work in garden
11						LUNCH	↓
12 noon						KIDS' soccer game	LUNCH
1						↓	Take kids to bday party
2	→	→	→	→	→	→	Party

3	Pick up kids	Orthodontist appt.	Pick up kids	Teachers' meeting ↓	Pick up kids, soccer practice	*(scribble)*	*(scribble)*
4	Help kids w/homework	Make Dinner	Soccer practice		Errands: Bank,	*(scribble)*	Make Dinner
5	Make Dinner	Make Dinner	Pizza Dinner	Pick up kids, Dinner	Cleaners, groceries ↓	Pick up Babysitter	Make Dinner
6	Dinner w/ Family	Dinner w/ Family	Supervise homework	Book Club	Take-out dinner	Kids' Dinner	Dinner with grandparents
7		Supervise homework, Bedtime *(scribble)*	*(scribble)*	Club	Family Movie	Dinner and Movie with	Read for
8	Kids' Bedtime	*(scribble)*	Kids' Bedtime		Night at home	Katie and Jack	Book Club
9							
10	TV News			↑		↑	
11							
Hours:							

Total Hours Worked Toward Goal: 4 1/2 hrs

present schedule, his goal was unattainable. By underestimating how much of his time was already spoken for, he was setting himself up for failure. He either had to revise his goal or revise his schedule.

Perhaps you are one of those people who have a lot of unscheduled time. Many people who work from home or work part-time or who are self-employed or unemployed find that they face large blocks of unstructured time. For procrastinators, this "free" time can generate a lot of anxiety, because it means they have to create their own structure in order to get anything done.

The un-schedule can also tell you something about how you are currently managing your time. A brilliant graduate student did not realize until he filled out his un-schedule that waking up at 8:50 for a 9:00 A.M. class was cutting it too close. No wonder he was always late for everything!

Sometimes people examine their commitments and discover how much of their time is taken up with social engagements and recreation. These procrastinators have planned their excuses ahead of time, so that when the moment comes, they feel they are meeting their obligations, and they may not recognize that they're procrastinating. "I keep planning so many social events after work that I never even have to decide if I'm going to start writing my book or not," said a magazine editor. "I just barely have time to get where I'm going."

Look closely at your un-schedule. Is there anything missing from your life? Some procrastinators don't allow themselves any recreation; since they're always behind, they feel they don't deserve any downtime. And those who do hop from one recreational event to another may not experience genuine pleasure in their frenetic activity if they are using fun events to escape their work. Amy, a realtor, realized, "I haven't included any fun! I feel so guilty about all the work I have to do that I don't think I should take any time out just to enjoy myself. No wonder I'm so tense all the time."

Some procrastinators schedule too much socializing and leave out time to be alone. Others withdraw from people and allow themselves too little social contact. What have you scheduled too little of? Time with your family? With friends? Physical activity? Leisurely reading?

Record and Reward

As you work on your behavioral goal or on any project, use the un-schedule to record your progress. After you have finished thirty minutes of work toward your goal, block off one-half of the appropriate hour on your un-schedule. If you work for an hour, block off the entire box. (Some people who really enjoy charts use different colors to track progress on different projects.) Then add up the blocks to get the total amount of time you spent that week working toward your goal. For example, Sonya worked toward her goal for an hour on Tuesday, a half-hour on Wednesday, and two hours on Saturday and Sunday, for a total of four and a half hours. (See pages 202–203 for Sonya's completed un-schedule.) If it's better for you to work in smaller increments of time, mark off a quarter of a box for every fifteen minutes you spend toward your goal.

Remember to record your progress *after* you have completed time spent toward your goal. You may find that your week does not develop quite as you'd predicted, so your blocks may appear at times you'd expected to use for something else. Keeping track of your progress toward your goal in this simple way has several benefits. First, when you record progress after you've made it, you focus on what you have accomplished. Instead of making a promise to yourself about when and how much you'll work, which can leave you feeling like a failure if you don't live up to it, you record what you have actually done, which is more likely to give you the experience of success. Monitoring your progress in this way helps you to see your glass as half-full, not half-empty. Second, the darkened blocks serve as a reward for your productive behavior. The sooner you record your progress after your work period, the more reinforcing the blocks become. One of the factors that has been shown to reduce procrastination is making a reward more immediate. Working for fifteen minutes or half an hour and then recording your effort provides a prompt reward after a short period of time.

As the week goes by, and you watch the number of blocks increase, you may feel motivated to continue. "These marks work like gold stars in grade school," commented one procrastinator who found the un-schedule especially helpful. "I get a sense of satisfaction every time I fill in a block, and I feel like doing more."

Rewarding progress after thirty minutes of work is also a good way to recognize that even a half hour of effort is worthwhile. You don't have to wait until you have all the time you need to finish a project in order to start the project. The un-schedule shows you when you have small bits of time available and helps you reward yourself for every half hour you use toward your goal.

Keeping track of the number of hours you worked toward your goal is a form of self-monitoring. Self-monitoring has been shown to increase the time spent on work and also to improve achievement.[4] Self-monitoring also helps procrastinators be more realistic about time. Counting up the number of hours you worked toward your goal is facing reality. You can't fool yourself into believing that you've accomplished an enormous amount when you see that you spent a half hour during your week on your goal. You also can't pretend that you haven't gotten anything done if you count up ten hours of effort. You may find that your feelings about what you've done don't match what the numbers tell you—you can work for ten hours and still not feel a sense of accomplishment. But if you've made a record of those hours, at least you have tangible proof before you to counter your disappointed feelings. This is an objective alternative to your subjective interpretation of how you spend your time.

TECHNIQUES TO IMPROVE YOUR TIMING

Practice Telling Time.   Can you accurately predict how long things actually take to accomplish? Sometimes people underestimate, thinking, "I can read *War and Peace* in two nights," or, "My tax return will only take a couple of hours." Sometimes procrastinators overestimate how much time is needed, putting off a project such as cleaning out the basement because they think, "I can't do that now—it will take forever." In both cases, the result is that they do nothing.

Brain chemistry affects our capacity to tell time accurately. When the neurotransmitter dopamine is in short supply, the clock in your brain that tracks time intervals is thrown off. The capacity to estimate how much time has passed also diminishes with age.[5] If your timing is off, you may have to practice telling time.

One way to counter wishful thinking and improve your ability to tell time is to compare your predictions about how long things take with what actually happens when you do them. For example, estimate how long it takes you from the time you hear the alarm in the morning to the time you leave your house, and then clock yourself. Or guess how long it will take you to answer your e-mails when you get to work, and then see how long it actually takes. Or measure how long it takes you to drive across town. One procrastinator, a New York City businessman, planned his drives to Long Island using the timetable, "It takes forty-five minutes without traffic." This might be true, but had he ever driven to Long Island *without* traffic?

Learn to Use Little Bits of Time. Alan Lakein made a great suggestion for procrastinators when he described the "Swiss cheese"[6] method of time management in his book *How to Get Control of Your Time and Your Life*. He recommends "poking holes" in a large task by using little bits of time instead of waiting for one large block of time. This technique can be an extremely helpful way for you to make a start on a project or to keep up some momentum once you have begun.

The significance of the Swiss-cheese technique is that it values any amount of time, no matter how small. The fact that your goal will require ten hours to accomplish does not mean you have to wait until you have a ten-hour block of time before you can start. There are a lot of crucial steps you can take in just fifteen minutes, or ten minutes, or even five minutes. If you're feeling overwhelmed, you can use one minute to make a list. If you've been avoiding the room where all your unfinished projects wait, you can just stand inside it for fifteen minutes, keep breathing, and get used to being there. If you have a lot of organizing to do, use a few minutes to locate your box of file folders.

Any step toward your goal is one more step than you would have taken if you'd continued to avoid it.

You may find small bits of time by surprise. If a colleague cancels an appointment that was supposed to last for a half hour, you have just been given thirty minutes. If you finish your phone calls ten minutes before you have to leave the office, those ten minutes can be put to use.

The Swiss-cheese method has several advantages of particular benefit to procrastinators. For one thing, it's realistic. It is more likely that you can find fifteen or thirty minutes here and there than a big block of free time. If you're waiting for a large chunk of free time, you can wait forever.

In addition, if you use a little bit of time, you have a natural limit. Setting a time limit for yourself is good practice for procrastinators. It helps you to counter the magical notion that one day when you have a lot of time you'll summon up all of your energy and just do it, until it's all done. This kind of time and this kind of effort rarely occur and even more rarely coincide.

Limiting your time working on a goal also makes it more tolerable. As difficult, unpleasant, or tedious as your task may be, you can probably stand anything for fifteen minutes. Horrible things can seem less horrible if you realize that getting started is not the beginning of an endless experience. And if you do manage to get even a little bit of a task accomplished, you're likely to feel good about it. Then the satisfaction you get from making progress can function as a reward. Remember that feeling good about accomplishing something releases chemicals in your brain that increase your sense of wellbeing.[7] You may be drawn to repeat the experience of working, so that you'll feel good again.

The Swiss-cheese method can be quite a contrast to the way you may have been using work to punish yourself. If you've put something off, you may sentence yourself to solitary confinement for a whole weekend in order to catch up. But the mere thought of such confinement can conjure up feelings of being chained to your desk while everyone else is watching football or going to the beach. The prospect of a lonely, arduous Sunday is aversive, so you avoid it. Ex-

perience confirms what research has shown: punishment is not a mo-
tivator.[8] You're better off using a little carrot rather than a big stick.

Working in small amounts of time is an especially helpful technique when your procrastination is a sign that you're involved in a
battle of wills, as we discussed in Chapter 4. If you put things off because you don't like feeling pushed around or controlled, your procrastination is saying, in effect, "You can't make me do this." Your
sense of freedom and autonomy is threatened if you go ahead and do
the work. But if you decide that you will be the one to set your own
time limits, that you will work for ten minutes or five minutes and no
longer, you can regain the sense of control you need and still move
forward.

Using small bits of time is effective. A college professor was so
pleased with this technique that she said, "I set my kitchen timer for an
hour and use this method for all kinds of projects, from grading papers
to cleaning closets. It gets me going, yet I know there's an end in sight!"
Others are not so easily converted. If you don't see tangible results right
away, you may discredit your initial steps, as if you'd taken none at all.
You may find that doing a little at a time is inglorious. It's not as
thrilling as being able to attack and conquer in one magnificent effort.
A lawyer who had difficulty implementing this technique told us, "I refuse to start anything unless I have enough time to finish it. I can see
that thinking big is counterproductive, but I do everything that way."
Once again, we are reminded that the "all-or-nothing" view is a constant obstacle for procrastinators. Using small portions of time is effective if you let yourself accept the value of "something."

Expect Interruptions and Disruptions. According to Murphy's
Law, "Anything that can go wrong will go wrong." But many procrastinators don't believe this rule of thumb will apply to them once
they have finally made up their minds to get down to work. You
probably can recall incidents when you've procrastinated and then
been in a real jam because things failed to go smoothly at the eleventh hour. Unexpected obstacles, like a phone call or a misplaced paper, can really throw you off balance. Why haven't you planned for

the possibility that something could go wrong? Why assume that your effort is the only factor to consider? Once you finally overcome your own resistance and are ready to work, you may expect the rest of the world to cooperate. Unfortunately the world doesn't always go along with your plan.

Tyler had a job interview at two on Monday afternoon. The week before the interview he knew he should take his suit to the cleaners, but he didn't get around to it. On Monday morning, after a late night spent looking over the financials of the company that might hire him, Tyler got up early and rushed his suit to the cleaners to meet the 7:30 A.M. deadline for a 1:00 P.M. pickup. At one-thirty, on the way to the interview, wearing his dress shirt, tie, good shoes, and jeans, Tyler stopped at the cleaners. They could not find his suit; maybe it was still in process, or maybe someone misplaced the ticket. Tyler rushed behind the counter to the cleaning area, frantically searching for his suit. The result: he had to cancel his interview at the last minute. Of course, he didn't get the job.

Unfortunately, the world doesn't always take notice of your burst of resolve, and things go wrong at their usual rate. There are limits to what you can control. You can't get to the airport on time if there is a big traffic jam. You can't get your data to your manager in time for his big meeting if your computer crashes, especially if you have also procrastinated on backing up your files. You can't study effectively all night if you're catching a cold. If you acknowledge in advance the possibility of random disaster, you are in a better position to take obstacles in stride instead of feeling frantic and thwarted, furious at the bad-luck gods or hating yourself.

Delegate.   Delegating is one way to increase your time efficiency. If you give some of your workload to someone else, then your burden is reduced, and you are free to concentrate on other tasks. The process of delegating involves identifying tasks you alone don't have to do, finding the best person who could do it, making clear what needs to be done, and keeping track of how they're progressing.

A consistent recommendation by time management experts is to prioritize your tasks and spend your time on only the most important things. Less important things can be delegated (or even set aside). Peter Drucker, the famous management expert, said, "First things first; second things, not at all."[9] Stephen Covey's third habit of highly effective people is, "Put first things first."[10] You should be spending your personal time on the most important things that require your attention and delegating things that are not your top priority.

This consistent advice makes sense. You'd think procrastinators would leap at the chance to lessen their burdens. But when we ask people to think specifically of a project they could actually give away, they usually object rather than feeling relieved. Why? Here are some reasons procrastinators have given for why they don't delegate.

"I should be able to do it all myself." Perhaps in your pursuit of perfection you believe you should never have to ask for help. So you interpret delegating to mean that you have failed to meet your responsibility or that you are less competent. "I thought of hiring someone to clean my house while I was involved in an important court case," said an attorney, "but I know other women who are organized enough to do it all, and I should be, too."

We don't think delegating is a failure. It's a skill. The real failure lies in stubbornly holding on to every item in your life, which results in only half of them getting done.

"I'm the only one who can do this right." This is another perfectionistic pitfall. Although there may be some things that you—and only you—can do, is that really true of *everything* on your list of unfinished chores? Even if someone else wouldn't do it in quite your way, it would be better to have it done in a different manner than to leave it undone altogether. If you delegate, you will not have total control. You may have to stand that loss for the sake of accomplishment.

"Delegating is a cop-out." You may feel too guilty to ask for help. You may believe that because you've been Very Bad, you now have to be Very Good to make up for it. You may feel that you don't deserve to be helped, so you can't delegate or rely on others.

Refusing help is a good way to procrastinate yourself into martyr-dom. "I was the only person on my committee who wasn't prepared for the meeting," reported a board member of a charitable organiza-tion. "I felt so terrible that I wouldn't talk to anyone about it. They did their work; why should they have to help me with mine? I wanted to be especially prepared the next time, but I wasn't, so I didn't go to the meeting. Then I left the board."

This stoic and self-punitive approach does not increase your pro-ductivity; it only increases the pressure and, thus, your suffering. Adding pressure is adding problems.

"I might delegate the wrong thing to the wrong person." Even if you agree in principle that there are some matters you could shift to someone else, you may procrastinate in deciding what to delegate and to whom. It's best to delegate to someone who has the ability to help you, who doesn't hold a grudge against you, and who isn't a pro-crastinator or a perfectionist. It also helps to release tasks that don't require your constant supervision, or you've defeated the purpose. But if you assume there is one right way to delegate, you will be un-able to make a decision while you consider every possible angle, look-ing for the perfect solution. Anything you pass along will lighten your load, whether it's mundane or important.

"I'd run out of distractions." Imagine yourself getting help with many of the tasks that now bog you down. What then? Without the pressure of all those urgent demands, you'd have less standing be-tween you and the really important things you've been avoiding. You'd be brought face-to-face with your fears. So if you are able to pare down your list of things to do, be forewarned that you may at first feel more anxiety than relief. But if you persevere, and if you confront and address your underlying fears, relief will probably come later.

Don't Spread Yourself Too Thin. We knew a college student, Ethan, who took eighteen course units, marched in the school band, played on an intramural soccer team, and frequently traveled home to see his girlfriend. He'd squeeze in studying while he commuted or between band practice and soccer practice. Although Ethan claimed that school was his top priority, he behaved as if it were at the bottom of his list.

Clearly, if Ethan really wanted to do better in school, he'd have to give something up—perhaps drop band or soccer and take fewer academic units. But when we suggested this to him, he refused. Ethan wanted to do it all.

Is being too busy the same thing as procrastinating? It can be, if like Ethan, you use your busyness to avoid something more important. When you make lots of commitments, not only are you setting the stage for procrastination, but you're also giving yourself a ready excuse: "I'm not really procrastinating; I'm just too busy to get everything done on time."

Take a hard look at your commitments (the un-schedule will be useful for this). Are you spread too thin? Is this a setup to procrastinate on something that matters? Aren't there things you really could give up? You may lose something in the process, but is it necessary for the sake of the greater goal?

We learned this lesson the hard way, when we tried to write the first edition of this book while working full-time. Guess what happened? We couldn't do it! In addition to being teased mercilessly about procrastinating, we felt very bad that we weren't making more progress. Finally, with great reluctance, we decided to try working only part-time and writing part-time. This proved to be successful. Although we missed our colleagues and our paychecks, we were able finally to have enough time to write.

Identify Your Prime Time. If you promise yourself that you'll do thirty minutes of exercise each morning before work, but you're not really a morning person and you barely make it to work on time as it is, you're setting yourself up for failure. We each have a natural daily biorhythm. Think about when during the day you have the most mental energy, when you are most physically energetic, when you feel most sociable, and when you feel depleted. There's no point in planning to spend every night after work writing your novel, if all you have the energy for is taking a nap or reading someone else's novel.

You probably recognize the problem here for procrastinators: identifying your prime time means acknowledging that some of your time is less than prime. It's admitting that you can't work at top capacity all the time or whenever you think you should. It means realizing that you have human limits.

Work on Balancing Your Perspective on Past, Present, and Future. It's important not to get stuck in time. If you're stuck in the past, you can't enjoy the present or plan for the future. If you're stuck in the present, you're at the mercy of the immediate moment, with no connection to past and future; you can't benefit from your experience. If you're stuck in the future, you're locked in a world of fantasy, either positive or negative, and all you do is plan or worry. In *The Time Paradox*, authors Zimbardo and Boyd emphasize the need to achieve a balance among these time orientations and offer many suggestions for resetting your time perspective clock.[11]

Enjoy Your "Free" Time. It is obvious that procrastinators have difficulty working effectively, but it is often overlooked that they also have difficulty relaxing. Even if you indulge in fun activities while you're procrastinating, chances are you're not fully enjoying them, because you know you're using them to avoid doing something else. Or, you may not even let yourself have these diversions because you feel unproductive and therefore undeserving. In either case, you're not having real fun.

Pleasure is so important in life. Try to plan for it, and give it to yourself without guilt or desperation. Play time is necessary for everyone, no matter how degenerate you feel you are. If you deprive yourself of true relaxation, you will run out of energy the way a car runs out of gas. And you will steal leisure time by procrastinating.

14

Learning to
Say Yes and No

Procrastination can be an indirect way to say no when we are unable to say no directly; it can also represent "stealing" time to spend on things we can't openly say yes to. Deciding what to agree to and what to refuse can be a challenge. In our consumer-driven, acquisition-oriented society, one word that characterizes modern life is "more." We have more information, more speed, more choices, more cars, more stuff, more TV channels, more mobility, more demands on our time. More, more, more. Yet, with this seemingly insatiable press for more, many of us end up feeling like we actually have less of what matters most: less downtime, less privacy, less opportunity to pursue our passions, less time with the people we love, less time for our creative pursuits. It is easy to get caught up in the push for more. Procrastination may be a reflection of our feeling overwhelmed by too much, or it may express a yearning for something we are missing. Instead of relying on procrastination, we think it is important to say yes consciously to what enhances life, to say no to what detracts from it, and to say it directly rather than using procrastination to say it for you.

LEARNING TO SAY YES TO HELPFUL PEOPLE AND ACTIVITIES

Say Yes to Support from Others

Procrastinators are usually ambivalent about asking for support from others. They may feel ashamed of waiting until the last minute, so they believe they don't deserve help. Some people are so convinced they can and should do everything by themselves that relying on someone else feels like failure. In some cultures, asking for help outside the family is shameful. Some procrastinators interpret asking for support as being rescued, hoping someone else will take over and finish the job for them. However, asking for support doesn't have to carry any of these meanings. Finding support can mean using your connections with other people to help you take actions that are important to you and move you forward. Let's look at some ways you can say yes to getting support from others.

Choose the Right People.   When you're looking for support, the first issue is to find the right people to help you. Social networks are a powerful influence: research has shown, for example, that smoking cessation and obesity are closely tied to whether the people around us stop smoking or are obese.[1] Look for people who are kind, encouraging, and nonjudgmental, but also realistic and able to focus on your task. Choose people who are on your side, who can see things from your point of view. Sadly, we sometimes yearn for help from the very people who are least able to give it. You may crave support and encouragement from a parent, spouse, manager, or sibling—only to find repeatedly that what they offer doesn't feel like support. "Whenever I'm in trouble, I call my dad," said one businesswoman. "If I have a problem at work, I think he'll know how to handle it. But instead, he criticizes me for having the problem in the first place. I probably shouldn't keep calling him, but each time I hope it will be different."

Think about who would be most helpful in which circumstances. We have a friend who is a terrific sounding board for our ideas. She has a tough intellectual mind and asks challenging questions that help us clarify our thoughts—once we know what we're talking about. But if we discuss our ideas with her when we're in the brainstorming phase, just starting to think, her skepticism and her eye for contradictions are demoralizing rather than helpful. Another friend is always ready for fun. On any given evening, he knows where there are several interesting parties, which old movies are playing in town, and where to find a free concert. It's great to plan rewards with him—but he's not a good working partner, since all he wants to do is play.

You can discuss your procrastination issues or your behavioral goal with a supportive person. Try to listen openly and nondefensively to feedback and suggestions. You never know when you'll hear an idea that could help you get going. Just having someone listen to your experience can be a great support, helping you feel less alone in your struggle.

Make a Public Commitment. Tell people what you're working on and when you're aiming for completion. People are more serious about a public commitment than one they keep to themselves, and the more public the promise, the more reluctant they are to change it.[2] Having to account to someone else makes it harder to abandon your goal or interrupt your steps toward that goal, because someone else knows your plan. You can no longer avoid your goal in secret. If you tell a friend that you're determined to lose ten pounds, for example, you'll probably find it harder to eat dessert. You know she'll check in with you and ask how you're coming along, and you won't want to confess that you ate two pieces of apple pie last night.

In addition to your friends, you can turn to the Internet for help. You will find chat rooms for procrastinators and help from Procrastinators Anonymous. We also recommend the Internet site, StickK.com to help you make a commitment and stick to it. Founded in 2008, the site was developed by two Yale University economists who understand the psychological and economic principles behind "commitment contracts."[3] People don't always do what they say they will do, but if they make their intentions public, and if they make a commitment of money, they are more likely to succeed. On the site, people make commitments to work toward goals they need help with, such as losing weight, exercising regularly, and stopping smoking. You can set up any goal you choose, post it publicly on the site (using your name or not), and connect with other people who are working toward similar goals. To increase your motivation even further, you'll be given the option to make a financial commitment to your goal. If you achieve your goal, you get your money back; if you don't, the money is donated to charity.

Make a Plan Together. You can talk with another person to create a plan for action. If, like most procrastinators, you are vague about what you need to do, the simple act of articulating your plan to someone else can help clarify your thoughts. You may realize that you're attempting too much, or you may discover that your plan seems more feasible as you explain it to someone else. Perhaps the next steps will become obvious as you talk it through.

Talking with someone whose strengths are complementary to yours may be especially helpful. If you're good at seeing the final outcome but can't figure out how to get there, talk with someone who's good with the nitty-gritty. If you're good at working out details but have a hard time seeing the big picture, talk with someone who thinks in grand fashion.

You might also benefit from hearing how someone else has approached and solved a problem you're grappling with. We once interviewed a prolific writer, comparing ideas about how to integrate writing with our other commitments. In contrast to our attempts to fit writing around the rest of our lives, he said, "I think of writing as my main priority. I work at it every day from nine till twelve, and I don't let myself be interrupted. I don't even answer the phone." We were startled. Not answer the phone? Actually let it ring when it could offer the possibility of a friendly chat, an invitation to escape, or a dire emergency? We could see from his clarity of purpose that we needed to change our perspective.

Keep in mind that if you ask for help, you're not obliged to take it. And don't be intimidated if the other person has insights you have overlooked. It's almost always easier to help someone else craft a plan than to design your own. When we work with groups of procrastinators, we ask people to formulate a goal and then discuss their plans with two other people. Over and over we see that procrastinators can be very levelheaded and realistic about another person's project, while remaining muddled and idealistic about their own. You might help someone else think through a project of theirs to discover some of your own creative organizational and time management skills. You could even imagine that one of your friends is facing your project and think about how you would offer help.

Ask for Help When You're Stuck.   When brain lock hits, it's time to call for outside help: if you've procrastinated yourself into a bind, chances are you can't easily see a way out. Rather than give up, this is a good time to ask for help. But it may also be a time when you feel so reprehensible that you're not sure you deserve to be helped. One procrastinator told us, "When I'm stuck, going around in circles, I hate myself so much that I don't even want to talk to other people, let alone ask them to help me. I feel unfit for human contact." It is precisely when you have sunk to the depths of self-loathing that support can bring you the greatest relief. Someone else can treat you decently even when you can't be decent to yourself. On the practical side, talking with someone else about your dilemma may offer a way out that you hadn't considered, enabling you to take a small step forward and realize that all is not lost.

Work Together.   Talking is great, but it has its limits. You still have to *do* something to make progress. One way to take action is to enlist a partner in a joint effort. We weren't sure that either of us could write this book alone, but we were much more optimistic about doing it together. (And we were right!) When two people are committed to the same goal, there is more incentive for each of you to live up to your commitment. If you don't, it's not only your life that's hurt, but someone else's, too.

Having a partner also helps because you can create intermediate deadlines together, and the closer the deadline, the more likely you are to take action. If you set up regular meetings with your partner, it gives you some impetus to get to work—even if you wait until the night before the meeting to do it. And it can be comforting to know that you're not the only one going through the agonies and deprivations of working hard. Our temptation to procrastinate would have been much more powerful had either of us been working alone. On a beautiful, sunny California day, when we were both sequestered indoors writing or rewriting, we knew that there was at least one other person in the Golden State who was not outside enjoying the weather.

You can work with a partner as an equal, as we are coauthors, or you can engage a partner specifically as a check on your individual progress. You could use your manager at work as a partner by setting up a regular time to discuss your progress on a project. A writer struggling with the draft of his first novel hired a friend to be his "editor." He arranged weekly meetings so that he would feel pressured to write something for his friend to read. A pair of procrastinating friends enlisted each other as task partners, setting up a regular schedule to check on their respective efforts. No matter how little you've actually accomplished, at the very least, meeting with your partner will be a consistent reminder to stay on track.

Parallel Play.   When children are toddlers, they go through a stage in which they engage in "parallel play." That is, they play beside each other with their own toys, rather than with each other. In the same way, you can arrange to work on your project with someone who works separately on his or her own task. For example, we know a group of people who hate to prepare their tax returns, so they get together every March for sessions they call "Tax Torture." Each person brings a laptop, plus a large box filled with the forms, checks, receipts, and papers he or she needs. Then they all sit down together at a large table, moaning and groaning, but gradually, they get their taxes done.

You can use parallel play to work on all kinds of things that you've been postponing. Two women, each feeling overwhelmed by the prospect of creating a family scrapbook, took turns going to each other's houses and worked side by side putting their scrapbooks together. An accountant arranged to meet a friend at the local library on Saturday mornings, so that both could catch up on work they hadn't finished at their offices. They agreed that their homes were distracting environments, and the library was a setting in which they could focus. By making a date to meet each other, people can help each other get their work done, and just as important, they can reinforce a social connection at the same time.

Social Rewards. Sometimes progress is its own reward, but more often people are a better reward. One woman who worked at home told her husband to call one hour before he left his office. If she made a dent in her work by the time he arrived home, they would go out to dinner together. She spent the hour between the call and the dinner reading rather boring background material assigned by her company. Looking forward to going out with her husband gave her the incentive she needed to spend time on drudgery.

You can use social events as rewards at every step toward a goal: call a friend after you've taken your first step and get some encouragement to continue; take a walk with someone when you need a break; go to the movies at the end of a long day; plan a holiday after you've completed a large project.

Say Yes to Time with People You Love. Too often, procrastination interferes with spending guilt-free time with the people who are most important. If you put off work at the office and bring home a bulging briefcase on weekends, you may not feel you can take time to have fun with your family and friends, but you miss out on precious experiences. Life is short. Use your work time for work and your family time for family. Remember to put first things first.[4] If time with people you love is a priority, fit your projects around them and not the other way around. And if you don't have friends, now is the time to make some. When you feel loved and connected, procrastination may not seem so seductive.

Say Yes to Personal Growth

Try New Challenges. Procrastination is often a way of retreating from challenges; instead, remember that tackling challenges can benefit you. Does this challenge stretch you? Does it help you develop and grow? New challenges keep you learning, learning keeps you vital, vitality keeps you feeling alive and happy. And new challenges are good for your brain. Remember that your brain changes every day. New challenges encourage your brain cells to grow and connect in more complex ways.

Do More of What You Love. Procrastinators get so focused on the dreaded tasks hanging over them or feel so guilty about all they haven't done, they often don't allow themselves to do things that give them joy. Whatever it is you love to do, do more of it. Whether it's planting a garden, learning a new language, reading to children, quilting with friends, closing a deal, raising money for a cause you believe in, cooking with your family, spending time in nature, reading novels, taking care of animals, playing or dancing to music, or creating art—if it makes you feel alive and enriched, add it to your life. These are the activities that make life worth living, and they deserve to have more time in your life, not less.

LEARNING TO SAY NO TO POINTLESS PURSUITS

Say No to Timewasters and Downers

It is as important to think about what you want to minimize or eliminate from your life as it is to think about what you want to include.

Learn to identify and say no to things that aren't helpful or connected to what really matters most. We all have things, people, and activities that weigh us down, tire us out, derail us, and diminish the quality of our lives. Yet for procrastinators, the prospect of getting rid of that which drags us down can be intimidating. Often we procrastinate by spending time on these peripheral or detrimental activities. More importantly, the process of deciding what to include and what to exclude can be difficult in and of itself, especially if you don't trust your judgment.

Say No to Empty Tasks.   There are plenty of tasks in life that we have to do even though we don't want to, such as paying taxes and maintaining the car. It's important to do those things that help your life run smoothly, even if they might feel aversive. But there's a difference between taking care of business and wasting time on empty tasks. If you're faced with doing something that doesn't move you in the direction you want to go, don't do it.

Empty tasks are those with the lowest priority relative to your current goals and values. One of the most frequently cited guidelines in time management is the "80/20 rule"[5]: 20 percent of your tasks are very important and yield the most results, and 80 percent of your tasks are not so important and don't contribute much. This is referred to as "the vital few and the trivial many."[6] Learn to say no to many of the trivial tasks and devote 80 percent of your time to completing those few vital tasks.

Do you really have to clear off your desk before you can begin to work on the computer? If the most vital issue is writing the copy for your marketing brochure so that you can have it printed and get your business going, then cleaning your desk can wait. However, if the most important issue is paying your mortgage before it's overdue, then cleaning off your desk to find your mortgage statement is vital. Recognizing empty tasks implies that you know what's important and what isn't. This can be difficult for procrastinators and for those with ADD or executive dysfunction. It's always worthwhile to ask yourself, "Should I be doing this right now?" and to say no to tasks that are trivial.

Say No to Unnecessary Commitments. It's so easy to become overcommitted. Procrastinators, living as they do in a world of high expectations and grand ideals, like to believe they can do it all. Being overcommitted provides an excuse for not doing everything—or anything—in a timely way. Unnecessary commitments infringe on the time we need for the most important things.

It can be hard to say no when other people ask us to do things— help them out, join their cause, provide a service. It boosts our ego when we are wanted and valued, especially if we're persuaded that we're the best person for the job, or the *only* person for the job. Sometimes we agree to do things because we want to please people, or we worry about offending them if we refuse. But agreeing to do things for the wrong reasons is ultimately unsatisfying and may lead to resentment and procrastination. Just say no.

Say No to the Wrong People. As you were growing up, your parents may have advised you to "choose your friends wisely." It is important to spend your time with people you can be open with, laugh with, trust, and turn to in times of trouble. It's also important to "choose your enemies wisely." You probably know people who make you feel worse instead of better. Maybe they are angry, downcast, critical, or dismissive. When you're with them, you find yourself shutting down and feeling drained, inadequate, or unlovable. If you recognize people like this in your life, it's time to think about reducing their impact on you. Can you say no? Can you have less contact with them? You are not obligated to make time for every person who wants time with you.

There may be some people who have a negative impact on you, but you can't say no to them altogether, especially if they are co-workers or members of your extended family. Perhaps you can limit the amount of time you spend with them or try to develop an internal buffer so that their negativity doesn't become yours. When Terry, a perpetually guilt-ridden procrastinator, asked her younger sister how she resisted the constant criticism and pressure from their mother, her sister said, "I just don't listen to her!" The thought of saying no to her mother in her mind had never even occurred to Terry.

Say No to Clutter

"Throw Out Fifty Things."[7]   We love this suggestion by Gail Blanke, a life coach who advises people to start with throwing out stuff and then move on to throwing out mental clutter. We all have fifty things we can get rid of, says Blanke, from single socks and earrings to clothes we haven't worn in years, from dried-out lipsticks to unidentifiable keys. Anything you don't know what to do with or why you have it, get rid of it. If you have clutter that makes you feel heavy, weighed down, or discouraged when you see it, throw it out. There is one important caveat, however: newspapers, magazines, and catalogues count as one thing, no matter how many you throw out. As you say no to fifty things, make a list of what you throw away; later, you can look back and feel proud of all you've discarded.

You can also look inside yourself for "things" to throw away. Are you holding on to old ideas, grudges, resentments, hopes, or dreams that don't fit who you are today? Are there regrets that fill your mind or disappointments that continue to haunt you? Are there beliefs about yourself, about other people, about success, failure, or life that no longer serve you? It's not easy to let go of emotional clutter, but when you finally give yourself permission to do so, you'll probably feel lighter, freer, and happier. Add the mental throwaways to the written list. Some of this emotional clutter probably contributes to your procrastination.

Say No to E-Addictions

Pull the Plug.   For periods of time, ban the Internet, Blackberry, cell phone, and e-mail, and say no to distractions in your environment. Choosing to be disconnected for a few hours or days may be disorienting and even anxiety-arousing ("I might miss something important!"), but most people feel liberated once they unplug. For example, Stanford Law School professor Lawrence Lessig, an expert on cyberlaw, "makes a deliberate decision to go off the digital grid— no blogging, limited email, few phone calls" for one month every year; on a smaller scale, when he needs to focus on writing, he unplugs his wireless router so that e-mail won't get in the way of his focusing on his work.[8] When you say no to e-mail, instant messaging, texting, blogging, and surfing the Internet, you'll find that you have a lot more time and mental space available to concentrate on what you need to do. Keep in mind that your brain cannot actually multitask (it takes 0.7 seconds each time you shift your attention).[9] So even if the meeting is tedious or the professor boring, unplug, turn off your cell phone or PDA, and listen to what's being said; otherwise, you can't really pay attention.

Go on a Low-Information Diet.   Do you really need to watch or listen to news reports four or five times a day? Do you really need to check the latest price comparisons on the Internet? Do you need to have e-mail updates for retail promotions, political groups, or every good cause you support? Say no to e-clutter. There is too much information coming in, far more than our brains can comfortably process. It's up to each one of us to set limits on how much information we take in, to keep ourselves buffered from an information glut that can pollute life rather than enhance it.

Say No to Video Games, Virtual Worlds, and Internet Porn.   All are mesmerizing, to be sure, but they are also addictive and draining if you do too much of them. It's like medicine—the right dose helps you feel better, but an overdose becomes poisonous. Check your fantasy dosage carefully. Besides being huge time wasters, these pursuits can take you away from healthy, intimate interactions with real people.

These suggestions for saying yes and no are only a beginning. We hope they will encourage you to think further about other yes and no choices you can make, about what you want and don't want in your life. When you claim the right to set parameters for how you spend your time, you will procrastinate less and make more space in your life.

15

Using Your Body to Reduce Procrastination

When we are procrastinating, whether we are running fast to avoid something or frozen in couch-potato mode, we lose contact with our most fundamental self: our biological being. Taking time to attend to your sensory experience and to cultivate bodily well-being can help you face what you've been putting off. Taking care of your body will not stop you from procrastinating overnight, but it can help you feel more balanced, steady, and at ease in body and mind. When you're in a state of physical and mental harmony, you are more prepared to handle the unfinished projects that are waiting for you.

GET GOING BY GETTING MOVING

For some of you, the idea that you can use exercise to help extricate yourself from the paralysis of procrastination may offer relief and a feeling of hope. Others may find the prospect unappealing and feel oppressed or trapped at the mere thought of putting on your walking shoes. Before you reach for the remote control or begin another computer game, however, we hope you'll at least consider taking steps to include exercise as a way to manage your procrastination. Like all our suggested techniques, exercise can help *if* you do it. If you find yourself putting off exercise along with everything else, in spite of the known benefits, think back to the fears we described in Part One. Fears of failure, success, and feeling controlled can undermine your readiness to integrate exercise into your life.

We have known for some time that, in addition to promoting general physical health, exercise can have a significant benefit in improving mood. If people who are depressed can get themselves to take a walk or go to the gym, they typically feel better. Exercise spurs the body to produce endorphins, hormones that promote feelings of pleasure and well-being. Whether we are depressed or not, exercise can help lift our spirits, as long as it is not used to excess.

There is now evidence that exercise, in addition to elevating mood, promotes the growth and regulation of the brain. In his book *Spark*, Harvard psychiatrist John Ratey wrote about the many ways exercise helps our brain.[1] We draw from his work in what follows.

When you exercise, says Ratey, not only do you feel better, but your brain works better: you learn faster, cognitive flexibility increases, you think more clearly, and memory is sharper. The blood that has been pumping through your body during exercise shifts almost immediately back to your brain when you stop, priming your brain for learning. In one research study, people learned new words 20 percent faster after exercising than before. In another study, after a Chicago school district instituted an early morning personal fitness session for students, its eighth graders scored first in the world on a standardized science test, besting students from such math and science powerhouses as Taiwan, Singapore, and Japan.[2]

Exercise stimulates the release of a growth factor known as brain-derived neurotrophic factor (BDNF). BDNF is like fertilizer for your brain (Ratey calls it Miracle-Gro), helping your neurons grow healthy and thick with branches that interconnect with as many as 10,000 other neurons.[3] In addition, BDNF stimulates the growth of new neurons, including new neurons in the hippocampus. As you may remember, the hippocampus is vital for memory storage, so it plays an important role in helping us put what's happening at any given moment into the broader context of what we have already experienced. With the help of our hippocampus, we can see the big picture.

This capacity to contextualize is crucial for the regulation of emo-tional upset. When you're in the throes of procrastination, filled with feelings of dread, anxiety, defiance, or fear, the threat detector of your brain, the amygdala, is activated. Normally, your hippocampus helps you put the threat in perspective, so that you don't get stuck in a cycle of fear. You can tell yourself, "I'm not going to lose everything if I don't pay this credit card bill on time; last time, I had to pay a late fee." However, as Ratey and others note,[4] chronic stress wreaks havoc on the hippocampus (it actually shrivels up as neurons die), reducing its effectiveness at remembering the past. As the threat detector gets stronger and you get more worked up, realistic thoughts become less accessible. It can then be literally terrifying to start writing that re-port, to work on the overdue tax return, or to go to the post office to pick up all the mail that has accumulated over the last six months.

Exercise not only "wards off the ill effects of chronic stress; it can also reverse them."[5] It has been demonstrated that in rats, a reduced hippocampus can actually grow back to its preshriveled state through exercise! Blood volume in the hippocampus increases by 30 percent after just three months of regular exercise.[6] So, get moving; it will help your brain help you get going. Here are some suggestions for how to do it.

Get (and Use) a Pedometer.   Health professionals recommend that we take 10,000 steps each day, which is roughly equivalent to walking five miles. Using a pedometer (which you wear at your hip) signifi-cantly increases the number of steps you are likely to take—by about a mile each day![7] When you wear a pedometer, every little step really does count. Walking more can help you feel better, sharpen your brain, and put you in a frame of mind to tackle those long-avoided tasks.

Take Exercise Breaks.   When you find yourself bogged down in a task or spinning your wheels fruitlessly trying to get started, take a short break. A break will interrupt the connections of a neural circuit that fills you with dread, anxiety, or self-loathing. What you do during your break matters, however. Instead of sitting down to watch your favorite

TV program or eating a bowl of ice cream, find some way to get your body moving. A walk around the block, ten minutes on the exercise bike, or dancing around your living room to your favorite music can get your blood moving and help your brain be ready to focus.

Do Something You Enjoy. It does not matter how you exercise; picking something that's fun for you does matter because exercise will be hard to sustain over time if you hate every minute of it. If you enjoy an activity that not only gives you a cardiovascular workout but also challenges your brain, all the better. Sign up for salsa lessons or set up tennis games with a friend. As your brain works to learn unfamiliar movements or anticipate the moves of your opponent or partner, you'll get the benefit of a double workout.

Exercise with a Friend. As with so many other hard-to-do tasks, finding a buddy to keep you company can increase your commitment and make the activity more fun. If you have a date to meet another person, you are more likely to get out of the house instead of giving in to the temptation to put your feet up and take a nap. Remember, too, that social contact is beneficial for your brain; it counters the stress hormones that are activated by isolation.

Exercise before Tackling a Difficult Project. When you get your blood pumping during exercise, that blood flows right to your brain when you stop. Your brain gets bathed with extra oxygen, BDNF, and endorphins, so you will be sharper mentally for an hour or so after your workout. Take advantage of that and plunge into one of your harder tasks right after you finish exercising.

Start Small. Yes, we know, we say this all the time, and it's as unappealing as ever. If you're interested in exercising, you might feel compelled to start by running three miles or playing full-court basketball, even if you've been sedentary for years. After all, small steps feel so *puny!* But with exercise, as with so much else, taking small steps is the best approach. While this strategy may not be as grand as your ideal vision, it is more realistic. People who start exercising too aggressively are not only at greater risk for physical injury but more likely to abandon the effort. It's much better to start slowly and progress bit by bit.

Exercise Your Brain. Like your muscles, your brain strengthens with exercise. It responds especially powerfully to novel challenges that demand your full attention and concentration, and stretch you to perform at progressively higher levels. Michael Merzenich, a researcher at UC-San Francisco, who was one of the first scientists to demonstrate brain plasticity throughout the life span, has developed programs of computer-based exercises for the brain. Merzenich has found that when people are challenged in performing auditory and visual tasks, brain speed and accuracy improve significantly and last over time. People who are 65–90 years of age can re-establish the brain functioning of people who are fifteen to twenty years younger![8] So do those brainteaser puzzles and learn a new language or how to play bridge. If you want to check out Dr. Merzenich's Web site, see http://www.positscience.com.

Exercise is the single most powerful thing you can do to optimize your brain function.[9] If you move your body and expand your brain, you can get going on other things you've been putting off.

MINDFULNESS: THEME AND VARIATIONS

Exercise gets your body moving, and that is one way to prime your brain to grapple with things you've been putting off. Another approach that helps prepare you for tackling delayed projects involves the exact opposite activity—slowing down so that you become "mindful."

Mindfulness refers to "paying attention on purpose, in the present moment, and non-judgmentally."[10] It is a meditative way of observing one's experience that has been practiced for over 2,500 years. It can be especially helpful to procrastinators because of its emphasis on moment-to-moment nonjudgmental awareness. Since "the overall tenor of mindfulness practice is gentle, appreciative, and nurturing," it serves as a counterpoint to self-criticism.[11] Practicing mindfulness is one way to develop a capacity to observe yourself with compassion rather than cruelty, to offer yourself gentle support rather than harsh demands, and to experience steady, balanced acceptance rather than anxious worry or guilt. Imagine how different your experience of yourself could be, and how, from a more peaceful frame of mind, you might approach the dreaded tasks you've been putting off.

There are physical benefits to mindfulness, too. Mindful practices have been linked with improved immune function, a reduction in cardiovascular disease, and a lessening of reactivity to stress.[12] Since procrastinators live with so much mental and physical stress, mindfulness as an approach to stress reduction is especially valuable.

Mindfulness-Based Stress Reduction.   Jon Kabat-Zinn has developed a system for teaching mindfulness practices that can be incorporated into modern life. His eight-week program, "Mindfulness-Based Stress Reduction,"[13] (MBSR) is taught in medical centers and clinics around the country and has been the subject of many research studies that demonstrate its effectiveness. A recent study at Harvard, for example, showed that regular mindfulness practice stimulates growth in the part of the brain (the anterior insula in the cortex) that is associated with feelings of compassion, kindness, openness, and receptivity.[14]

As with most mindfulness practices, MBSR begins with sitting in a comfortable position and focusing on your breathing. Just taking a moment to pay attention to this fundamental and essential activity of your body immediately takes you out of the automatic, pressured mental and physical activities most of us engage in throughout the day. Many people find that as they focus on their breathing, without intending to change anything, they begin to breathe in more slowly and fully, and they exhale more deeply.

Paying nonjudgmental attention to your breathing and to body sensations extends to noticing your thoughts without judging them.[15] In mindful practice, you observe your thoughts, whatever they are, as they come and go, as they change from moment to moment. Paying attention to your thoughts in this gentle, observant manner will allow you to know more about yourself without a harsh attitude, and you might even feel gratitude just for the experience of being alive in mind and body.

The Sacred Pause. One way to incorporate mindful awareness into tiny moments throughout your day is to make use of the "sacred pause."[16] It is both utterly simple and remarkably difficult to do. The idea is to stop for just a moment, deliberately and consciously, before engaging in an activity or taking the next step. For a few short seconds, pause and just notice your breathing and the sensations in your body. Reconnect as fully as you can to the present moment. For a few short seconds, you don't have to do anything else or be anywhere else, ruminating about the past or anticipating the future. For a few short seconds, you simply discontinue whatever you are doing, becoming "wholeheartedly present, attentive, and often physically still."[17] You can even do it right now, in this present moment. Stop reading and just be aware of what you are experiencing.

The sacred pause can be especially helpful for procrastinators. When you start to experience a buildup of anxiety, dread, guilt, self-blame, or terror, use the sacred pause to come back to the present moment, when you are simply connected to your body. When you are ready to take a step toward your behavioral goal, use the sacred pause to quiet yourself for just a moment before making that phone call, opening that file, writing that sentence, or paying that bill. Each time you use the sacred pause, you are de-linking the familiar, well-honed neural circuit of procrastination just a bit, giving yourself a chance to approach the next moment in your life in a slightly different way—more open, more balanced, and perhaps, eventually even more confident that you can handle whatever comes your way.

Heartmath. By focusing (mindfully) on your heart, you can regulate your own heart rhythm. A smooth, ordered heart rhythm is experienced as a feeling of harmony, energy, or ease and is associated with positive emotions. Negative feelings, however, are linked with jerky, disordered heart rhythms and a sense of inner disturbance,[18] which is what you probably feel when you're angry at yourself for procrastinating or frantic in the anxious push toward a deadline.

In just one or two minutes, you can regulate your heartbeat. Begin by focusing your attention on your heart, perhaps by touching your hand to the center of your chest, where your heart lies behind your breastbone. As you breathe, imagine the air flowing in and out of your heart, slowly and gently finding your own rhythm until your breathing feels smooth and balanced. Five to six breaths per minute is a calming rate for most people, but it's important that you find the rhythm that feels best to you. As you continue to breathe and feel your heart rhythm, recall a positive feeling from some time in your life when you felt good, and just enjoy that feeling for a moment.[19]

You can choose an attitude or feeling that you wish to cultivate and focus on that feeling with each breath. For example, you might think to yourself, "Breathe calm," "Breathe courage," "Breathe forgiveness," or, "Breathe balance." This "attitude breathing,"[20] like the sacred pause, may be especially helpful when you're feeling overwhelmed, stressed, or scared, or when you're in the midst of a highly charged situation. "Breathe steadiness," perhaps, or, "Breathe purpose." Or you might help yourself lessen the emotional significance, and thus the tension, that is linked to a task by breathing, "Take the significance out" or, "Breathe neutral."[21]

Benson's Relaxation Response.   The "attitude breathing" we just described is a version of the original work done by Dr. Herbert Benson over thirty years ago. Dr. Benson, a Harvard cardiologist and pioneer in mind-body medicine, developed a deceptively simple stress management technique that also focuses on the breath.[22] All you have to do is breathe in and out, slowly and regularly, using deep belly breathing. Each time you exhale, repeat a word you find soothing. In Benson's original teaching and research studies, he had people say the word "One" with each exhalation, but any word will work, as long as it's easy and calming to you. Some words people like to use are "Peace," "Ease," "Calm," and "Warm." Try to do this for ten to twenty minutes, twice a day. The more you do it, the easier it will be, and the more quickly you will be able to relax yourself when you are stressed.

Beyond exercise and mindful practice, there are many other ways to take care of your biological self that will reduce stress and help you feel more balanced and more able to tackle whatever you've been putting off. If you're trying to take these steps but keep procrastinating, we once again recommend that you consider what underlying anxieties might be stopping you. We also recommend you use these tips in moderation, because any of them can be used to procrastinate on something else!

- Get enough sleep. Take short naps if necessary.
- Eat foods that will nourish your brain and body.
- Limit your use of caffeine, alcohol, and other substances.
- Have good sex, preferably with someone you love.
- Get a pet. Dogs will keep you walking, and both dogs and cats have a positive effect on blood pressure and cardiovascular health.[23]
- Call a friend, or better yet, get together and laugh a lot; this will lower stress hormone levels in both of you.
- Play and make time for fun.

As you experiment with these suggestions, remember that, as with all new learning, repetition is helpful. You are, among other things, forging new neural pathways in your brain, and it is only through repetition that those neurons will begin to fire together and then wire together. So don't give up; every little bit will help.

16

Tips for Procrastinators with ADD and Executive Dysfunction

It is very common for people with attention deficit disorder (ADD) and executive dysfunction (ED) to have problems with procrastination. Although our previous suggestions for managing procrastination are effective, in this chapter we offer additional help for those who have ADD or ED. Even if you don't have these issues, we hope you will read this chapter, because some of these ideas might be useful for you as well.

We want to remind you that ADD and some ED difficulties are primarily problems with inhibition, meaning that it is difficult to manage impulses and distractions, one of the main factors that lead to procrastination.[1] It's hard to stop yourself from paying attention to all the novel stimulation you experience—ideas, thoughts, sounds, sensations, urges, and other people. Being distracted and unfocused makes it hard to organize, persevere, and follow through, so procrastination is rampant. It takes effort to rein in distractibility and get yourself back on track. It's important to develop strategies that reduce the number of competing distractions and remind yourself to return to the task you're trying to complete.

In this chapter, we highlight some principles that have been shown to be helpful to people with ADD and give specific suggestions that are based on each principle. In addition, we hope you'll use your experience and creativity to generate your own strategies and solutions. We encourage you to look at the many books and Internet resources available on ADD and executive dysfunction, some of which are included in our chapter notes.

START WITH THE EXTERNAL, MOVE TO THE INTERNAL

As we learn new behaviors and skills, the typical progression is to start with a lot of external support, then gradually fade that support as we internalize the behavior, and eventually do it independently without external cuing or structure. For example, parents teach children by talking them through tasks, helping them think about time (by explaining a clock or a calendar), or guiding them through a sequence of steps. Gradually, most children begin to talk out loud to themselves as they do the job. ("First you get your paper and pencil. Now write your name at the top of the page. Now write the title."). As they gain more proficiency, children subvocalize; that is, they talk to themselves very quietly, almost under their breath. Eventually, this vocal function becomes completely internalized, an inner voice of guidance and support that the child doesn't even think about consciously. This same process holds true for adults as well: we begin learning new skills with some supervision, then gradually need less and less, as we are able to practice new behavior on our own. And we talk to ourselves, out loud or internally; we self-monitor.

The capacity to self-monitor is an important executive function.[2] We use it to talk ourselves through the steps of a task, help ourselves stay on track, adjust to new situations, regulate our emotional state, and know how we're doing as we go. However, many people with ADD or ED have trouble with self-monitoring; their brains don't do this easily. Therefore, providing external supports is especially important and may be needed for long periods of time before internalization is in place. You might ask someone to help you map out a strategy and then check in about your progress, or practice talking yourself through the steps you want to take.

POINT OF PERFORMANCE HELP

You can set up, be clear about, and really want to achieve a significant, realistic behavioral goal, but if your working memory doesn't perform very well, when you get ready to take your first step five minutes later, you've completely forgotten what you intended to do! Or, you get ready to start working on your goal, and something unexpected catches your eye. Perhaps you see an interesting magazine cover, or you remember a book title somebody mentioned, and you look that up when you open up your laptop instead of going directly to your work file. There's not necessarily a deep inner conflict at work, such as we described in Chapters 2 through 5, when we discussed the fears that usually underlie procrastination. You just don't remember—and it's not because you have early-onset Alzheimer's disease. It may be because your brain is simply not good at remembering and staying on track.

Barkley's recent summary of research on adults with ADD[3] stresses that an essential strategy for approaching tasks is to get point of performance help. Just having a plan in place is probably going to be insufficient to help you follow through. You need something outside yourself to remind you when and where you are going to take action, that is, at the point of performance, or since we are talking about procrastination, at the point of avoidance. There are many choices for point of avoidance help, including the following.

Visual reminders in your environment can be very effective. Notes, drawings, arrows, lists—anything you can use to remind yourself visually of your task can be helpful. For example, if you plan to work at your computer, stick some Post-it notes on the screen with reminders about the steps of your behavioral goal. Lenora has her clinical practice in Silicon Valley, and she has worked with many tech-savvy people who create reminders that come up periodically on their computer screens, so if they've wandered off in some other direction surfing the

Net or reading the news, an automatic cue pops up to help them get back on track.

Visual reminders may also be helpful if posted elsewhere in your environment to remind you to start working on your goal. Notes are especially helpful in places you go to mindlessly and frequently—on the bathroom mirror, on the TV screen, on the front door, on the steering wheel of your car, on your pillow. We know one procrastinator who puts notes inside his refrigerator and finds it helpful!

Auditory reminders can be used in a similar way. If you have a smart phone or a watch with alarm functions, you can use them to set reminders for the time you plan to take the next step toward your goal. You can also set a kitchen timer to remind you when to start a goal, or to delineate a specific amount of time you plan to work (for example, fifteen minutes), so that you know you only have to focus for a short period of time before you can pursue the next appealing distraction. If auditory cues are helpful for you, you might want to check out the Web site www.watchminder.com for an array of products designed to help people monitor time. You can, for example, get a watch that will signal you at predetermined intervals, reminding you to refocus your attention.

A real, live person may also be a terrific point of performance helper, as long as that person knows what you need (focus, reminding) and is able to provide that help with compassion and love. Whether the person is your partner, a buddy, a colleague, a coach, a therapist, or an employee, what matters is that you feel comfortable and accepted and that the other person can be an external source of the motivation and focus you have trouble providing for yourself. For some specific ideas about how to get help from another person, check out Chapter 14.

THE IMPORTANCE OF
STRUCTURE AND ROUTINE

If you have ADD or ED, every decision point represents a potential diversion from whatever path you are on.[4] Each time you have to choose what to do, you face the possibility that you'll get carried off in a whole different direction or mired in the muck of indecision. Either way, you're derailed, which is a perfect setup for procrastination. However, if you have habitual structures and routines in place, you greatly reduce the likelihood of getting off track, because you simply do what you always do, no questions asked. Rather than looking at structure and routine as a prison that deprives you of your freedom and creative individuality, try to think of it as a way to help you get the mundane parts of life taken care of, so that you can be free to be that unique, creative, spontaneous person you are (without sabotaging yourself by procrastinating).

Make (and Use!) Lists.   Get your ideas and plans out of your head and down in writing in a place that works for you. Carry a notebook, use your Blackberry, keep a whiteboard in your kitchen or office, send yourself e-mails—anything that helps you remember what you had in mind to do. And write it down before you forget! One variation of list-writing is to write a short list, no more than five items in very large print, of things you want to do *today*. If it works better for you, write out a short list of what you want to do *tomorrow* before you go to bed at night. Be sure to put the list in a prominent place where you can't miss it. Then, when you get up in the morning, you're ready to go without having to think (or decide).[5]

Keep a Basket by Your Front Door for Your Keys.   This simple suggestion[6] can save you a lot of time and aggravation. If you develop the routine of dropping your keys in the basket every time you come into your home, you won't be late for the job interview or for the meeting with your manager because you were frantically looking everywhere for the misplaced keys. As Ned Hallowell says so succinctly, "The devil *does* reside in the details in the land of ADD."[7] Even though dealing with details may seem boring, it is important so that the rest of your life will flow smoothly. Try to think of creative routines that will help you take care of those details, so you don't have to think about them, and they aren't subject to choice-point distractions; for example, auto-pay routine bills, and use Quicken or some other software to track and categorize expenditures.

Set a Regular Time.   Have a set time each day (or week) to take care of routine tasks or activities.[8] Set up regular exercise times with a friend, a trainer, or in a class, so you don't have to debate with yourself each time you consider breaking a sweat. Pick a time to sort your mail and throw away junk mail (without looking at it); even if you can't think of a regular time to do it, think of an activity you do regularly that you might use to "piggyback" your mail sorting; for example, you could decide that every time you take out the trash or recycling, you'll sort your mail first. If you have routines for taking care of these activities, you'll be much less likely to put off doing them.

KEEP IT SHORT

For ADD, shorter is better than longer, because it's more realistic. If that's how your attention works, so be it. Make "short" your ally in getting things done.

Use One Minute.   Do very small bits of your task in very small bits of time. Instead of following our standard recommendation to spend fifteen minutes taking a step toward your goal, spend one minute. Yes, you *can* do something even in just one minute.[9] Pick a piece of clothing up off the floor and put it away. Throw away something, anything, from one of your piles. (If you pick out and discard one item from a pile each time you pass by, you'll be surprised how quickly the pile shrinks!) Send a quick text message or e-mail to stay in touch with a friend or relative. Wash a dish. Write a check. Open your résumé file and just look quickly at the last version. Open a box in the garage, but don't even think about sorting—just see what's inside.

Think Like a Waiter.[10]   Keep moving. Clean up as you go. Clear off the dirty dishes before putting the next course on the table. This is one way to make use of your fast-moving brain, and it will help keep you from becoming completely overwhelmed by the accumulation of stuff, both literal and figurative. When something comes in, handle it right away, and then get rid of it. Move on to the next thing. Don't let to-do items sit on your "waiter's table" like the cold, crusted-over remains of a customer's dinner.

DON'T TRY TO GET GOOD AT WHAT YOU'RE BAD AT. GET BETTER AT WHAT YOU'RE GOOD AT.

This is important advice from Ned Hallowell and coauthor John Ratey.[11] Nothing is more frustrating and demoralizing than trying to make yourself do something that your brain just doesn't do well. Many procrastinators long to be self-disciplined, like people they see around them who do what they need to do, even when they don't want to do it. Procrastinators try over and over, disappointed with themselves when they "fail," feeling that if they simply tried harder, then they would be like everybody else. While we certainly wouldn't advocate throwing in the towel every time something is hard for you, it is important to be able to recognize the reality of your limits (like Jane's .03 percentile on spatial relations). If your brain is highly distractible and self-discipline is always a struggle, perhaps there are better ways to get some things done than trying to get yourself to be what you aren't.

Delegate, Delegate, Delegate.   Find partners whose strengths complement yours, so they can do (and enjoy) the things that are hard for you, and vice versa. One man is terrific at generating ideas and finding ways to connect people to one another, but he's terrible at following through on the details to bring his ideas to fruition. He's found his place in a marketing firm, meeting new clients and coming up with wonderfully creative, "out of the box" ideas. But other people follow up and figure out how to implement the ideas the clients like best.

You might even hire people to do things you have trouble with, like one procrastinator who drove himself crazy for years trying to get his taxes in order. Although he is an intellectual powerhouse with an international reputation, he could never find all the receipts, tax papers, and financial documents he needed to give to his accountant, and every year he agonized, looking in drawers (office, kitchen, clothing, any type of drawer), shoeboxes, clothes' pockets, folders, files, and piles throughout his house. He never knew if he'd gotten everything, so he lived in dread of finding an errant receipt or 1099 form tucked away in a jacket pocket. This struggle filled him with shame. He finally decided to bite the bullet and hire a bookkeeper. He now throws all financial papers (including receipts) into a single box, and once a month, the bookkeeper stops by his house, takes the box, and sorts, organizes, and records everything. It costs him the price of a nice dinner each month, but it's well worth it. He lives with a feeling of lightness that he hasn't experienced for decades.

Just be "Good Enough" at Organization.   Getting organized is an issue that brings many procrastinators (with or without ADD) to a grinding halt. The alluring vision of the perfectly ordered office, the ready-to-entertain-guests-at-a-moment's-notice home, or the show-off-to-the-neighbors spotless garage can tie you up in knots so quickly that you never get to the projects that make working in that office or living in that home worthwhile. Ned Hallowell borrows psychoanalyst Donald Winnicott's concept of the "good enough mother"[12] and applies it to organization: You don't have to be perfect; you only have to be good enough, doing just enough organizing to allow your life to work reasonably well. So rather than spending (wasting?) lots of time researching the ideal organizing system and figuring out how to implement it perfectly, make sure you have places for the really important stuff, that you have routines for handling that really important stuff, and then don't panic if you can't see the top of your desk for a while.

What Are You Good At?   Whether or not you have ADD or ED, think about your strengths, about what you're good at. Are you a creative thinker? Someone who's good at synthesizing ideas? A good storyteller? Good with kids? Great with dogs? Able to find your way in unfamiliar places without a map? Think, too, about what you love to do. What energizes you and fills you with joy? Dancing to funky music? A hard-fought game of tennis? Winning an important account for your company? Trying out new recipes and having friends over for dinner? Talking to people and finding out what makes them tick? (That's something *we* love!) Whatever it is, do more of it. Find your strengths and follow them. Get better at the things you like and do well. Fill your life with people and activities that make you happy and give you a sense of meaning, purpose, and connection to the larger world around you.

As Hallowell says, managing ADD (and, we would add, procrastination) is not just a matter of figuring out where you're having trouble and figuring out how to cope with that. It's also a matter of figuring out how to live joyfully.[13] We couldn't agree more.

17

Neither Here nor There
Procrastination and the Cross-Cultural Experience

If you have moved from one culture to another, there are special pressures that may contribute to your procrastination. In this chapter, we consider issues that are pertinent to cultural changes and ask you to think about how these issues might apply to you. We'll also offer some additional suggestions that may help you counter the pull of procrastination.

In making a cultural shift, people may move from one country to another. They may also move from one socioeconomic or educational class to another, such as those who are first in their family or community to attend college, referred to as "first-generation college students." These changes involve complex psychological, social, and emotional experiences that pose multiple challenges. Some people respond to this extra layer of pressure and complexity by procrastinating and avoiding experiences that would further distress or overwhelm them.

THE IMMIGRANT EXPERIENCE

Alexi is a Russian physicist who immigrated to the United States ten years ago. Unable to find a job in his profession, he works as a computer software designer. He is unhappy with his job but needs a steady income, and it's difficult to get a new job when he is competing with native speakers who have made connections through school or work. He complains, "This work is not challenging and it's not what I'm trained to do. My manager is twenty years younger than I am and knows a lot less than I do. I don't take this job seriously, so I'm always late." Alexi feels powerless about his work situation, which is affected by his immigrant status, and his procrastination reflects his dissatisfaction and allows him to feel he has some measure of control.

If you are an immigrant or the child of immigrants, you are part of a large wave of migration. As globalization extends its reach, more and more people are moving from one country to another; in 2006, approximately 200 million people lived for at least one year outside their country of origin.[1] The global workforce quadrupled between 1980 and 2008.[2] In 2005, one in eight people in the United States was an immigrant; by 2050, it is estimated that ratio will increase to nearly one in five.[3] The United States is experiencing the largest wave of immigration in its history. Distinct from past waves of immigration, the current one is bringing many who are highly educated to our shores. Between 1995 and 2005, immigrants founded or co-founded 25 percent of all high-tech companies, and since 2000 foreign graduate students have outnumbered U.S.-born students in the fields of engineering, physical sciences, and math.[4] In 2006, the University of California found that 54 percent of all students had a parent who was born in another country, and at UC-Berkeley and UCLA over one-fourth of the students were immigrants themselves.[5]

While immigrants can have a vast range of experiences, all share the experience of leaving behind a homeland.[6] Some leave the homeland temporarily to attend school or to work on a specific project for a limited time. Others move permanently and may never again return to live at home. Some people leave their home country voluntarily, legally or illegally; some leave in fear, as refugees, to escape poverty or religious, ethnic, or political persecution. Some families immigrate together; more often families split up. While some immigrants are highly educated and come from economically advantaged backgrounds, others have only known poverty and come to the new country with little or no education. Many face a language barrier; all face the challenge of adapting to a new culture with different social rules, different family norms, different expectations about work, and different perspectives about time and timeliness.

The closer you are to the actual immigration event, the greater the adjustment to the new country and culture, and the greater the potential conflict between the language, rituals, and values of the old country and those of the new. Whether you are an immigrant or the child or grandchild of immigrants, issues of adjustment, acculturation, and assimilation play a role in your sense of who you are, how you approach life, your sense of belonging, how you think of yourself in relation to the culture in which you now live and work, and your attitudes toward timeliness and asking for help. These issues and attitudes affect the likelihood that you will procrastinate.

THE FIRST-GENERATION COLLEGE STUDENT EXPERIENCE

Like immigrants, first-generation college students enter a new culture when they step onto a college campus. If you've grown up in a world in which no one has gone to college, then you may as well be going to another country when you go to college. You are, in essence, an immigrant. And, as is true for immigrants, it's easy to feel that you are different from others, leading to doubts about whether you really belong.[7] Even if you were the smartest kid in your high school, if your school was in a disadvantaged neighborhood, you may find that you are no longer at the top of the heap; in fact, you may struggle just to stay *in* the heap.[8] You may not realize that this recalibration of self in relation to a more selective pool of competitive students is a nearly universal experience for college freshmen: everyone has to face a new distribution of talent and find a new place among the others. For first-generation students, the adjustment to increased competition in college may be much more intense.

Most first-generation students do not have the same level of academic and social preparation for college as those whose parents attended college and enjoyed the benefits that higher education can bring: higher income, professional career tracks, work habits and study skills that are important for college success, knowledge of "the system," and a network of interpersonal connections that opens doors and creates opportunities.[9] And although your parents may encourage you, support you, and feel proud of you, they may not know how to help you make your way in this environment, which is like a foreign country to them. All of a sudden, you're a stranger in a strange land.

Paolo was the only child of working-class parents who had not attended college. In classes with students from prep schools who were taking notes on the latest laptop, he felt surrounded by education and privilege; he was intimidated but intrigued by these new surroundings. Wanting to fit in left him feeling neglectful of his parents. He began to procrastinate on his schoolwork for the first time.

We can see how easy it is for first-generation students to begin a pattern of avoidance: holding onto ties to old relationships, yet wanting to develop new ones creates uncertainty, confusion, and guilt. In addition, the less you're academically prepared, the harder the tasks will be; the harder the tasks, the more aversive they feel—and the more aversive the tasks, the more likely you are to procrastinate, especially if there's no one you feel you can call on to help you figure things out. It's no surprise, then, that first-generation students are more likely to withdraw or repeat courses than others, and they are far less likely to complete an undergraduate degree than other students.[10]

CHALLENGES OF CHANGING CULTURES

Loss. People who move from one culture to another, for whatever reason and with whatever hopes and dreams for a new life, always leave a lot behind. They leave a homeland along with an identity associated with that home place. They leave behind family, friends, pets, neighbors, colleagues, and all the years of familiar social support these people provide. They leave behind familiar institutions and ways of navigating through them—everything from how you pursue education to how you get a job, from how you shop for clothing and groceries to how you pay taxes or deal with the police. They leave behind their language, food, climate, and music. They leave behind traditions and values that are known, supported, and shared by an entire culture. Moving away marks a significant break from the past, and although there may be many positive feelings associated with the move, there are also significant feelings of loss. This is true whether you leave a country, a state, a city, or a neighborhood.

The sense of loss may be intense if the people who remain behind are unable to relate to the person's experiences in the new culture. It's difficult to understand a different world if you've never been there. For the first-generation student, this may mean that relationships with old friends and family seem strained and awkward; people back home might say, "You've changed," maybe even, "You're pretty full of yourself these days." It may be harder to relate to each other or find shared interests. There may be uncomfortable feelings on both sides—guilt, envy, a feeling of abandonment, a sense of growing distance.

Wherever there is awkwardness and discomfort, there lurks the possibility of procrastination: students may put off contact with family members and old friends. They may also procrastinate on schoolwork, sabotaging their academic progress as a way to minimize the separation from their old community. Some even flunk out and have to move back home.

A different experience of loss is faced by immigrants who, although they have high-level educational and professional backgrounds, face career obstacles in their new country. They may not yet be completely fluent in the new language, or they may face employment discrimination or a lack of job openings in their field, leading them to take jobs that are far beneath their skill level or knowledge base. Some people may be able to accept an occupational demotion and set about developing new skills and new contacts as quickly as they can. Others may feel so demeaned by the loss of job status that they procrastinate, retreating from new challenges and limiting their future options.

Culture Shock.   Immigrants always experience some degree of culture shock. Even when the home country is relatively similar to the new country, inevitably there are differences that require adjustments. Most immigrants struggle for a time as they learn to adapt to their new culture. Life feels unpredictable, and many people experience a "fatigue that results from having to remain consciously focused on what one would normally take for granted."[11] Being constantly alert is stressful, and over time, this can lead to the following signs of cross-cultural distress:[12]

- feelings of helplessness or intense homesickness
- the wish to depend on others of the same nationality or background
- delaying or refusing to learn the language of the new country
- excessive anger in response to minor frustrations
- excessive worry about being cheated, robbed, or injured
- excessive worry about physical health, sanitation, or food safety
- worry about cultural differences, such as family values
- staring off into space

We would add that procrastination may become part of the picture of distress, as people experiencing culture shock may have less energy to meet the confusing demands of a new culture and tend to avoid difficult situations and feelings.

Caught between Cultures.   When you take a step into a new world and you still have one foot back in the old one, you are straddling the divide. Having taken a step away from your old culture, you're no longer quite part of it, yet as much as you want and feel ready to join the new culture, you may find that you are not fully embraced by it. As a result, you may feel that you are "living in two vastly different worlds while being fully accepted in neither."[13] For undocumented immigrants, the stress of having no secure place is exacerbated. First-generation students often feel alienated and out of place, especially if they belong to a racial minority. This experience of alienation can lead to feelings of inadequacy or resentment, and as we have seen, these feelings can lead to procrastination.

It's Harder Than I Expected.   Moving into a new culture is hard, often much harder than people expect. The discrepancy between the new life you imagined and the reality you encounter can be the first "obstacle" that sends you into a tailspin of delay. First-generation students attest that it is harder to stay in college than it is to get into college, because both the academic and social pressures are much greater than they anticipated.[14] Similarly, immigrants may find that their dreams of equal treatment and economic opportunity are frustrated when they confront language barriers, overt or subtle discrimination, and economic struggles in addition to all the cultural changes they face.

Self-doubt.   Encountering more obstacles than you expect can plunge you into the depths of self-doubt. "Maybe I'm not really college material." "Maybe I don't belong here; I should go back home." "I'm not smart enough to make it." Self-doubt erodes your confidence and willingness to try new things and take risks. If you're plagued by fears that you're not smart enough and you're never going to be, you're likely to retreat from hard tasks—why study or take steps to get a job if you're convinced you're going to lose out anyway? On the other hand, if you expect to benefit from your experience, even if you don't pass the test or get the job, you will gain something.[15]

Additional Responsibilities.   Immigrants and first-generation students tend to work long hours, often for low wages, doing their best to build a better life. Immigrants may work multiple jobs to support their families or to send money back to the family in their home country. First-generation students are likely to work more than twenty hours a week while in college, attend school within fifty miles of home, and live at home rather than in a campus dormitory.[16] Because they work not only to pay for school but also to help support the family, students often let homework slide, which then impacts academic performance.

As they fall behind on their schoolwork, they feel increasingly discouraged and overwhelmed, and they are likely to procrastinate more and more as the term progresses. Both immigrants and first-generation students often are motivated to improve not only their own lives but the lives of family members. Going to college is not viewed as "solely an individual pursuit, but rather as the culmination of generations of effort and progress in their families and communities."[17] Many young people feel an obligation to make up for the sacrifices and hardships endured by their parents by doing well in school, but this pressure can lead to perfectionism and procrastination.

Isolation.   The more isolated people are, the more likely they are to feel depressed and the greater their difficulty in achieving success in the new culture. If you have trouble with procrastination, being isolated will make it harder for you to overcome it. Isolated first-generation students are more likely to drop out of school; immigrants are more likely to get caught in a downward spiral that isolates them even further. Isolation leaves you alone with your doubts about yourself and your decisions, increasing your uncertainty about how to navigate a foreign bureaucratic system, whether it's a government or an academic institution.

Suggestions for Countering Procrastination

Make Social Connections.   Our recommendation to seek support in managing procrastination is doubly important for immigrants and first-generation college students and is probably the most important suggestion we can make. Having a sense of belonging is a central human need.[18] Social isolation and lack of motivation are more likely if you feel you don't belong. Look for social, religious, or interest groups in your neighborhood and join in. Any connections you form with other people, whether they are from your homeland or the new land, will help you feel more comfortable in your new culture.

Social connections are especially important during the first year at college, because students are at much greater risk for dropping out at this time. So join a group—a club, a sports team, a fraternity or sorority, a service group, a study group. Attend events sponsored by your academic department. Look for people you can talk to about your experience, whether they are from your home culture or the new culture. Keep in mind that making use of social supports is strongly associated with college success for *all* students.[19]

Develop Your "College Knowledge."[20]   Don't be afraid to use your advisor to help you figure out how to find your way through the maze of college demands. Most colleges and some high schools offer study skills programs that teach time management, identifying priorities, goal-setting, and even managing procrastination![21] These programs can help you learn how to navigate the college bureaucracy—where to submit paperwork, how to get financial aid, where to find out about special events and opportunities.[22] You might choose to participate in these programs for the opportunity to develop relationships with people on campus—people you can turn to when you are feeling stuck, frustrated, lonely, or caught in a cycle of delay.

Pay Attention to Time.   Different cultures have vastly different attitudes toward time, and it's important to learn the expectations, rules, and attitudes toward time and timeliness in your new culture. Awareness of differences in time perception is critical in cross-cultural business, academic, and social environments. What does it mean to be "on time" in the new culture? What does it mean to be "late" for meetings, appointments, classes, and deadlines? Don't assume that time means the same thing in your new culture. Find out before you get into embarrassing situations and time trouble.

Learn to Speak and Write the Local Language.   This one endeavor can change your life and open up many opportunities for your future. Sometimes people don't want to learn the local language. Starting over in a new language takes people back to feeling like children, unable to communicate in an intelligent or sophisticated way. People may see learning a language as a test they are not sure they will pass;

they put off learning the new language so they won't feel ashamed or humiliated. This is a pessimistic view that keeps you from growing and learning.[23] Yet neuroscientists suggest that one of the best ways to keep your brain active in adulthood is to learn a new language.[24] Try to think of learning the language as an opportunity to get better at not just speaking the language but living life in your new home.

Persist Past Obstacles. We have emphasized how difficult it is for many procrastinators to keep going when they encounter obstacles. As an immigrant or first-generation student, you face many obstacles, so it's especially important that you not give up when you run into difficulties. For first-generation students, the first semester of college life is a particular challenge; those first months on campus are often overwhelming, confusing, and daunting. It's important not to take too heavy an academic load; one first-generation student took four intensive reading courses in her first semester and felt like a failure when she couldn't keep up. It's hard to overcome the obstacle of initial academic failure, but it can be done if you don't take it as a sign of inadequacy and if you learn from your experience. If you don't do well in a class, remember that it's not the end of the world. Join a study group (a big factor in academic success) or find a student who will tutor you in exchange for something you do well, like computer help or car repairs. And if you find yourself procrastinating, see your procrastination as a signal to pay attention to your anxieties and learn what it might be telling you.

Stay Connected to Your Family. It is understandable that people who are caught between cultures often want to extricate themselves from the pull of families, long-standing traditions, and old-fashioned ideas. You want to embrace the promise of the new culture and if your family is afraid of your assimilation, it's easy to see why you would want to distance yourself. A clash is especially likely if you shift from a culture that emphasizes family and community to a culture that emphasizes individual interests and development.

There's no simple way to navigate your way through this painful conflict. But we believe that families are an important source of social and emotional connection. Helping other family members learn more about your new culture may ease the tension. For example, when parents are involved in the college transition process, they are more able to understand what their children are going through and are better able to be appropriately supportive.[25] We encourage you to look for ways to maintain ties with your past, so that you can keep the richness of your heritage even as you explore the possibilities for a new life.

Consider Meeting with a Therapist. If you continue to struggle with procrastination or other issues that interfere with your progress and satisfaction, consider consulting a therapist. Even if your home culture judges it shameful to admit to distress you can't solve on your own, it is better to face that stigma than to continue to suffer and diminish your current life and your future. An immigrant professional woman in her midforties struggled with this conflict, saying to her first therapist, "No one in my community back home would ever see a therapist. But my husband suggested that I think of seeing you as being like talking to a wise aunt, and that feels a lot better." People who have thought of therapy as something that's only for severe problems or who thought they could only trust a traditional healer are often surprised and relieved to find that a therapist can be a healer, too.

18

Living and Working
with Procrastinators

We address this chapter to those of you whose lives are affected by someone else's procrastination. Whether or not you, too, are a procrastinator, if you live or work with someone who always puts things off, you probably get into struggles, trying vainly to motivate the procrastinator to take action, only to become frustrated. It can be painful to watch someone you care about making a mess of her life, not knowing how to help. There is no simple solution for procrastinators, and there is no simple answer for those of you who are close to them. But we have ideas about what helps and what doesn't.

THE CYCLE OF MUTUAL FRUSTRATION

I'm so fed up with Jamie not doing his homework. I've tried everything, and I'm absolutely at my wit's end. He's ruining his life! He can't see it, but I can. But he won't listen to me.

Mike always promises to do things to help out around the house, but he never follows through. He puts off doing the things I ask, saying he's not ready or it's not a good time to start. Or he gets partway through and then leaves an unfinished mess for the rest of the family to deal with. I'm sick of it!

> My assistant is making my life harder instead of easier. She does every-
> thing at the last minute. Her work is sloppy, and I have to spend time
> correcting it. I've told her to change or else, but it doesn't do any good.
> I don't get it.

Living or working with a procrastinator is hard: their chronic lateness, inaction, failure to follow through on commitments—it's so
exasperating and difficult to understand, especially if you are an organized person who handles responsibilities efficiently.

It's also frustrating because procrastinators are often indirect
about what they are—or are not—doing, so you can be fooled into
thinking that things are better than they really are. The procrastinator either does not want to tell you or is unable to tell you what is
really going on. This can leave you feeling deceived or betrayed, setting the stage for tension and conflict in your relationship.

It's easy to be drawn into a cycle of frustration. Things usually
start out with good intentions, but the relationship can deteriorate
quickly. The basic struggle always centers on one essential problem:
you want the procrastinator to do something, and he doesn't do it.
Let's take a closer look at what often happens.

Stage 1: Encouragement

When people first become aware that a procrastinator is having difficulty getting work done, they usually offer encouragement: "I know
you can do it." "Once you start, you'll see that it's not so bad." If you
are not a procrastinator, you know you need to have a plan and put
it into action with the deadline in mind. You know you have to do
something to get started, even if it is unpleasant, imperfect, or frightening at first. So when a procrastinator is stuck, you may assume that
with your clear thinking and encouragement, he will finally see the
logic in what you are saying and will get going.

Unfortunately, the procrastinator usually does not hear your encouragement as support. Instead, it may be taken as pressure to perform or interpreted as your attempt to be in control. You can't assume

that your good intentions will be well received. This is particularly true for encouragement that reminds the procrastinator of her intelligence, talent, or skill. "You're so smart. Of course you will do a terrific job." Deep down, even the most talented procrastinator probably feels inadequate, and such statements, although well meant, reinforce this underlying insecurity.

A procrastinator may humor you and say yes, sound appreciative, vow to take action—and do nothing. He seems agreeable, but in reality she ignores you. Other procrastinators will immediately reject any encouragement you offer. Some respond with, "Yes, but . . . " recognizing the validity of what you are saying and then coming up with all the reasons why it won't work for them. "You're right, I ought to just make a start, but I've got a lot of other things to do first." Or, "Narrowing the scope of this report probably would make it a lot easier to do. But it just wouldn't be the same." Whether the procrastinator reacts to your support with apparent agreeableness, stymies you with a "Yes, but," or rejects your help altogether, the end result is that your encouragement usually fails to get the procrastinator moving.

Stage 2: Disappointment

When it becomes clear that your efforts to be helpful have not worked, it's easy to feel disappointed and let down. You've put out a lot of effort to help, and your advice has gone unheeded. This may leave you feeling as though you've done all the work while the procrastinator has taken it easy.

You might feel disappointed with yourself, thinking that the procrastinator would have been able to make progress if you had just done a better job of helping; you could have been more encouraging or thought of a better suggestion, or you could have been more available to help. In essence, you are taking on the burden of responsibility for the procrastinator's continued inaction.

At this point, most people address the situation by trying even harder to help. They offer more encouragement and better advice, hoping that this will get the procrastinator moving and ease their own disappointment.

It doesn't work.

The procrastinator will sense your disappointment and feel worse than ever. In addition to worrying about facing the task itself, he now must worry about *you*. Soon, the procrastinator will silently begin to resent your investment in his progress—you become another expectation to live up to, another person to hide from. Eventually, he will withdraw from you, attempting to shut out both your disappointment and your renewed efforts to help.

Stage 3: Irritation

Irritation and anger often follow on the heels of disappointment. You begin to view the procrastinator's inaction as being willfully motivated or directed against you. Your efforts have all been thwarted; the procrastinator's passivity is incomprehensible.

Irritation can derive from several different sources. You may, for example, be furious because the procrastinator, who has rejected every effort you've made to help, is still stuck, reciting the same tales of woe you heard at the outset. By now he is likely to be angry, too, telling you, directly or indirectly, to "get off my back." Frustration is especially likely if what isn't done affects your welfare, or if you feel you are watching your procrastinator self-destruct, risking dismissal from school, loss of a job, financial ruin, legal retribution, or deterioration of physical health. It may make you feel better to scold your procrastinator for messing up, because at least you're doing *something*—even if it only makes things worse—and not just standing by helplessly.

Stage 4: Standoff

At this point, both you and the procrastinator are caught in an impasse. You are entrenched in the position of trying to get the procrastinator moving; the procrastinator is by now equally entrenched in the position of determined resistance. Tension can hang in the air like a thick, dark cloud, with resentment brewing on both sides. Over a long enough period of time, such a standoff can destroy what was once a satisfying relationship and lead to a rupture or to gradual estrangement in a marriage, a parent-child relationship, a friendship, or a business partnership. Unfortunately, the chasm sometimes grows so immense that the relationship is impossible to repair.

NEGOTIATING WITH A PROCRASTINATOR

How can you interact with a procrastinator and still maintain a relationship that is basically positive for you both? There are some general considerations that can make life easier for both you and your procrastinator. First, we'll identify some approaches to avoid, because they don't work.

What Doesn't Work

Saying, "Just Do It!" This phrase is the bane of the procrastinator's existence. When you say "just do it," you emphasize the procrastinator's inability to do what everyone else seems to be able to do, making the procrastinator feel worse.

Nagging and Being a Watchdog. When you continually remind a procrastinator about what needs to be done or check up on her progress, you will be perceived as a watchdog—and resented for it. You may be placated with promises, but the procrastinator will feel so resentful of your watchfulness (however altruistically motivated) that she may slow down further just to stay out of your vigilant oversight or to get back at you.

Using Criticism, Ridicule, or Threats of Extreme or Exaggerated Consequences. You may believe that if you shame procrastinators enough, especially in public, they will be motivated to start working. The father of one procrastinator made predictions of doom about his son's future at family gatherings: "If you don't make more of an effort in school, you'll never get a job. And without a job you can't support a family. Nobody wants a loser—and that's what you'll be." These kinds of comments do not help procrastinators take action. They only succeed in humiliating people who already feel ashamed of themselves, further eroding their confidence and prompting them to retreat from you and avoid tasks all the more.

Doing It Yourself.   You should never—except in rare cases—come to a procrastinator's rescue by doing the task yourself. It may be tempting to swoop in and take over, especially if you can see there will be significant consequences if the procrastinator doesn't get something done. But in becoming the magic solution you only perpetuate the problem, reinforcing the expectation that you or someone else will come to the rescue at the last minute. And you risk getting stuck in a perpetually sticky situation, as the procrastinator engages you in a provocative game—how close must she come to disaster before you will finish the job?

Saying "I Told You So!"   If indeed things turn out the way you predicted, you may be tempted to remind the procrastinator that you were right. But if you act on that impulse, it won't help. Whether or not she can admit it, the procrastinator already knows that you were right and feels bad. Saying, "I told you so!" is like rubbing salt into an open wound. You may feel vindicated, but it will further alienate the procrastinator from you.

Attitudes That Can Help

Unfortunately, there is no one guaranteed method for dealing with a procrastinator. Nevertheless, there are some general attitudes that can ease life for both of you.

Promote a Growth Mindset.   Most procrastinators are focused on outcomes and performance from the point of view of a Fixed Mindset, meaning that they see intelligence and talent as fixed entities that are set at birth.[1] With this perspective, everything they do in life, in school, at work, on the playing field, and even at home has the potential to reveal how smart or talented they really are. Therefore tasks become tests and carry the risk of failing, which leads many people to put off doing them. A Fixed Mindset leads people to retreat from bigger challenges. (See Chapter 2 for more about mindsets.) You can provide a tremendous service to your procrastinator by combating Fixed Mindset thinking and advocating a Growth Mindset: cultivate and convey the attitude that life is about learning, that tasks are opportunities to practice and improve, and that it can be fun and exciting to challenge yourself.

It is particularly important to develop your own Growth Mindset if your child is struggling with problems related to schoolwork. Beware the temptation to focus primarily on grades or to emphasize your child's intelligence above all else. Instead, compliment your child on how much effort he made, how hard he worked, or how much he learned. Notice how much better he is at doing something now than before. Ask about what was interesting at school, rather than about what grade he got on the test. If things didn't go well, help your child think about what he learned that would help him do better next time. This approach will help both you and your procrastinator take the pressure off the outcome and respect the process. And that will make procrastination less necessary as a protective strategy. A better outcome is more likely in the long run with an emphasis on the process. Pleasure in learning reinforces more learning.

Maintain Your Individual Perspective.   It's easy to forget that you and your procrastinator are separate individuals and to feel instead as though the procrastinator's problems are your own. You may develop a strong personal investment in the procrastinator's success, as if you need the procrastinator to perform well in order for you to feel good about yourself. But your spouse and children are not you, and their performance does not represent the only measure of whether you are a good partner or parent.

Carol—at her wit's end with her sixteen-year-old son, Jamie—had lost perspective. She felt totally responsible for him. If Jamie didn't do well in school, it meant that she had failed as a mother. Unfortunately, this only made things worse for both of them. Carol's over-investment in his performance became an additional source of pressure for Jamie, as well as generating tremendous tension in their relationship. Even if Carol succeeded in making Jamie sit with his schoolbooks for an hour a day, only Jamie himself could read the printed page and synthesize it in his brain. You, too, must remind yourself that your power over your procrastinator is limited. You can try to influence your procrastinator to do what you want, but you can never make him or her take action. Like it or not, he is his own separate person.

Be Aware of Possible Neurocognitive Differences. It is quite possible that your procrastinator lives with a brain that operates very differently from yours. His brain may have some executive functions that don't work well, such as the capacities for planning, organizing, or self-monitoring. Perhaps your procrastinator doesn't have a good working memory, or he may have ADD and be unable to stop himself from being distracted by every little thing when he tries to focus. Brains are wired differently. Your procrastinator may not be *able* to focus, track, sequence, or plan the way you do. Rather than assuming your procrastinator is uncooperative, slothful, or somehow morally deficient, you can help by learning about ADD and ED and offering (not lecturing) to be supportive in the practical ways your procrastinator needs. Just because *you* can see the steps that are necessary to begin and complete a task doesn't mean that a procrastinator with ADD or ED will know or remember exactly how to approach and effectively work on it.

Be Collaborative. In order to offer your help and have it be accepted, you have to set up a two-way collaboration. This is a very different dynamic from nagging, pushing, punishing, or scolding. You and your procrastinator can come to an agreement on your role and then you have to stick to it. Ask how you can be of help and provide only what is requested. Offer to demonstrate how you might approach a complex task with a distant deadline, but do so as a partner, not as a dictator.

Be Flexible about Your Strategy.   All too often, when a strategy has failed to yield the desired results, people try the same thing over and over again, with increased insistence. Instead, it would be more helpful to do something fundamentally different from previous efforts.

Carol tried many ways to get Jamie to stop procrastinating on his homework. For a time she nagged him: "Don't forget the science test you have on Friday." "You should start on your paper before it's too late." Jamie usually responded by sulking or by ignoring Carol altogether. When nagging didn't work, Carol tried to bribe him: "If you do an hour of homework every day for a month, I'll buy you an iPhone." Didn't work. Next, Carol attempted to motivate Jamie with guilt. "After all your father and I have done for you—can't you even do your schoolwork?" Still no success. Finally, Carol tried to threaten Jamie with moralistic doom: "You've got to learn how to discipline yourself. How will you ever make it through life if you can't do basic math?"

What Carol failed to realize was that her different strategies were all variations of the same basic tactic. She was pushing Jamie to take action, whether by nagging, threatening, or bribing; everything she'd been doing was aimed at convincing Jamie to do his homework— and nothing had come of it but conflict and resentment. Jamie was always either angry or withdrawn in sullen silence. Carol felt she was losing her son.

In desperation, Carol tried something novel. She decided to stop pushing Jamie to study. Rather than pressuring him to do his homework, Carol said to him, "It's part of growing up to learn to make decisions for yourself. You have to decide how important school is to you and how it fits into your life. I want our relationship to be about how we can enjoy each other, not about me nagging you to do your homework." So Carol no longer brought up the subject of homework. Even if her worst fear came true and Jamie never opened a book, Carol vowed to herself that she would hold her tongue and focus on positive experiences they could share.

This new stance was very different. By taking this stance, Carol stepped out of a futile power struggle and let Jamie live his own life. She was relieved to find that, after she made this shift in her own behavior, her relationship with Jamie became friendlier. And Jamie, on his own, even gradually started to do his homework—not immediately, not without struggles, not without angst for everyone, but he was managing, and more importantly, Carol felt she finally was beginning to get her son back.

Remember What's Most Important.   Think about what's most important to you about a relationship. No one wants to see a child fail a course, a spouse lose a job, a promising employee get demoted, or a manager create chaos in a department, all because of procrastination. But is it worth it to be in an angry stalemate with your spouse or child, or to remain loyal to an employee who doesn't help your business, or to work for a manager who can't manage? You have to decide what's most important for you and what matters most in your relationship with someone who is a chronic procrastinator. Then focus on that, rather than on trying to eliminate procrastination.

Specific Techniques

With these general principles in mind, we now focus on specific ways of interacting with a procrastinator that can help you avoid the notorious power struggle or standoff. Because having a child who is a procrastinator is so painful and frustrating, we begin with a summary of our suggestions, focusing on the parent-child relationship.

A Summary of Suggestions for Parents
1. Help your child set small goals.
> Teach your child to break a task down into component steps.
> Every task can be broken down into steps.
> Any task can *only* be done one step at a time.

Set up short intervals for working—ten or fifteen minutes at a time.

And, if fifteen minutes is too long, use five minutes!

2. Help your child learn to tell time.

Practice being realistic, rather than wishful.

Practice predicting how long a task will take.

Work backwards from the end point to gauge when to begin.

Look at time commitments and think about how much time is actually available.

Teach your child to use a timer. (Buy a timer if you don't have one!)

3. Set clear limits and consequences.

What exactly must be done and what exactly are the consequences of not doing it?

Instead of setting a time to *start* a task (e.g., homework), decide the time by which the task must be *completed*.

Consider a written "contract."

Enforce consequences matter-of-factly and consistently.

4. Encourage appropriate rewards.

Reward effort, creativity, and persistence, rather than outcome.

It's important to reward steps taken, not just completion of the final step.

Rewards come after completion of a goal and steps taken along the way.

Convert "excuses" into "rewards"—e.g., "You're hungry, so just do fifteen minutes on your paper, then have something to eat."

5. Remember whose task this is: Who owns the job? Your child, *not you!*

Your child is not an extension of you.

Your child's performance is not a reflection of your value; manage your own feelings of disappointment, competitiveness, embarrassment, or envy.

Never do for your child what your child can do for him or herself.

Do not rescue! Let your child live with the consequences.

(If you choose to help your child out on occasion, use a "time trade" so your child pays you back for your time by doing something for you.)

6. Respect your child's need for autonomy.

Be as flexible as you can within your limits. Offer choices whenever possible.

Choose your battles; is it really more important to win or to be right than to maintain the relationship and help your child develop in his own way?

7. Combat perfectionism whenever you see it—your child's, and yours too.

Talk about mistakes, and admit your own with humor and good grace.

Beware grandiosity; acknowledge human limitations and flaws.

8. Talk about fears—your own, as well as your child's.

Fear is a universal human experience. There are reasons for feeling afraid.

We can take action even though we are afraid.

"Courage is the mastery of fear, not the absence of fear."

9. Listen to what your child tells you with curiosity, not judgment.

Refrain from saying, "Why don't you just do it?" or some variant, especially if said with exasperation, disbelief, condescension, or other similar tone.

Never, *ever* demean, humiliate, ridicule, or express contempt for your child or your child's procrastination. (Watch out for eye-rolling.)

No matter how hard it is to understand, procrastination serves a purpose and this must be respected. Without judgment, it will be easier to help your child learn to manage difficult feelings and to act in spite of them.

10. Check for underlying issues that might be involved and need professional treatment. Possibilities include:

Depression, ADHD, Bipolar Disorder, Oppositional/Defiant Disorder,

Anxiety Disorder (including Social Phobia, Panic Disorder, Obsessive-Compulsive Disorder), Sleep Disorder (be especially alert for Sleep Apnea)

Some of these techniques are also effective if the procrastinator in your life is your partner or employee. In your interactions with adult procrastinators, try to function as a consultant and not as a director. Offer your support, be a sounding board, and help procrastinators be realistic, but don't try to decide things for them or judge their moral character. The most important strategies are:

Establish Clear, Specific Limits, Deadlines, and Consequences. It's best to do this collaboratively. Then, if the task isn't completed by the deadline, you can implement (nonpunitively) the consequences. If the procrastinator refuses to collaborate with you, you can set deadlines and consequences unilaterally, then follow through. Be as straightforward, calm, and matter-of-fact as possible, and try not to react impulsively out of frustration, resentment, or despair. Take time out to settle yourself down before approaching the procrastinator to talk things over.

Help the Procrastinator Be Concrete and Realistic. Procrastinators often set extremely vague and unrealistic goals. They think about what they'd *like* to accomplish rather than what is possible, given the limitations of their time and energy and the disruptions that are likely to occur. By being vague about their goals, they are much less likely to follow through. Be alert for attitudes such as, "No problem—won't take me any time at all," or, "That's way too complicated—it will take me years to do it right!" Then ask questions that help counter this tendency to view tasks unrealistically. "What's actually involved in this project?" or, "How much free time do you have this week?" These questions will help the procrastinator to stop and consider whether his assessment of the situation is realistic.

Help the Procrastinator Set Small, Interim Goals. You can help your procrastinator think through a set of minigoals, a series of steps that must be accomplished in order to reach the larger, final goal. Procrastinators tend to think about the end point of a goal but forget about the steps they'll need to take to get there. You can provide valuable assistance by pointing out steps the procrastinator has overlooked (such as allowing for commute time), or by clarifying the separate parts of a task that make up the whole.

Reward Effort and Progress along the Way. Procrastinators usually don't think they've achieved anything until they've reached their final goal, which means they derive no satisfaction from progress made along the way. No wonder they feel so discouraged.

Progress of any kind deserves to be recognized and rewarded. Effort counts, too—not only the outcome—so be sure to give lots of praise to any effort your procrastinator makes. "You've worked hard preparing for your presentation." "You've put in so much effort on this. Good for you."

You can also participate in activities that reward the procrastinator at points along the way. Take your procrastinator out to lunch or dinner for accomplishing a difficult step; arrange an evening at the movies *after* she has spent two hours working; have the procrastinator take a break with you and go for a walk. (But don't let the break go on too long!) Your procrastinator will begin to value and appreciate what she has done, even before reaching the final goal. This is an invaluable lesson, because it makes working toward a goal a reinforcing experience rather than a demoralizing one.

Tell the Procrastinator Directly If You Do Get Angry. There will certainly be times when the procrastinator's delaying irritates or frustrates you. Let the procrastinator know specifically what she has done that upsets you and discuss how the delay has affected you. Be clear, but try not to be punitive. You could say, for example, "You told me you would compile a list of people to contact and have it ready for this meeting. You haven't done it, and it's holding up everything else we want to do. I am annoyed that you didn't do your part." Indirect expressions of anger such as sarcastic comments, emotional withdrawal, or nonverbal behaviors, such as rolling your eyes or using a harsh tone of voice, won't get you anywhere.

Let Procrastinators Know That They Are More to You Than Just Their Performance. If you really want to be of help to procrastinators, let them know that you value other qualities besides productivity. What about his boundless generosity or insatiable curiosity, her great sense of humor or sensitivity to the personal dilemmas of other people? Your procrastinator may have a talent for cooking, an eye for design and color, or a knack for repairing anything that isn't working.

Procrastinators can appreciate these qualities in other people, but they have trouble valuing the same qualities in themselves. They believe they are what they do. Their worth as people depends solely on how well—or poorly—they perform. You can let procrastinators know that your esteem and respect for them extend beyond their success or failure, perhaps even helping them come to a new definition of what success and failure actually mean.

Consider Yourself. An important question to ask yourself is: What could happen to you if the procrastinator doesn't get around to doing something? Are there substantial consequences that could significantly impact your life or put you at risk? If the procrastinator is your business partner, for example, you may stand to lose revenues and clients, be the target of a lawsuit, or damage your professional reputation. Or if your spouse is an unreliable partner and unable to move forward in life, your own life progress may be compromised.

In such situations, you need to think about how to take care of yourself. If you've tried everything, and your procrastinator's behavior still leaves you at risk, you may have to take unilateral action— you either do the work yourself, hire somebody else to do it, or in extreme cases, end the relationship. You might dissolve the business partnership or fire an employee if you feel the procrastinator is too unreliable. You might decide to break up a close relationship or leave your marriage if you feel that the procrastinator's delays have caused more trouble than you can bear. Although it may be very difficult to end a relationship with someone who's been an important part of your life, sometimes it's the best option you have.

———

We know it can be difficult to live and work with procrastinators, but it can also be wonderful. Many procrastinators are intelligent and creative; many have a strong independent streak and want to put their individual stamp on things. All are sensitive and anxious about being good enough, strong enough, or capable enough. If you can remember that under the surface there is a vulnerable, uncertain person who wants to be accepted and loved, perhaps you will find it easier to make room in your heart for someone who is struggling with human imperfections.

Epilogue

So, procrastination really is like a dandelion, isn't it? Lots of tangled roots and very difficult to eradicate completely. To help you untangle the roots of your procrastination, we've offered many perspectives on why people procrastinate. We hope you will take a close look at those psychological roots that are relevant for your unique story.

But as we've said, it's not enough to untangle procrastination's roots. You still have to do something to keep it from dominating your life, and for this, we've made a variety of suggestions on how you can take action. Our hope is that you will embrace the opportunity to try something new—play with a fresh way of thinking and experiment with different approaches to those projects that await you. We're not advocating a grand relandscaping, but rather pulling out the dandelions, one at a time, so that your garden isn't completely taken over, and there's space to grow other plants you will enjoy.

We hope that, after reading this book and trying out new behaviors, you will feel less plagued by procrastination and that it will no longer be a central organizing principle of your life. But we also hope that your drive to overcome procrastination will not rule out pleasure, fun, and simple enjoyment. We are reminded of a tombstone epitaph:

> Got everything done.
> Died anyway.

We have no illusions that ending procrastination guarantees happiness. Happiness comes from living well, according to your values. It comes from being connected to other people and to your innermost self. It comes from being able to accept that you are who you are and that what is, is, whether procrastination is part of your life or not, like being able to enjoy your garden—even with a few dandelions.

APPENDIX A

Procrastination
Twenty-five Years of Research

When we published the first edition of our book, ours was only the third self-help book on procrastination, and there were virtually no research studies on the subject. Since then, procrastination has been the focus of hundreds of social psychology research studies and is being explored in other related fields such as neuropsychology, behavioral economics, and neuroeconomics. Psychologists have typically been concerned with identifying individual personality traits of procrastinators and the characteristics of tasks that are put off. Behavioral economists have tried to explain why so many of us postpone making good economic decisions and doing things that are clearly in our best financial interests, like saving money or paying bills on time. The Procrastination Research Group at Carleton University in Ottawa, Canada, maintains an updated bibliography of relevant research, which is available on the Internet.

A comprehensive review of procrastination research was published in January 2007 by Piers Steel, a psychologist at the University of Calgary Haskayne School of Business.[1] After integrating the results of hundreds of psychology research studies, most of which were done with college students, Steel proposed four factors that are likely to increase the tendency to procrastinate:

- low confidence in one's ability to succeed;
- expecting that the process and/or outcome will be unpleasant;

- the reward is too far away to feel real or meaningful;
- difficulties in self-regulation, including impulsiveness and distractibility.

Steel summarizes, "We are more likely to pursue goals that are pleasurable and that we are likely to attain . . . and we will most likely procrastinate any tasks that are unpleasant in the present and offer recompense only in the distant future."[2]

CHARACTERISTICS OF PROCRASTINATORS

Poor Self-regulation.   The personality traits that researchers find to be most strongly correlated with procrastination seem self-evident, part of what defines the very nature of procrastination itself. The three characteristics that bear the strongest statistical relationship to procrastination are:

1) the "intention-action gap," which refers to a failure to act upon one's intentions (even though procrastinators *plan* to work as hard as anyone else, or harder);
2) low "conscientiousness," which refers to not doing one's duty, having difficulty with purposeful planning and perseverance, and experiencing low motivation for achievement unless work is intrinsically engaging; and
3) poor self-discipline, referring to a lack of self-control in planning and organization.[3]

Also closely correlated with procrastination are distractibility (being easily derailed by distractions) and impulsiveness (making unplanned decisions to procrastinate and not being future-oriented). Taken together, these traits constitute what Steel calls "self-regulatory failure," which he found to be the single factor that is most significantly related to procrastination. Procrastinators repeatedly choose "short-term benefits over long-term gains, reflecting a core component of poor self-regulation."[4]

Although self-regulation helps us ignore distractions and temptations, it is difficult to achieve and maintain. Self-regulation is the central problem for people with ADD and executive function difficulties,[5] which is why these disorders and procrastination so often go hand in hand. But even people who don't have ADD struggle with self-regulation. One study related self-regulation to the experience of autonomy. In questioning college students, researchers found that the more a task was felt to be intrinsically rewarding, that is, students experienced pleasure and satisfaction while doing it, the more likely they were to maintain consistent progress. When the motivation for doing a task was less autonomous—if it was being promoted by someone else, or if it was difficult to see the point of doing it—the more likely students were to procrastinate.[6] Even believing that something was important to their own future did not make it intrinsically rewarding. "No matter how important students consider their courses to be for achieving their future life goals, they are still likely to procrastinate if they are not genuinely interested in the course material. Thus, procrastination appears to be a motivational problem that requires that a very high threshold of autonomy be reached before it can be overcome."[7] You have to be highly motivated to do the things in life that you are not really interested in, and it's easy to make excuses and put off these less compelling tasks.

Another perspective suggested by research on self-regulation is that we have a limited capacity to control our behavior, and this capacity can be depleted after we have had to exercise a lot of self-control.[8] As you exert self-control to deal with one difficult thing, you lessen the amount of self-control available for handling the next difficult thing. If self-control is a limited resource, there are bound to be failures in self-control, especially if you are coping with stress, managing negative feelings, or resisting temptations that occur closely together in time. There have to be periods when self-control is relaxed in order to build up your strength for the next time. It's difficult to maintain self-control all the time—just ask anyone on a diet or in a 12-step program! Although "self-regulatory failure" carries judgmental connotations of a lack of will power, overindulgence, and general moral lassitude, it's important to remember that there are many explanations for why someone might have poor self-regulation, none of which relate to moral failings.

Worry, Anxiety, and Mood. A cluster of personality traits that can affect self-regulation involves worry, anxiety, and mood. Steel[9] found these factors to be less strongly correlated with procrastination than the self-regulatory factors just described, but they were related nonetheless. Depressed mood can lead to procrastination, since the lethargy and low energy associated with depression interfere with taking action.[10] Depression is also linked to low self-confidence, and both low self-confidence and low self-efficacy (doubting your ability to do well) have been shown to be related to procrastination.[11] Fear of failure, which appears to be a combination of low self-confidence, anxiety, and perfectionism, is also repeatedly linked to procrastination.[12] With less confidence in themselves and in their ability to complete projects, especially when being evaluated, procrastinators are more likely to give up when they encounter an obstacle.[13] Ironically, procrastinators create their own obstacles all the time, an example of what some researchers call "self-handicapping."[14] Waiting too long to start a task is an example of self-handicapping, as is the tendency to spend too much time on impossible projects. Procrastinators are much more likely than nonprocrastinators to persist on projects if they are likely to fail.[15]

In contrast, some procrastinators are too optimistic; they worry too little. They may be overly optimistic about how long it takes to complete a task, consistently underestimating how much time they need.[16] Some are "socially active optimists"[17] who use the distraction of social activity to procrastinate and have fun doing it. Outgoing and extroverted, they are overly confident about postponing now and being successful later.

There has been some controversy about how perfectionism is related to procrastination. Most clinicians observe that procrastinators are likely to be perfectionists. Yet after Steel's overview of the procrastination research, he concluded that perfectionism was inconsistently and weakly related to procrastination.[18] Few people reported that perfectionism contributed to their procrastination,[19] and in some studies, people who scored high as perfectionists scored the same or lower than nonperfectionists on ratings of procrastination.[20] Steel notes that this finding is discrepant with clinical observations and is not in agreement with the consistent finding that fear of failure, which is correlated with perfectionism, is indeed a factor in procrastination. Steel's conclusion that perfectionists procrastinate less because they do better and avoid delaying was widely covered by the media when his review of the research on procrastination was published in 2007.[21]

We think this discrepancy between clinical and research findings may be due in part to the fact that clinicians see people who come for counseling, and who are more likely to be what Dr. Kenneth Rice refers to as *maladaptive* perfectionists.[22] Steel seems to be describing Rice's *adaptive* perfectionists,[23] people who recognize that they have high standards and believe their performance lives up to their standards, so they are satisfied with their performance and with their lives.[24] By contrast, maladaptive perfectionists have high standards but they are disappointed with their performance; they experience self-criticism, self-doubt, and excessive concerns about making mistakes and are less satisfied with their lives.[25] With these anxieties, they are more likely to seek professional help.

In addition, the majority of studies in Steel's overview used questionnaires that relied on the respondents to identify whether or not they were perfectionists. In our experience, most procrastinators don't identify themselves as perfectionists, and therefore, when they are answering a questionnaire, they are unlikely to endorse items that reflect perfectionism. They invariably protest, "I'm not a perfectionist; I never do anything perfectly." These procrastinators don't recognize that the attitude of perfectionism comes through in their very disclaimer. Over and over again, we find that when we look below the surface, perfectionism is alive and well in the procrastinating mind.

Personality Traits That Are Not Related to Procrastination. Some personality traits have been found to have little or no relation to procrastination. "Rebellion against control" was found to be unrelated to procrastination, acknowledged by fewer than 5 percent of respondents.[26] Other traits unrelated to procrastination include "openness to experience" (intellectual curiosity, creativity and imagination, appreciation of art and beauty), "agreeableness" (cooperation, consideration for others, concern with social harmony, optimism, honesty, trustworthiness), "sensation-seeking" (there's a weak link here with risk-taking), and intelligence.

We wish to offer an important caveat here about the nature of statistics in research that draws conclusions based on collective data from large numbers of people. For example, when Steel says that rebelliousness has not been found to relate to procrastination, he means that this is true in general for most of the people who were studied. However, he is careful to note that for the individual for whom rebelliousness is an issue, everything becomes a battle, and procrastination is one way to express rebellion.[27] As clinicians, we can't emphasize this point enough. We know someone who feels rebellious about nearly everything, including brushing his teeth (flossing is out of the question, as is doing his taxes—he is years behind). So, if you are an individual who feels your independence is threatened by any request, then for you, rebelliousness is indeed related to procrastination. Statistical conclusions don't apply to everyone.

TASK AVERSIVENESS

Many research studies have focused on the nature of the task as a way to understand procrastination. There is strong, consistent support for the finding that tasks that are seen as aversive trigger procrastination.[28] In the workplace, people procrastinate when they feel their jobs don't allow them enough autonomy, when they don't see the significance of what they're doing, when they don't get much feedback about their work, or when they feel frustrated, resentful, or bored with the task.[29] In academia, students procrastinate when they find a task unpleasant, boring, or uninteresting. "The more people dislike a task, the more they consider it effortful or anxiety producing, the more they procrastinate," concludes Steel, so "one possible reason why some people procrastinate is simply that they find more of life's chores and duties aversive."[30]

We think this research about the nature of the task may have more to do with the nature of people. A task is not inherently and universally boring or anxiety producing. One person's aversion is another person's delight. Furthermore, it is true that many people complete tasks even though the tasks are aversive to them. Thus, while it makes common sense that people put off doing things they find unpleasant, the more interesting question to us is: Why is this particular task unpleasant for this particular person, leading to avoidance, even when the task is important and the consequences are significant? For procrastinators, an aversive task becomes an *avoided* task. Why this is the case has not been addressed by the research to date.

Another concern we have about the research on task aversiveness and procrastination is that most of the studies have relied on college students answering questionnaires about why they procrastinate. There are two limitations to data generated in this way. First, the data are limited to a particular population, college students, who may or may not be similar to a more general population of procrastinators. One must be careful about generalizing from these data to a broader population. Second, answers on questionnaires are of limited help in understanding complex and often unconscious motivations. For example, one of Steel's findings was that 45 percent of procrastinating college students said that they "really dislike" writing term papers.[31] Yet many students who don't like writing term papers do write them and turn them in on time. So we're back to the question of *why*. Is this student someone who lacks writing skills or who is writing in a language other than his native tongue, so he dreads getting back yet another paper with a lot of criticism and a poor grade? Or is the student a gifted writer who feels pressure to get an A+ on every paper, seeing anything less than a top grade as a failure? Or does the student struggle with getting organized, finding the right materials, and developing an idea for the paper and therefore feel completely overwhelmed? Thus, the finding that "task aversiveness" correlates with procrastination leaves a lot to be explained and is not particularly useful in helping people overcome their aversion to unpleasant tasks.

The issue of unconscious motivation is also significant when we consider task aversiveness. Maybe students know why they "really dislike" writing term papers and maybe they don't. We have found over and over again that even when students have clear, conscious ideas about why they delay, there are almost always other issues below the surface that play a major role in their procrastination. As we noted in our chapter on neuroscience and procrastination, it is now widely accepted that much of mental life occurs outside of conscious awareness. People often don't know what is going on in their minds; some psychological issues are unremembered, subtle, and not readily apparent; some issues are uncomfortable to acknowledge, leading people to disavow them. Therefore we suggest that it is a mistake to rely exclusively on conscious reporting of likes and dislikes as full explanations for why people procrastinate. Contrary to Steel's suggestion that procrastinators may "simply" find many of life's demands aversive, we believe that it's not simple at all. We think it's unrealistic to expect that students would necessarily be able to identify the fears that interfere with success and happiness in response to a simple questionnaire. Like the woman who avoided shaking hands after being pricked by a pin (see Chapter 7), students (and others) may have no conscious recollection of painful experiences in the past that make a particular task aversive to them today.

PROCRASTINATION AND HEALTH

Because procrastinators compromise their well-being in many ways, procrastination has serious consequences for health. Students who put things off are more likely to eat poorly, sleep less, and drink more alcohol than students who do not.[32] At the end of the academic term, student procrastinators are more likely to go to the health service with complaints of colds, flu, and stomach problems.[33] In the general population, procrastinators report higher levels of stress, suffer more acute health problems, and practice fewer wellness behaviors than nonprocrastinators.[34] People who are less "conscientious" are more likely to engage in all of the major behaviors that lead to premature mortality—less physical activity, poor diet, consumption of tobacco, alcohol, and drugs, risky driving and sexual activity, violence and suicide.[35] People who think procrastination is nothing but a joke are so wrong: procrastination can kill.

THE CONTRIBUTION OF
BEHAVIORAL ECONOMICS

Daniel Kahneman won the 2002 Nobel Prize in Economics for demonstrating that people do not always make rational economic decisions. His theories about irrational economic choices have become the basis for the field of behavioral economics, a marriage of psychology and economics. Psychological motives, Kahneman suggests, determine people's economic behavior and "more often than not, individual decisions are based on context, faulty reasoning and perception, rather than on [rational] cost-benefit analysis."[36] How choices are framed, rather than the actual or relative value of the choice, is a major influence on the decisions people ultimately make[37] and therefore is a significant factor in the decision to procrastinate.

Future Discounting.   A factor that has been strongly linked to procrastination is the time interval to task completion (or reward). If the end point of the task you are facing is far off in time, you are more likely to delay getting started on it; the closer the end is, the more likely you are to be productive. In psychological research, this finding holds true for pigeons[38] and monkeys,[39] as well as students.[40] This behavior has also been researched by economists, as they seek to understand why people put off important financial tasks, such as saving money for retirement. Economist George Akerlof suggests that people are likely to overemphasize the importance of present events and to underrate the importance of future events. He calls this tendency "future discounting."[41] Even if the present event (checking e-mail) is clearly less important to your well-being than the future event (meeting next month's work deadline), you decide to do the more immediate thing and put off the future task. The reason that present events take on more apparent value is that they seem more "salient"[42] or vivid, especially in contrast to less immediate, pallid events in the far-off future. Procrastination occurs when the future pales in comparison to the present. You want to save money for a future down payment on a house, but the immediate saliency of having a big-screen TV for the playoffs wins out. You want to impress your manager with your quarterly numbers, but the immediate pleasure of winning at Internet poker entices you to leave the report for a later date.

Certainly, it is a "human tendency to grab immediate rewards,"[43] even when those immediate rewards may have delayed costs. If you choose to play video games, for example, the reward is immediate and the cost of not doing your work is delayed. Other actions may have immediate costs and delayed rewards, such as when you struggle at first to learn a foreign language, but later feel delighted when you are able to converse with people in another country. The experience of immediate pain or pleasure will have more salience than any pain or pleasure associated with future outcomes. If an action involves an immediate cost, people tend to procrastinate. If there is an immediate reward, they go for it.

Choices Based on Timing, Not Reason.   Another variable affecting decision making is that the procrastinator's evaluation of the significance of a task varies greatly over time and changes dramatically as the task deadline approaches, even though the actual importance of a task does not really change. In other words, preferences are influenced by timing rather than by reason.[44] If you have a project due next Monday, you may not view it as important on Thursday, but come Sunday night, it will probably seem very important indeed. Thus, procrastinators tend to be very inconsistent in their assessment of the importance of tasks, and this inconsistency makes it difficult to work steadily toward future goals.

Irrational Optimism.   Finally, some people are more realistic about what they will do next time than others. Those who are "correctly pessimistic" about their future behavior recognize that they are going to have "self-control problems in the future."[45] They anticipate that they may not have more time later and know that the task will be just as difficult then as now, so they'd better get started. People who are "irrationally optimistic,"[46] however, do not anticipate that it's going to be just as difficult to get started in the future. They fail to realize that they're going to have just as much trouble working later and incorrectly assume that they have plenty of time or that it will be easier later. We think irrational optimism is related to a person's sense of the continuity of self across time (see Chapter 6) and to the need to maintain a grandiose self-image (see Chapter 2). And, of course, we come up against the problem of accepting reality—the reality that you're not going to be magically different two weeks from now, the reality that projects take time to complete, the reality that pleasure in the present may cost you pain in the future.

What behavioral economists are telling us is that these ways of looking at present versus future events, and of assessing ourselves in this time frame, are natural human inclinations. Everyone tends to discount the future. Everyone is more engaged by immediate reward. Everyone makes decisions that are not rational.[47] And yet, there are ways to fight the natural tendency to procrastinate. You can recognize that you're likely to discount the value of something that seems far off in the future and remind yourself about its value to you in the long-term. You can make a goal more real and vivid by knowing exactly what is involved in the task, when it is due and by setting short-term interim goals to get you there. You can admit that you're just as likely to want to procrastinate later as you are now, that the task is not going to be done by a different, nonprocrastinating version of yourself. And you can make your goal less vague and more immediate by taking action—any action—toward the goal *now*.

RESEARCH ON WHAT TO
DO ABOUT PROCRASTINATION

With these findings in mind, researchers have delineated a number of important strategies for reducing procrastination.[48] Since task aversiveness is a major component of procrastinating, looking for ways to mitigate it might help reduce procrastination.[49] Perhaps boring tasks could be made more challenging or difficult. Or, a task with a long-term reward might be "piggy-backed" or "fused" with one that has immediate satisfactions, such as participating in a study group (social fun) to prepare for a final exam (long-term goal).[50] The Tax Torture group we describe in Chapter 14 is an example of this fusion of the aversive and the pleasurable.

Increasing one's expectancy of success is another way to decrease procrastination on a given task. Watching other people complete the task successfully can help, as can experiencing "actual performance accomplishments."[51] Thus, improving skills needed for a particular task may increase the feeling of self-efficacy and thereby help decrease procrastination.[52] The technique we and so many others recommend of breaking down a large goal into small steps may help increase the frequency of actual performance accomplishments, because the achievement of small goals along the way can be experienced as successes. Having small, interim goals with interim deadlines also makes the task more salient.

Steel also describes "learned industriousness,"[53] which is the process of changing the value of a task, so that effort toward a goal becomes reinforcing in and of itself. This is consistent with the work of Carol Dweck (see Chapter 2), who emphasizes the importance of intrinsic motivation as part of a "Growth Mindset" and the experience of reward and pleasure in the process of working rather than in the performance outcome.[54] To our minds, this is a crucial aspect of de-linking self-worth from performance, which we believe is central to freeing people from the mire of procrastination.

Given the distractibility, impulsiveness, and self-control struggles of so many procrastinators, Steel suggests the technique of stimulus control to reduce the availability of distractions that tempt people to stray from their tasks.[55] This refers to changing environmental cues to support important goals and banish temptations. Turning off or delaying access to e-mail might be one way to banish a very common and compelling temptation. Studying in a quiet library corner rather than in a popular café is another example of stimulus control. We offer suggestions that use stimulus control in Chapter 14, "Learning to Say Yes and No."

Another suggestion is to create routines that serve to reduce the number of decisions one must make to get tasks done (see Chapter 16). This strategy is based on the observation that the greater the number of choice points a task requires, the greater the likelihood of procrastination.[56] Eliminating choice allows people to follow a course of action with little or no thought,[57] and so prevents them from becoming bogged down in decision making. Keeping strict time schedules is one example of such "automaticity."[58]

Finally, Steel notes that the research indicates that goal-setting does reduce procrastination.[59] Setting daily goals and making contracts for periodic work completion are useful antiprocrastination devices. These are examples of creating short-term, incremental, behavioral goals to help with the achievement of a larger, long-term goal, a process we have stressed for over twenty-five years in our clinical practice.

CONCLUSION

We are pleased that virtually all of our clinical ideas have been validated by social science research. Our central idea that procrastination is linked to lack of confidence and vulnerable self-esteem has been supported, and our assertions about the relationship between fear of failure and procrastination have also been corroborated. Many of our suggestions for overcoming procrastination are now supported by scientific evidence, especially the suggestion that procrastinators approach a task by breaking it down into small, manageable steps. (Everyone agrees on this strategy!) Our observation that procrastinators underestimate how long it will take to accomplish a task has been demonstrated by research, and our suggestion to enjoy rewards along the way, rather than wait until the elusive, far-off end of a project, is now backed up by both psychologists and economists.

Much has been learned about the complex behavior of procrastination over the past twenty-five years, and we look forward to the research yet to come. However, we once again stress that the most important research is that which you do yourself. Looking honestly at your own personal motivations for procrastinating, making an effort to use our suggested techniques, and seeing what works for you is, in the end, the only research that really matters.

APPENDIX B

A Short List of Techniques for Managing Procrastination

1. **Identify a *behavioral* goal** (observable, specific, and concrete), rather than setting a vague, global one.

NOT: "I want to stop procrastinating."

INSTEAD: "I want to clean out and organize my garage by September 1."

2. **Set a *realistic* goal.** Think small, rather than large, and choose a *minimally acceptable* goal rather than an ideal goal. Focus on one (and only one!) goal at a time.

NOT: "I'll never procrastinate again!"

INSTEAD: "I'll spend an hour a day studying for my Math class."

3. **Break your goal down into small, specific minigoals.** Each minigoal is more easily reached than the big goal, and small goals add up to a big goal.

NOT: "I'm going to write the report."

INSTEAD: "I'll spend thirty minutes working on a plan for my spreadsheet tonight. Tomorrow I'll spend another thirty minutes filling in the data, and then the next day, I'll spend an hour writing a report based on the data."

4. **Be realistic (rather than wishful) about time.** Ask yourself: How much time will the task actually take? How much time do I actually have available?

NOT: "I have plenty of time to do this tomorrow."

INSTEAD: "I'd better look at my calendar to see when I can start. Last time, it took longer than I thought."

5. Just get started! Instead of trying to do the whole project at once, just take one small step.

Remember: "The journey of a thousand miles begins with a single step."

NOT: "I've got to do it all in one sitting."

INSTEAD: "What is the *one first step* I can take?"

6. Use the next fifteen minutes. You can stand *anything* for fifteen minutes. You can *only* accomplish a task by working at it fifteen minutes at a time. So, what you can do in fifteen minutes *is* of value.

NOT: "I only have fifteen minutes, so why bother?"

INSTEAD: "What part of this task can I do in the next fifteen minutes?"

7. Expect obstacles and setbacks. Don't give up as soon as you hit the first (or second or third) obstacle. An obstacle is just a problem to be solved, not a reflection of your value or competence.

NOT: "The professor isn't in his office, so I can't work on my paper. Think I'll go to a movie."

INSTEAD: "Even though the professor isn't in, I can work on my outline until he gets back."

8. When possible, delegate (or even dump!) the task. Are you really the *only* person who can do this? Does this task really have to be done at all?

Remember, no one can do everything—not even you.

NOT: "I am the only one who can do this correctly."

INSTEAD: "I'll find the right person for this task so that I can work on a more important project."

9. Protect your time. Learn how to say no. Don't take on extra or unnecessary projects.

You can choose not to respond to what's "urgent" in order to attend to what's *important*.

NOT: "I have to make myself available to anyone who needs me."

INSTEAD: "I don't have to answer the phone while I'm working. I'll listen to the message and call back later when I've finished."

10. Watch for your excuses. Instead of using your excuse as an automatic reason to procrastinate, use it as a signal to spend just fifteen minutes on your task. Or use your excuse as a reward for taking a step.

NOT: "I'm tired (depressed/hungry/busy/confused, etc.), so I'll do it later."

INSTEAD: "I'm tired, so I'll just spend fifteen minutes working on my report. Then I'll take a nap."

11. Reward your progress along the way. Focus on effort, not on outcome. Watch out for all-or-nothing thinking: the cup can be half-full just as well as half-empty.

Remember, even a small step is progress!

NOT: "I can't feel good until I've completely finished."

INSTEAD: "I took some steps and I've worked hard. That feels good. Now I'm going to watch a movie."

12. Use your procrastination as a signal. Stop and ask yourself: "What message is my procrastination sending me?"

NOT: "I'm procrastinating again and I hate myself."

INSTEAD: "I'm procrastinating again: What am I feeling? What does this mean? What can I learn?"

Remember: YOU HAVE A CHOICE. YOU CAN DELAY OR YOU CAN ACT.

You can act, even though you are uncomfortable.

The legacy of the past does not have to control what you do in the present.

You can take pleasure in learning, growing, and challenging yourself.

You do not have to be perfect to be of value.

APPENDIX C

Notes and Sources

A NOTE TO OUR READERS

1. Steel, P. (2007). The nature of procrastination: A meta-analytic and theoretical review of quintessential self-regulatory failure. *Psychological Bulletin, 133*(1), 65–94.

2. Steel, op. cit.

PART ONE. UNDERSTANDING PROCRASTINATION

1. Meissner, W. (2007). *Time, self, and psychoanalysis.* New York: Jason Aronson.

2. Doidge, N. (2007). *The brain that changes itself.* New York: Penguin.

1. PROCRASTINATION: NUISANCE OR NEMESIS?

1. *The new shorter oxford English dictionary* (Vols. 1–2) (1973/1993). Oxford, England: Clarendon Press.

2. Ferrari, J. R., Johnson, J. L., & McCown, W. G. (1995). *Procrastination and task avoidance: Theory, research, and treatment.* New York: Plenum Press, p. 4.

3. Johnson, S. (1751). *Rambler* 134. Retrieved February 21, 2007, from www.samueljohnson.com/ram134.html.

4. "Morning Edition—Last word in business." National Public Radio report July 21, 2008.

5. Steel, P. (2007). The nature of procrastination: A meta-analytic and theoretical review of quintessential self-regulatory failure. *Psychological Bulletin, 133*(1), 65–94.

6. Ferrari, J. R. (2004). Trait procrastination in academic settings: An overview of students who engage in task delays. In H. C. Schouwenburg, C. H. Lay, T. A. Pychyl, & J. R. Ferrari (Eds.) (2004), *Counseling the procrastinator in academic settings* (pp. 19–27). Washington, D.C.: American Psychological Association, p. 23.

7. Steel (2007), op. cit.

8. Steel (2007), op. cit., p. 77.

2. FEAR OF FAILURE:
THE PROCRASTINATOR ON TRIAL

1. Frost, R. O., Heimberg, R. G., Holt, C. S., Mattia, J. L., & Neubauer, A. L. (1993). A comparison of two measures of perfectionism. *Personality and Individual Differences, 14,* 119–128.

2. Slaney, R. B., Rice, K. G., & Ashby, J. S. (2002). A programmatic approach to measuring perfectionism: The Almost Perfect Scales. In G. L. Flett, & P. L. Hewitt (Eds.) (2002), *Perfectionism: theory, research, and treatment* (pp. 63–88). Washington, D.C.: American Psychological Association.

3. Slaney, Rice, & Ashby (2002), op. cit.

4. Rice, K. G., & Ashby, J. S. (2007). An efficient method for classifying perfectionists. *Journal of Counseling Psychology, 54*(1), 72–85.

5. Burns, D. (1980). The perfectionist's script for self-defeat. *Psychology Today*; Burns, D. (1980/1999). *Feeling good: The new mood therapy.* New York: Avon Books.

6. Slaney, R. B., Rice, K. G., & Ashby, J. S. (2002), op. cit.

7. Jones, E. E., & Berglas, S. (1978). Control of attributions about the self through self-handicapping strategies: The appeal of alcohol and the role of under achievement. *Personality and Social Psychology Bulletin, 4,* 200–206; Lay, C. H., Knish, S., & Zanatta, R. (1992). Self-handicappers and procrastinators: A comparison of their practice behavior prior to an evaluation. *Journal of Research in Personality, 26,* 242–257; Ferrari, J. R., & Tice, D. M. (2000). Procrastination as a self-handicap for men and women: A task-avoidance strategy in a laboratory setting. *Journal of Research in Personality, 34,* 73–83.

8. Dweck, C. (2006). *Mindset: The new psychology of success.* New York: Random House.

9. Ibid., p. 40.

10. Ibid., p. 16.

11. Sarton, M. (1987/1993). *At seventy.* New York: W. W. Norton, p. 10.

3. FEAR OF SUCCESS:
HELLO PROCRASTINATION, GOOD-BYE SUCCESS

1. Lay, C. H. (2004). Some basic elements in counseling procrastinators. In H. C. Schouwenburg, C. H. Lay, T. A. Pychyl, & J. R. Ferrari (Eds.) (2004), *Counseling the procrastinator in academic settings* (pp. 43–58). Washington, D.C.: American Psychological Association, p. 45.

2. Freud, S. (1914). Those wrecked by success. *The standard edition of the complete psychological works of Sigmund Freud, Vol. XIV (1914–1916): On the history of the psycho-analytic movement, papers on metapsychology and other works.* (pp. 316–331). London: The Hogarth Press.

3. Kolodny, S. (2000). *The captive muse.* Madison, CT: Psychosocial Press, pp. 80–81.

4. Fisch, R., Weakland J., & Segal, L. (1982). *The tactics of change: Doing therapy briefly.* San Fransicso: Josey-Bass.

5. Balint, M. (1968/1992). *The basic fault: Therapeutic aspects of regression.* London: Tavistock Publications.

6. Improving education for immigrant students: A guide for K-12 educators in the Northwest and Alaska. (2001). Northwest Regional Educational Laboratory, p. 29. Retrieved on May 21, 2008, from www.nwrel.org/cnorse/booklets/immigration/4.html.

6. DO YOU KNOW WHAT TIME (IT) IS?

1. Meissner, W. (2007). *Time, self, and psychoanalysis.* New York: Jason Aronson.

2. Griffith, J. (1999/2004). *A sideways look at time.* New York: Jeremy P. Tarcher/Penguin.

3. Zimbardo, P., & Boyd, J. (2008). *The time paradox: the new psychology of time that will change your life.* New York: Free Press.

4. National Institute of Mental Health. (2007). Cell networking keeps brain's master clock ticking. Retrieved May 25, 2007, from www.NIMH.NIH.gov/science-news/2007.

5. Sato, F., Kawamoto, T., Fujimoto, K., Noshiro, M., Honda, K. K., Honma, S., et al. (2004). Functional analysis of the basic helix-loop-helix transcription factor DEC1 in circadian regulation. Interaction with BMAL1. *European Journal of Biochemistry,* 271, 4409–4419. Retrieved February 18, 2008, from www.ncbi.nlm.nih.gov/pubmed/15560782?dopt=Abstract.

6. Van Wassehnhove, V., Buonomany, D. V., Shimojo, S., & Shams, L. (2008). Distortions of subjective time perception within and across senses. Retrieved February 19, 2007, from www.plosone.org/article/info:doi%2F10 .1371%2Fjournal.pone.0001437.

7. Meaux, J., & Chelonis, J. (2003). Time perception differences in children with and without ADHD. *Journal of Pediatric Health Care, 17*(2), 64–71.

8. Zimbardo, P., & Boyd, J. (2008), op. cit.

9. Akerlof, G. (1991). Procrastination and obedience. *American Economic Review, 81*(2), 1–19.

10. Ibid.; Joireman, J., Strathman, A., & Balliet, D. (2006). Considering future consequences: An integrative model. In L. J. Sanna, & E. C. Chang (2006), *Judgments over time: The interplay of thoughts, feelings, and behaviors.* Oxford, England: Oxford University Press.

11. University of Cincinnati. (2002). E-briefing, "A timely look at time." Dec 20. Retrieved May 25, 2008, from www.uc.edu/news/ebriefs/time02.htm.

12. Rousseau, G., & Venter, D. (2004). Measuring time perception in a cross cultural environment. Retrieved May 25, 2008, from http://smib.vuw .ac.nz:8081/.

13. Lombardi, R. (2003). Knowledge and experience of time in primitive mental states. *The International Journal of Psychoanalysis, 84*, 1531–1549.

14. Our timeline is drawn from Calvin Colarusso's series of articles about the development of a time sense in different life stages. The summary article is Colarusso, C. (1998). The development of time sense: In late adolescence and throughout the life cycle. *The Psychoanalytic Study of the Child, 53*, 113–140.

15. Priel, B. (1997). Time and self: On the intersubjective construction of time. *Psychoanalytic Dialogues, 7*, 431–450.

16. Hagglund, T. (2001). Timelessness as a positive and negative experience. *The Scandinavian Psychoanalytic Review, 24*, 83–92.

17. Griffith, J. (1999/2004), op. cit.

18. Bion, W. R. (1965). *Transformations: Change from learning to growth.* London: Heinemann.

19. Priel, B. (1997), op. cit.

20. Maroda, K. (1987). The fate of the narcissistic personality: Lost in time. *Psychoanalytic Psychology. 4*, 279–290.

21. Loewald, H. (1972). The experience of time. *The Psychoanalytic Study of the Child, 27*, 401–410.

22. Atwood, M. (2000). *The blind assassin: A novel.* Toronto: McClelland and Stewart.

23. Colarusso, C. (1998), op. cit.

7. CURRENT NEUROSCIENCE: THE BIG IDEAS

1. Doidge, N. (2007). *The brain that changes itself.* New York: Viking; Restak, R. (2003). *The new brain: How the modern age is rewiring your mind.* Emmaus, PA: Rodale Press.

2. Ibid.

3. Restak, R. (2003), op. cit.

4. Diamond, M., & Hopson, J. (1998). *Magic trees of the mind: How to nurture your child's intelligence, creativity and healthy emotions.* New York: Penguin; Doidge, N. (2007), op. cit.; Restak, R. (2003), op. cit.

5. Doidge, N. (2007), op. cit., p. 223.

6. Ibid., p. 242.

7. Pascual-Leone, quoted in Doidge (2007), op. cit., p. 209.

8. Ibid., p. 242. Italics original.

9. Damasio, A. (1999). *The feeling of what happens.* New York: Harcourt, Inc.

10. Damasio, A. (1999), op. cit.

11. Ibid.

12. LeDoux, J. (1996). *The emotional brain.* New York: Simon & Schuster, p. 267.

13. Solms, M., & Turnbull, O. (2002). *The brain and the inner world*, p. 79. Italics original.

14. Cozolino, L. (2006). *The neuroscience of human relationships.* New York: W. W. Norton, p. 133; Doidge, N. (2007), op. cit.; LeDoux, J. (1996), op. cit.; Solms, M., & Turnbull, O. (2002), op. cit.

15. Cozolino, L. (2006), op. cit.

16. LeDoux, J. (1996), op. cit., p. 250–252; Solms, M., & Turnbull, O. (2002), op cit., p. 134–135.

17. Cozolino, L. (2006), op. cit.; Le Doux, J. (1996), op. cit.; Solms, M., & Turnbull, O. (2002), op. cit.

18. LeDoux, J. (1996), op cit., p. 181–182; Solms, M., & Turnbull, O. (2002), op cit., p. 164.

19. Cozolino, L. (2006), op. cit., p. 317–319; LeDoux, J. (1996), op cit., p. 265.

20. Freud, S. (1923). The ego and the id. *The standard edition of the complete psychological works of Sigmund Freud, Vol. XIX* (1923–1925): *The ego and the id and other works,* pp. 1–66.

21. Doidge, N. (2007), op. cit., p. 232, 235.

22. Goldin, P., McRae, K., Ramel, W., & Gross, J. (2008). The neural bases of emotion regulation: Reappraisal and suppression of negative emotion. *Biological Psychiatry, 63*(6), 577–586.

23. Cozolino, L. (2006), op. cit.

24. Bion, W. (1959). Attacks on linking. *International Journal of Psychoanalysis, 40,* 308–315.

25. Gross, J. (2001). Emotional regulation in adulthood: Timing is everything. *Current Directions in Psychological Neuroscience,* 10, 214–219; Ray, R., Ochsner, K., Cooper, J., Robertson, E., Gabrieli, J., & Gross, J. (2005). Individual differences in trait rumination and the neural systems supporting cognitive reappraisal. *Cognitive, Affective, & Behavioral Neuroscience,* 5(2), 156–168.

26. Goldin et al. (2008), op. cit.

27. Schwartz, J. (1996). *Brain lock: Free yourself from obsessive-compulsive disorder.* New York: Harper Collins.

28. Solms, M., & Turnbull, O. (2002), op. cit., p. 137.

29. Kandel, E. (2006). *In search of memory.* New York: W. W. Norton.

30. Winnicott, D. W. (1974). Fear of breakdown. *International Review of Psycho-Analysis, 1,* 103–107.

31. Cozolino, L. (2006), op. cit.

32. Kandel, E. (2006), op. cit.; Solms, M., & Turnbull, O. (2002), op. cit.

33. Cozolino, L. (2006), op. cit.

34. Ibid.

35. Sapolsky, R. (1992) *Stress, the aging brain, and the mechanisms of neuronal death.* Cambridge, MA: MIT Press.

36. Cozolino, L. (2006), op. cit.; Solms, M., & Turnbull, O. (2002), op. cit.

37. Cozolino, L. (2006), op. cit.

38. Steel, P. (2007). The nature of procrastination: A meta-analytic and theoretical review of quintessential self-regulatory failure. *Psychological Bulletin. 133*(1), 65–94.

39. Keltner, D. (2007). "Understanding Social Intelligence" conference presentation, sponsored by the Institute for Brain Potential, in Palo Alto, California, Oct. 26, 2007.

40. Cozolino, L. (2006), op. cit.

41. Iacoboni, M., Woods, R., Brass, M., Bekkering, H., Mazziotta, J., & Rizzolatti, G. (1999). Cortical mechanisms of human imitation. *Science, 286,* 2526–2528; Ramachandran, V. S. (2000). Mirror neurons and imitation learning as the driving force behind "the great leap forward" in human evolution, *Edge* no. 69, May 29; Rizzolatti, G., Fadiga, L., Gallese, V., & Fogassi, L. (1996). Premotor cortex and the recognition of motor actions. *Cognitive Brain Research, 3,* 131–141; University of California–Los Angeles (2005, February 25). UCLA Neuroscientists Pinpoint New Function for Mirror Neurons. *Science*

Daily. Retrieved August 28, 2008, from www.sciencedaily.com/releases/2005/02/050223163142.htm.

42. Emde, R. (1988). Development terminable and interminable: I. Innate and motivational factors from infancy. *International Journal of Psychoanalysis, 69,* 23–42, quoted in L. Cozolino (2006), op. cit., p. 85. Italics original.

43. Cozolino, L. (2006), op. cit., p. 14.

44. Ibid.

45. Siegel, D. (2007). *The mindful brain: reflection and attunement in the cultivation of well-being.* New York: W. W. Norton.

46. Davidson, R. J. (2004). Well-being and affective style: Neural substrates and biobehavioural correlates. *Philosophical Transactions Royal Society London, B, 359,* 1395–1411.

47. Davidson, R. J. (2000). Affective style, psychopathology, and resilience: Brain mechanisms and plasticity. *American Psychologist,* 1196–1214; Siegel, D. (2007), op. cit.

48. Cozolino, L. (2006), op. cit.

49. Ibid.

50. Ibid.

51. Davidson, R. J. (2004), op. cit.; Siegel, D. (2007), op. cit.

52. Siegel, D. (2007), op. cit.

53. Ibid., p. 78.

8. PROCRASTINATION AND YOUR BRAIN

1. Goldberg, E. (2001). *The executive brain.* New York: Oxford University Press.

2. Dawson, P., & Guare, R. (2004). *Executive skills in children and adolescents.* New York: Guilford Press; Goldberg, E. (2001), op. cit.

3. Packer, L. Retrieved Jan 18, 2008, from www.tourettesyndrome.net/ef.htm.

4. Barkley, R., Murphy, K., & Fischer, M. (2008). *ADHD in adults: What the science says.* New York: Guilford Press; Dawson, P., & Guare, R. (2004), op. cit.

5. Anderson, P. (2002). Assessment and development of executive function during childhood, *Child Neuropsychology. 8*(2), 71–82.

6. Dawson, P., & Guare, R. (2004), op. cit.; Gioia, G. A., Isquith, P. K., Guy, S. C., & Kenworthy, L. (2000). *Behavior rating inventory of executive function.* Odessa, FL: Psychological Assessment Resources; Packer, L. Retrieved Jan 18, 2008, from www.tourettesyndrome.net/ef.htm.

7. Faraone, S. (2007). Neurobiology and genetics of ADHD: An expert interview with Stephen V. Faraone, Ph.D. Retrieved Sept. 25, 2008 from http://www.medscape.com/viewarticle/557612; Surman, C. (2008). ADD in adults: not just a childhood disorder. Conference presentation, sponsored by Shire Pharmaceuticals, San Francisco, CA, Sept. 20, 2008.

8. Barkley, R. (2000). *Taking charge of ADHD*. New York: Guilford Press; Barkley, R., et al. (2008), op. cit.; Hallowell, E., & Ratey, J. (1995), *Driven to distraction: recognizing and coping with attention deficit disorder in childhood through adulthood*. New York: Simon and Schuster; Hallowell, E., & Ratey, J. (2005). *Delivered from distraction: Getting the most out of life with attention deficit disorder*. New York: Ballantine; Sarkis, S. M. (2006). *10 simple solutions to adult ADD: How to overcome chronic distraction and accomplish your goals*. Oakland, CA: New Harbinger Publications.

9. Barkley, R., et al. (2008), op. cit.; Hallowell, E., & Ratey, J. (1995), op. cit.; Hallowell, E., & Ratey, J. (2005), op. cit.

10. Ritter, M. (2007, March 27). It's something we all do. *San Jose Mercury News*, p. 3A.

11. Barkley, R., et al. (2008), op. cit.

12. Ibid., p. 51.

13. Bronowski, J. Referenced in Barkley, R. (2008), op. cit., p. 51.

14. Barkley, R. (2008), op. cit., p. 51.

15. Meaux, J., & Chelonis, J. (2003). Time perception differences in children with and without ADHD. *Journal of Pediatric Health Care, 17*(2), 64–71.

16. Barkley, R., et al. (2008), op. cit., p. 52.

17. Ritter, M. (2007, March 27), op. cit.

18. Grady, C., Springer, M., Hongwanishkul, D., McIntosh, A., & Winocur, G. (2006). Age-related changes in brain activity across the adult lifespan. *Journal of Cognitive Neuroscience, 18*, 227–241.

19. Barkley, R., et al. (2008), op. cit.

20. Ibid.

21. Shaw, P., Rapoport, J., & Evans, A. (2007). ADD at the far end of a continuum of normal traits. *Proceedings of the National Academy of Sciences*, Nov. 12, 2007.

22. Hallowell, E., & Ratey, J. (2005), op. cit., p. 60.

23. Barkley, R., et al. (2008), op. cit.; Hallowell, E., & Ratey, J. (2005), op. cit.; Ratey, J. (2008). *Spark: The revolutionary new science of exercise and the brain*. New York: Little Brown.

24. Barkley, R., et al. (2008), op. cit.; Shaw, P., Rapoport, J., & Evans, A. (2007), op. cit.

25. Restak, R. (2003). *The new brain*. Emmaus, PA: Rodale Press, p. 45.

26. Schwartz, E. (1994). Interrupt-driven, *Wired* magazine, as quoted in Restak, R. (2003), op. cit., p. 45.

27. Restak, R. (2003), op. cit., p. 48.

28. Kramer, P. (2005). *Against depression.* New York: Penguin.

29. Ibid.

30. Hollon, S., Jarrett, R., Nierenberg, A., Thase, M., Trivedi, M., & Rush, A. (2005). Psychotherapy and medication in the treatment of adult and geriatric depression: Which monotherapy or combined treatment? *Journal of Clinical Psychiatry, 66*(4), 455–468.

31. Ratey, J. (2008), op. cit.

32. Rosenthal, N. (2006). *Winter blues.* New York: Guilford Press.

33. Ibid.

34. Ibid., p. 78.

35. Ibid.

36. Schwartz, J. M. (1996*). Brain lock: Free yourself from obsessive-compulsive disorder.* New York: Harper Collins.

37. Ibid.

38. Neziroglu, F., Bubrick, J., & Yaryura-Tobias, J. A. (2004). *Overcoming compulsive hoarding.* Oakland, CA: New Harbinger Publications.

39. Ibid., p. 37.

40. Saxena, S., Brody, A. Maindment, K., Smith, E. Zohrabi, N., Katz, E., Barker, S., & Baxter, L. (2004). Cerebral glucose metabolism in obsessive-compulsive hoarding. *American Journal of Psychiatry,* June, *161,* 1038–1048.

41. Saxena, S. (2007). Is compulsive hoarding a genetically and neuro-biologically discrete syndrome? *American Journal of Psychiatry, 164*(3), 380–384.

42. Sapolsky, R. (1994). *Why zebras don't get ulcers.* New York: W. H. Freeman and Co.

43. Sapolsky, R. (1992). *Stress, the aging brain, and the mechanisms of neuronal death.* Cambridge, MA: MIT Press.

44. Kramer, P. (2005), op. cit.; Sapolsky, R. (1992), op. cit.

45. Flaherty, A. (2004). *The midnight disease: The drive to write, writer's block and the creative brain.* Boston: Houghton-Mifflin.

46. Dement, W., & Vaughn, C. (2000). *The promise of sleep.* New York: Bantam Dell.

47. Dahl, R. E. (1999). In K. L. Wahlstrom (Ed.), *Adolescent sleep needs and school starting times* (pp. 29–34). Bloomington, IN: Phi Delta Kappa Educational Foundation, quoted in Dawson, P., & Guare, R. (2004), op. cit., p. 85.

48. Dement, W., & Vaughn, C. (2000), op. cit.

49. Ibid.

50. Kramer, P. (2005), op. cit.

51. Flaherty, A. (2004), op. cit., p. 147.

9. HOW YOU CAME TO BE A PROCRASTINATOR

1. Kagan, J., & Snidman, N. (2004). *The long shadow of temperament.* Cambridge, MA: Harvard University Press.

2. Ibid.; Cozolino, L. (2006). *The neuroscience of human relationships.* New York: W. W. Norton.

3. Steel, P. (2007). The nature of procrastination: A meta-analytic and theoretical review of quintessential self-regulatory failure. *Psychological Bulletin, 133*(1), 65–94.

4. The immigrant experience (2001). Northwest Regional Educational Laboratory. Retrieved May 20, 2008, from www.nwrel.org/cnorse/booklets/immigration/4.html.

5. First in my family: A profile of first-generation college students at four-year institutions since 1971 (2007). UCLA Higher Education Research Institute. Retrieved May 20, 2008, from www.gseis.ucla.edu/heri/PDFs/pubs/briefs/FirstGenResearchBrief.pdf.

6. Pally, R. (2007). The predicting brain: Unconscious repetition, conscious reflection and therapeutic change. *International Journal of Psycho-Analysis, 88*(4), 861–881, p. 861. See also Hawkins, J. (2004). *On intelligence.* New York: Henry Holt.

7. LeDoux, J. (1998). *The emotional brain.* New York: Simon and Schuster.

8. Rice, K. G., & Ashby, J. S. (2007). An efficient method for classifying perfectionists. *Journal of Counseling Psychology, 54*(1), 72–85.

9. Khan, M. (1964). Ego distortion, cumulative trauma, and the role of reconstruction in the analytic situation. *International Journal of Psycho-analysis, 45*, 272–279.

10. Winnicott, D. W. (1953). Transitional objects and transitional phenomena: A study of the first not-me possession. *International Journal of Psycho-Analysis, 34*, 89–97; Bettelheim, B. (1987). *A good enough parent.* New York: Alfred A. Knopf.

11. Tronick, E. Z., & Gianino, A. (1986). Interactive mismatch and repair: Challenges to the coping infant. *Zero to Three.* February, 6(3), 1–6.

12. Lewicki, P., Hill, T., & Czyzewska, M. (1992). Nonconscious acquisition of information. *American Psychologist, 47*, 796–801; See also Cozolino, L. (2006), op. cit.; Solms, M., & Turnbull, O. (2002). *The brain and the inner world.* New York: Other Press.

13. Cozolino, L. (2006), op. cit., p. 132.

14. Main, M., Kaplan, N., & Cassidy, J. (1985). Security in infancy, childhood, and adulthood: A move to the level of representation. In I. Bretherton, & E. Waters (Eds.) (1985), Growing points of attachment theory and research. *Monograph of the Society for Research in Childhood Development, 50,* Serial No. 209 (1–2), 66–104.

15. Ibid.

10. LOOKING AHEAD TO SUCCESS

1. Fisch, R., Weakland J., & Segal, L. (1982). *The tactics of change: Doing therapy briefly.* San Fransicso: Josey-Bass.

2. The top 10: The most influential therapists of the past quarter-century. (2007). Retrieved January 18, 2007, from www.psychotherapynetworker.com/index.php?category=magazine&sub_cat=articles&type=article&id=The%20Top%2010&page=6.

3. Doidge, N. (2007). *The brain that changes itself.* New York: Penguin Books, p. 198.

4. Goleman, D. (1998). *Working with emotional intelligence.* New York: Bantam Books, p. 317.

5. Ibid.

6. Eifert, G. H., & Forsyth, J. P. (2005). *Acceptance and commitment therapy for anxiety disorders: A practitioner's guide to using mindfulness, acceptance, and value-guide behavior change strategies.* Oakland, CA: New Harbinger Publications, p. 153.

7. Ibid., p. 171. See also Hayes, S. (2005). *Get out of your mind and into your life: The new acceptance and commitment therapy.* Oakland, CA: New Harbinger Publications, pp. 153–163.

8. Siegel, D. J. (2007). *The mindful brain: Reflection and attunement in the cultivation of well-being.* New York: W. W. Norton.

PART TWO. OVERCOMING PROCRASTINATION

1. Prochaska, J. O., DiClemente, C. C., & Norcross, J. (1992). In search of how people change. *American Psychologist, 47,* 1102–1114.

2. For more information, see www.prochange.com.

3. Hargrove, M. D. (1997). Michael D. Hargrove, Bottom Line Underwriters. Retrieved April 24, 2008, from www.mysuccesscompany.com.

4. Dweck, C. (2006) *Mindset: The new psychology of success.* New York: Ballantine.

5. Steel, P. (2007). The nature of procrastination: A meta-analytic and theoretical review of quintessential self-regulatory failure. *Psychological Bulletin, 133*(1), 65–94.

6. Doidge, N. (2007) *The brain that changes itself.* New York: Penguin, p. 223–224.

7. Giroux, R. Flannery O'Connor: The complete stories. Retrieved May 20, 2008, from http://speakingoffaith.publicradio.org/programs/faithfired bylit/giroux-intro.shtml.

8. Jackson, Y. H. (Ed.). (2006). *Encyclopedia of Multicultural Psychology.* New York: Sage Publishers, p. 223.

9. Cloutterbuck, J., & Zhan, C. (2006). Ethnic elders. In K. D. Melillo, & S. C. Houde. *Geropsychiatric and mental health nursing* (pp. 69–81). Sudbury, MA: Jones and Bartlett Publishers.

10. Seligman, M. (1995). The effectiveness of psychotherapy: The *Consumer Reports* study. *American Psychologist, 50*(12), 965–974.

11. Eels, T. D. (1999). Psychotherapy versus medication for unipolar depression. *Journal of Psychotherapy Practice and Research, 8,* 170–173.

12. Etkin, A., Pittenger, C., Polan, H., & Kandel, E. (2005). Toward a neurobiology of psychotherapy: Basic science and clinical applications. *Journal of Neuropsychiatry and Clinical Neurosciences, 17,* 145–158, in N. Doidge (2007), op. cit., p. 233.

13. Doidge, N. (2007). *The brain that changes itself.* New York: Viking.

12. SETTING AND ACHIEVING GOALS

1. Dweck, C. S. (2006). *Mindset: The new psychology of success.* New York: Ballantine.

2. Doidge, N. (2007). *The brain that changes itself.* New York: Penguin, p. 106–107.

13. LEARNING HOW TO TELL TIME

1. http://thinkexist.com/quotation/failing_to_plan_is_planning_to_fail/252276.html.

2. Lakein, A. (1973). *How to get control or your time and your life.* New York: Signet, p. 25.

3. Fiore, N. (1989/2007). *The now habit: A strategic program for overcoming procrastination and enjoying guilt-free play.* New York: Tarcher/Putnam (1989), Penguin (2007).

4. Shunk, D. H., & Zimmerman, B. J. (2003). Self-regulation and learning. In W. M. Reynolds, & G. E. Millers (Eds.), *Handbook of psychology, Vol. 7: Educational Psychology*. Hoboken, NJ: Wiley.

5. Meck, W. H. (2005). Neuropsychology of timing and time perception. *Brain and Cognition, 58*(1), 1–8.

6. Lakein, A. (1973), op. cit., p. 104.

7. Doidge, N. (2007). *The brain that changes itself.* New York: Penguin, p. 106–107.

8. Drucker, P. F. (1967/2006). *The effective executive: The definitive guide to getting the right things done.* New York: Harper Collins.

9. Covey, S. R. (1989/2004). *The 7 habits of highly effective people: Powerful lessons in personal change.* New York: Free Press.

10. Zimbardo, P., & Boyd, J. (2008). *The time paradox: The new psychology of time that will change your life.* New York: Free Press.

14. LEARNING TO SAY YES AND NO

1. Christakis, N. A., & Fowler, J. H. (2007). The spread of obesity in a large social network over 32 years. *The New England Journal of Medicine, 357*(4), 370–379. July 26, 2007; Christakis, N. A., & Fowler, J. H. (2008). The collective dynamics of smoking in a large social network. *The New England Journal of Medicine, 358*(21), 2249–2258. May 22, 2008.

2. Deutsch, M., & Gerard, H. B. (1955). A study of normative and informational influences upon individual judgment. *Journal of Abnormal and social Psychology, 51,* 629–636. More currently, Ashraf, N., Karlan, D., & Yin, W. (2006). Tying Odysseus to the mast: Evidence from a commitment savings project in the Philippines. *Quarterly Journal of Economics, 121*(2), 635–672.

3. Ian Ayres, Professor at Yale Law School and Yale School of Management, and Dean Karlan, Assistant Professor of Economics at Yale University. (Jordan Goldberg, personal communication, April 2008.)

4. Covey, S. R. (1989/2004). *The 7 habits of highly effective people: Powerful lessons in personal change.* New York: Free Press.

5. Juran, J. The non-Pareto principle—mea culpa. From *Quality Progress* magazine, 1972. In K. S. Stephens (Ed.) (2005), *Juran, quality, and a century of improvement.* The Best on Quality Book Series of the International Academy for Quality, Vol. 15. pp. 185–190. Milwaukee, WI: ASQ Quality Press. Retrieved March 15, 2008, from http://management.about.com/cs/general-management/a/Pareto081202.htm.

6. Although the 80/20 rule is attributed to the Italian economist Vilfredo Pareto, who observed in 1906 that 20 percent of the people owned 80 percent of the wealth, it was Joseph Juran, a quality management pioneer in the U.S. in the 1930s and 1940s, who recognized this as a universal principle of "the vital few and the trivial many." Retrieved March 15, 2008, from http://management.about.com/cs/generalmanagement/a/Pareto08102.htm.

7. Blanke, G. (2009). *Throw out fifty things: Clear the clutter, find your life.* New York: Springboard Press.

8. Cassidy, M. (2008). Let's take a holiday from the Net, *San Jose Mercury News.* July 4, 2008.

9. Restak, R. (2003). *The new brain: How the modern age is rewiring your brain.* Emmaus, PA: Rodale Press, p. 55.

15. USING YOUR BODY TO
REDUCE PROCRASTINATION

1. Ratey, J. (2008). *Spark: The revolutionary new science of exercise and the brain.* New York: Little Brown.

2. Ibid., p. 14.

3. Kramer, P. (2005). *Against depression.* New York: Penguin.

4. Kramer, P. (2005), op. cit.; Ratey, J. (2008), op. cit.; Sapolsky, R. (1992). *Stress, the aging brain, and the mechanisms of neuronal death.* Cambridge, MA: MIT Press; Sapolsky, R. (1994). *Why zebras don't get ulcers.* New York: W. H. Freeman and Co.

5. Ratey, J. (2008), op. cit., p. 79.

6. Ibid.

7. Bravata, D., Smith-Spangler, C., Sundaram, V., Gienger, A., Lin, N., Lewis, R., Stave, C., Olkin, I., & Sirard, J. (2007). Using pedometers to increase physical activity and improve health: A systematic review. *Journal of the American Medical Association, 298*(19), 2296–2304.

8. Merzenich, M. (2008). Brain plasticity-based therapeutics. Conference presentation, sponsored by the Psychoanalytic Institute of Northern California, San Francisco, CA, Sept. 20, 2008.

9. Ratey, J. (2008), op. cit., p. 245.

10. Kabat-Zinn, J. (2005). *Wherever you go there you are.* New York: Hyperion Books, p. 4.

11. Ibid., p. 5.

12. Siegel, D. (2007). *The mindful brain: Reflection and attunement in the cultivation of well-being.* New York: W. W. Norton.

13. Kabat-Zinn, J. (1990). *Full catastrophe living.* New York: Bantam Dell.

14. Lazar, S., Kerr, C., Wasserman, R., Gray, J., Greve, D., Treadway, M., McGarvey, M., Quinn, B., Dusek, J., Benson, H., Rauch, S., Moore, C., & Fischl, B. (2005). Meditation experience is associated with increased cortical thickness. *NeuroReport, 16,* 1893–1897.

15. Kabat-Zinn, J. (1990), op. cit.; Kabat-Zinn, J. (2005), op. cit.; Siegel, D. (2007), op. cit.

16. Brach, T. (2003). *Radical acceptance: embracing your life with the heart of a Buddha.* New York: Bantam Books, p. 71–72.

17. Ibid., p. 51

18. Childre, D., & Rozman, D. (2005). *Transforming stress.* Oakland, CA: New Harbinger Publications, p. 14.

19. Ibid., p. 43–45.

20. Ibid., p. 99.

21. Ibid., p. 107.

22. Benson, H. (2000). *The relaxation response.* New York: Harper Collins.

23. Baker, L. (2004, February 12). Deconstructing the pet-effect on cardiovascular health. SUNY *Buffalo Reporter, 35*(22). Retrieved April 26, 2008, from www.Buffalo.edu.reporter.

16. TIPS FOR PROCRASTINATORS
WITH ADD AND EXECUTIVE DYSFUNCTION

1. Steel, P. (2007). The nature of procrastination: A meta-analytic and theoretical review of quintessential self-regulatory failure. *Psychological Bulletin, 133*(1), 65–94.

2. Dawson, P., & Guare, R. (2006). *Executive skills in children and adolescents.* New York: Guilford Press.

3. Barkley, R., Murphy, K., & Fischer, M. (2008). *ADHD in adults: What the science says.* New York: Guilford Press.

4. Barkley, R., et al. (2008), op. cit.; Hallowell, E., & Ratey, J. (2005). *Delivered from distraction: Getting the most out of life with ADD.* New York: Ballantine; Ratey, N. (2008). *The disorganized mind.* New York: St. Martin's Press; Sarkis, S. (2006). *10 simple solutions for dealing with adult ADD.* Oakland, CA: New Harbinger Publications.

5. Kohlberg, J., & Nadeau, K. (2002). *ADD-friendly ways to organize your life.* New York: Brunner-Routledge.

6. Hallowell, E., & Ratey, J. (2005), op. cit.; Kohlberg, J., & Nadeau, K. (2002), op. cit.

7. Hallowell, E., & Ratey, J. (2005), op. cit., p. 308

8. Ibid.; Kohlberg, J., & Nadeau, K. (2002), op. cit.; Ratey, N. (2008), op. cit.; Sarkis, S. (2006), op. cit.

9. Kohlberg, J., & Nadeau, K. (2002), op. cit.

10. Ibid., p.11

11. Hallowell, E., & Ratey, J. (2005), op. cit.

12. Winnicott, D. W. (1953). Transitional objects and transitional phenomena. *International Journal of Psychoanalysis, 34,* 89–97.

13. Hallowell, E., & Ratey, J. (2005), op. cit., p. 177–186.

17. NEITHER HERE NOR THERE:
PROCRASTINATION AND THE CROSS-CULTURAL EXPERIENCE

1. Slocum, J. (2006, Nov. 29). "International Migration Trends" speech to MacArthur Foundation Initiative on Global Migration and Human Mobility. Retrieved May 23, 2008, from www.macfound.org.

2. Migration: Open up. (2008, Jan. 3). *The Economist.* Retrieved May 20, 2008, from www.economist.com/specialreports/displaystory.cfm?story_id=10286197.

3. Passel, J., & Cohn, D. (2008, Feb. 11). "Immigration to Play Lead Role in Future US Growth" Pew Research Center Publication. Retrieved May 23, 2008, from http://pewresearch.org.

4. Schramm, C. (2007, Dec. 26). Unleash the little guys. Retrieved May 20, 2008, from www.newsweek.com/id/82041/page/3.

5. Douglass, J., Roebken, H., & Thomson, G. (2007). The immigrant university: assessing the dynamics of race, major and socioeconomic characteristics at the University of California. Center for Studies in Higher Education. Retrieved August 20, 2008, from cshe.berkeley.edu/publications/docs/ROPS.ImmigrantUniv.CSHE.19.07.pdf.

6. *The immigrant experience. Improving education for immigrant students: A guide for K-12 educators in the Northwest and Alaska.* (2001, July). Northwest Regional Educational Laboratory. Retrieved May 20, 2008, from www.nwrel.org/cnorse/booklets/immigration/4.html.

7. Ostrove, J., & Long, S. (2007). Social class and belonging: Implications for college adjustment. *The Review of Higher Education, 30*(4), Summer, 363–389.

8. Chen, X. (2005). First-generation students in postsecondary education: A look at their college transcripts. Washington, D.C.: National Center for Education Statistics; Engle, J. (2007). Postsecondary access and success for first-generation college students. *American Academic,* January; Engle, J., Bermeo, A., & O'Brien, C. (2006). *Straight from the source: What works for*

first-generation college students. Washington, D.C.: The Pell Institute for the Study of Opportunity in Higher Education. December; Higher Education Research Institute. (2007, May).

9. First in my family: A profile of first-generation college students at four-year institutions since 1971. (2007 May). UCLA Higher Education Research Institute. Retrieved May 20, 2008, from www.gseis.ucla.edu/heri/PDFs/pubs/briefs/FirstGenResearchBrief.pdf.

10. Chen, X. (2005). op. cit.

11. *The immigrant experience*, op. cit., p. 23.

12. Ibid.

13. Rendon, L. (1992). From the barrio to the academy: Revelations from a Mexican American "scholarship girl." In L. Zwerling, & H. London (Eds.) (1992), *First Generation College Students: Confronting the Cultural Issues*. (p. 56–64). San Francisco: Jossey-Bass, p. 56.

14. Engle, J., et al. (2006), op. cit., p. 6.

15. Dweck, C. (2006). *Mindset: The new psychology of success*. New York: Ballantine.

16. First in my family (2007), op. cit.; Engle, J., et al. (2006), op. cit.

17. Engle, J., et al. (2006), op. cit., p. 22.

18. Ostrove, J., & Long, S. (2007), op. cit.

19. Engle, J., et al. (2006), op. cit.

20. Ibid.

21. Tuckman, B., Abry, D., & Smith, D. (2002). *Learning and motivation strategies: Your guide to success*. Englewood Cliffs, NJ: Prentice-Hall; Tuckman, B. (2007). Evaluating a program for enhancing the study skills and academic performance of urban high school students. Paper presented at the annual meeting of the American Educational Research Association, Chicago.

22. Engle, J., et al. (2006), op. cit.

23. Dweck, C. (2006), op. cit., p. 171–178.

24. Doidge, N. (2007). *The brain that changes itself.* New York: Viking.

25. First in my family (2007), op. cit.; Engle, J., et al. (2006), op. cit.; El-Ghoroury, N., Salvador, D., Manning, R., & Williamson, T. (1999). A survival guide for ethnic minority graduate students. APA Online. Retrieved May 20, 2008, from www.APA/org/apags/diversity.

18. LIVING AND WORKING WITH PROCRASTINATORS

1. Dweck, C. (2006). *Mindset: The new psychology of success*. New York: Ballantine.

APPENDIX A: PROCRASTINATION:
TWENTY-FIVE YEARS OF RESEARCH

1. Steel, P. (2007). The nature of procrastination: A meta-analytic and theoretical review of quintessential self-regulatory failure. *Psychological Bulletin. 133*(1), 65–94.

2. Steel, P. Procrastination Central Home Page. Haskayne School of Business, University of Calgary, Canada. Retrieved September 10, 2007, from http://procrastinus.com/research/theories.

3. Steel, P. (2007), op. cit.

4. Tice, D. M., & Baumeister, R. F. (1997). Longitudinal study of procrastination, performance, stress, and health: The costs and benefits of dawdling. *Psychological Science, 8,* 454–458.

5. Barkley, R., Murphy, K., & Fischer, M. (2008). *ADHD in adults: What the science says.* New York: Guilford Press; Hallowell, E. M., & Ratey, J. J. (2005). *Delivered from distraction: Getting the most out of life with attention deficit disorder.* New York: Ballantine.

6. Senecal, F., Koestner, R., & Vellerand, R. (1995). Self-regulation and academic procrastination: An interactional model. *Journal of Social Psychology, 135,* 607–619.

7. Ibid., p. 617.

8. Muraven, M., & Baumeister, R. F. (2000). Self-regulation and depletion of limited resources: Does self-control resemble a muscle? *Psychological Bulletin, 126*(2), 247–259.

9. Steel, P. (2007), op. cit.

10. Strongman, K. T., & Burt, C. D. B. (2000). Taking breaks from work: An exploratory inquiry. *Journal of Psychology, 134,* 229–242.

11. Briody, R. (1980). An exploratory study of procrastination. (Doctoral dissertation, Brandeis University, 1980). *Dissertation Abstracts International, 41,* 590.

12. Steel, P. (2007), op. cit.

13. Micek, L. (1982). Some problems of self-autoregulation of volitional processes in university students from the point of view of their mental health. *Sbornik Praci Filosoficke Fakulty Brnenske University, 31,* 51–70. Cited in Steel (2007), op. cit.

14. Jones, E. E., & Berglas, S. (1978). Control of attributions about the self through self-handicapping strategies: The appeal of alcohol and the role of underachievement. *Personality and Social Psychology Bulletin, 4,* 200–206; Smith, T. W., Snyder, C. R., & Handelsman, M. M. (1982). On the self-serving

function of an academic wooden leg: Test anxiety as a self-handicapping strategy. *Journal of Personality and Social Psychology, 42*, 314–321.

15. Lay, C. H. (1990). Working to schedule on personal projects: An assessment of person-project characteristics and trait procrastination. *Journal of Social Behavior and Personality, 5*, 91–103.

16. McCown, W. (1986). Behaviour of chronic college-student procrastinators: An experimental study. *Social Science and Behavioural Documents, 17*, 133.

17. Steel, P. (2007), op. cit., p. 77.

18. Ibid.

19. Haycock, L. A. (1993). The cognitive mediation of procrastination: An investigation of the relationship between procrastination and self-efficacy beliefs. (Doctoral dissertation, University of Minnesota, 1993). *Dissertation Abstracts International, 54*, 2261.

20. Enns, M. W., & Cox, B. J. (2002). The nature and assessment of perfectionism: A critical analysis. In G. L. Flett, & P. L. Hewittt (Eds.), *Perfectionism: Theory, research, and treatment* (pp. 33–62). Washington, D.C.: American Psychological Association; Slaney, R. B., Rice, K. G., & Ashby, J. S. (2002). A programmatic approach to measuring perfectionism: The Almost Perfect Scales. In G. L. Flett, & P. L. Hewitt (Eds.), *Perfectionism: theory, research, and treatment* (pp. 63–88). Washington, D.C.: American Psychological Association.

21. Borenstein, S. (2007, January 12). Study is a put off: Scientists research why procrastination is getting worse. *USAtoday.com*. Retrieved April 17, 2007, from www.usatoday.com/tech/science/2007–01–12-procrastination-study_x.htm.

22. Slaney, R. B., Rice, K. G., & Ashby, J. S. (2002), op. cit.

23. Frost, R. O., Heimberg, R. G., Holt, C. S., Mattia, J. L., & Neubauer, A. L. (1993). A comparison of two measures of perfectionism. *Personality and Individual Differences, 14*, 119–128.

24. Rice, K. G., & Ashby, J. S. (2007). An efficient method for classifying perfectionists. *Journal of Counseling Psychology, 54*(1), 72–85.

25. Ibid.

26. Kachgal, M. M, Hansen, L. S., & Nutter, K. J. (2001). Academic procrastination prevention/intervention: *Journal of Developmental Education, 25*, 14–24.

27. Steel, P. (2007), op. cit.

28. Ibid.

29. Ibid.

30. Ibid., p. 75.

31. Ibid.

32. Hitti, M. (2004). It's never too late to stop procrastinating. Retrieved March 5, 2008, from www.webmd.com/balance/guide/its-never-too-late-to-stop-procrastinating.

33. Tice, D. M., & Baumeister, R. F. (1997), op. cit.

34. Sirois, F. M. (2007). I'll look after my health, later: A replication and extension of the procrastination-health model with community-dwelling adults. *Personality and Individual Differences, 43*(1), 15–26.

35. Bogg, T., & Roberts, B. W. (2004). Conscientiousness and health-related behaviors: A meta-analysis of the leading behavioral contributors to mortality. *Psychological Bulletin, 130,* 887–919.

36. Cynkar, A. (2007). A towering figure. *Monitor on Psychology, 38*(4). Retrieved June 9, 2007 from www.apa.org/monitor/apr07/towering.html.

37. Kahneman, D., & Tversky, A. (1979). Prospect theory: An analysis of decision and risk. *Econometrica, XLVII,* 263–291.

38. Mazur, J. E. (1998). Procrastination by pigeons with fixed interval response requirements. *Journal of Experimental Analysis of Behavior, 69,* 185–197.

39. National Institute of Mental Health *Science News* Online (2004). Brain's reward circuitry revealed in procrastinating primates. August 10. Retrieved March 1, 2008, from www.nimh.nih.gov/science-news/2004/brains-reward-circuitry-revealed-in-procrastinating-primates.shtml. Referring to Liu, Z., Richmond, B. J., Saunders, R. C., Steenrod, S., Stubblefield, B. K., Montague, D. M., & Ginns, E. I. (2004). DNA targeting of rhinal cortex D2 receptor protein reversibility blocks learning of cues that predict reward. *Proceedings of the National Academy of Sciences of the United States of America, 101*(33), 12336–12341.

40. Schouwenburg, H. C., & Groenewould, J. T. (2001). Study motivation under social temptation; Effects of trait procrastination. *Personality and Individual Differences, 30,* 229–240.

41. Akerlof, G. A. (1991). Procrastination and obedience. *American Economic Review, 81*(2), 1–19.

42. Ibid.

43. O'Donoghue, T., & Rabin, M. (1999). Doing it now or later. *American Economic Review, 89*(1), 103–124.

44. Ibid.

45. Ibid.

46. Ibid.

47. Brafman, O., & Brafman, R. (2008). *Sway: The irresistible pull of irrational behavior.* New York: Doubleday.

48. Schouwenburg, H., Lay, C., Pychyl, T., & Ferrari, J. (2004). *Counseling the procrastinator in academic settings.* Washington, D.C.: American Psychological Association.

49. Steel, P. (2007), op. cit.

50. Ainslie, G. (1992). *Picoeconomics: The strategic interaction of successive motivational states within the person.* New York: Cambridge University Press.

51. Bandura, A. (1997). *Self-efficacy: The exercise of control.* New York: Freeman

52. Steel, P. (2007), op. cit.

53. Eisenberger, R. (1992). Learned industriousness. *Psychological Review, 99,* 248–267.

54. Dweck, C. (2006). *Mindset: The new psychology of success.* New York: Ballantine.

55. Steel, P. (2007), op. cit.

56. Silver, M. (1974). Procrastination. *Centerpoint, 1,* 49–54.

57. Bargh, J. A., & Barndollar, K. (1996). Automaticity in action: The unconscious as repository of chronic goals and motives. In P. M. Gollwitzer, & J. A. Bargh (Eds.), *The psychology of action: Linking cognition and motivation to behavior* (pp. 457–481). New York: Guilford Press; Karoly, P. (1993). Mechanisms of self-regulation: A systems view. *Annual Review of Psychology, 44,* 23–52.

58. Kuhl, J., & Goschke, T. (1994). A theory of action control: Mental subsystems, modes of control, and volitional conflict-resolution strategies. In J. Kuhl, & J. Beckmann (Eds.), *Volition and personality: Action versus state orientation* (pp. 93–124). Gottingen, Germany: Hogrefe & Huber.

59. Steel, P. (2007), op. cit.

Index